Winifred M. Brennan

130
3
39 00
3

Previewed Dictation

With Previews Written in
Gregg Shorthand Simplified

Charles E. Zoubek

THE GREGG PUBLISHING COMPANY

Business Education Division, McGraw-Hill Book Company, Inc.

New York   Chicago   San Francisco   Dallas   Toronto   London

PREVIEWED DICTATION

Shorthand Plates Written by
CHARLES E. ZOUBEK

PUBLISHED BY THE GREGG PUBLISHING COMPANY
Business Education Division of the McGraw-Hill Book Company, Inc.
Printed in the United States of America

PREFACE

Previewed Dictation is a compilation of 175 five-minute dictations counted at speeds ranging from 50 through 150 words a minute, distributed as follows:

1– 20	counted for dictation at	50	words a minute
21– 40	counted for dictation at	60	words a minute
41– 60	counted for dictation at	70	words a minute
61– 80	counted for dictation at	80	words a minute
81–100	counted for dictation at	90	words a minute
101–120	counted for dictation at	100	words a minute
121–140	counted for dictation at	110	words a minute
141–160	counted for dictation at	120	words a minute
161–170	counted for dictation at	130	words a minute
171–174	counted for dictation at	140	words a minute
175	counted for dictation at	150	words a minute

Previewed Dictation contains the following features:

1. Each take is preceded by a thorough preview in Gregg Shorthand Simplified of the more difficult words and phrases that appear in the take. The words and phrases in the preview are given in the order in which they occur in the take, and the minute of the take in which they occur is indicated. The teacher may, therefore, present the entire preview if he wishes to dictate the take as an exercise in sustained dictation; or he can present a minute or two of the preview at a time if he is developing speed by the minute-step plan described later in this Preface.

A type transcript immediately follows each shorthand preview.

2. The takes within each speed are arranged according to their difficulty as determined by their actual syllable intensity, which is given at the end of each take.

3. The takes are counted by the Standard word of 1.4 syllables. This method of counting, which is used in counting all Gregg dicta-

tion material, equalizes to a considerable extent the difficulty of dictation material.

4. All the takes at the speeds from 50 through 100 words a minute
are on business-letter material. The first ten takes at 110 words a
minute are also on business-letter material; but, beginning with take
No. 131 at 110 words a minute, carefully selected *Congressional
Record* material is used.

5. Immediately preceding take No. 131 (page 198), a list of
shortcuts for frequently used *Congressional Record* expressions is
given.

There are, of course, various ways in which the material in *Previewed Dictation* may be used for speed development purposes. The
plan that the author has found most effective is that originated by
Louis A. Leslie—the minute-step plan, which is briefly described here.

Assuming that the class is able to write a first reading of a 1-min-
ute dictation at about 60 words a minute and that a 60-word dictation in this book is being practiced, then the procedure would be
about as follows:

1. Place on the blackboard the preview indicated for the first 100
words, or approximately 2 minutes of the dictation, taking not more
than 60 to 90 seconds to get the preview on the blackboard and to
have a quick reading drill. These previews are read as the teacher
points quickly at random; they are not written by the student.

2. Dictate the first 60 words in 1 minute. Have the pupils who
got the dictation raise their hands after each dictation. Whenever more
than half the pupils raise their hands, the piece may be redictated about
10 words a minute faster.

3. Take perhaps 15 seconds to have the pupils read the preview
quickly from the blackboard.

4. Dictate in a minute 75 words; that is, the 60 words previously
dictated and an additional 15 words. Ask how many got it. Have students read back.

5. Have the pupils read again from the blackboard the preview in
not more than 10 to 15 seconds.

6. Redictate the material, this time 90 words in the minute.

7. Have the preview reread from the blackboard and redictate the
material, this time 100 words in the minute. Not all students may get

this fourth dictation, but urge them to keep on and write as much of it as they can get.

8. Repeat steps 1–7 for the next 100 words of the 5-minute dictation.

9. Then dictate at approximately 100 words a minute the first 200 words of the take. Ask the students to read back about half of this dictation.

10. Repeat steps 1–7 for the next 200 words. (This will carry you partly into the next 60-word dictation.)

11. Finally, redictate the entire 400 words, at 80 words a minute in this case, although the speed will vary with the class and with the difficulty of the material. This will require about one and one-half 5-minute 60-word dictations.

Actually, the teacher will probably never dictate each minute-take exactly four times. If the dictation is composed of easy matter with good phrasing, it may be worth dictating four times to give the pupils practice in writing at the high speed that is possible on this type of material. If the dictation is composed of more difficult material, it may not be worth dictating more than twice. Thus, instead of dictating four groups four times each, actually the four groups will be dictated probably a total of twelve times rather than sixteen, as might be indicated by the rigid application of the schedule given above.

When this procedure is used, it will be possible to give effectively just one full 5-minute dictation in a 45-minute period. On some days, when other things, such as more reading back, have to be done, it may be impossible to have the final 5-minute dictation; but an attempt should always be made to include it in order to tie together all the single minutes. Not more than one dictation out of four or five should be read back.

Perhaps the most powerful motivating device that is available to the shorthand teacher is the Gregg Credentials service. This service provides a series of incentives, not too far apart, from the very early stages of the student's study of shorthand to the point where he is an expert writing 200 words a minute.

One feature of this Credentials service is the Gregg Shorthand Speed Tests consisting of a series of tests from 60 to 200 words a minute. This speed-test service was inaugurated in 1924, and since that time more than two million awards have been granted to students in all parts of the world.

The tests at 60, 80, 100, 120, and 140 words a minute are available monthly in *The Business Teacher,* which is sent without charge to teachers of business subjects; the tests at 160, 175, and 200 words a minute are issued six times a year and are sent to teachers on request only.

Another valuable Gregg Credential service is the *Business Education World* Transcription Tests, which appear in the *Business Education World.* These tests should be given after the student has passed the Gregg Shorthand Speed Tests at 80, 100, and 120 words a minute, respectively. Transcription certificates are granted only on mailable transcripts. More and more schools are making the Gregg Shorthand Speed Test Certificate and the B. E. W. Transcription Certificate requirements for graduation from the shorthand course.

CHARLES E. ZOUBEK

CONTENTS

PART I

50 WORDS A MINUTE

1

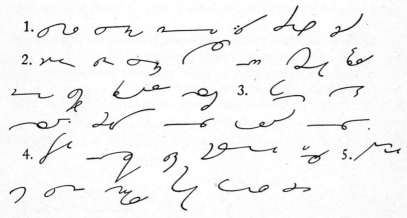

Key: (1) Agree, I am sure, one of the most, ahead, generation, we want. (2) Strong, young, anxious, to make, in the world, develop, spirit, summer, activities, children, carefully. (3) Program, themselves, gardening, first time, many of the, learned, many of them. (4) Beds, engaged, useful, fundamentals, overnight. (5) Directors, confident, again, co-operate, valuable, please write, Sincerely yours.

Dear Mrs. Smith: You will agree with me, I am sure, when I say that | one of the most important tasks ahead of us is to see that the present | generation does not grow up with the feeling that the world owes | it a living. We want the present generation to grow up as a (1) group of strong young men and women who will be anxious to make their own | way in the world. To develop this spirit in boys and girls is the purpose | of our summer camps.

The activities at all our camps are based on | teaching children the fun of working. Under our carefully worked out (2) program, the boys and girls learn how to help themselves.

This past summer, | gardening was stressed at our camps. For the first time, many of the children had | the experience of watching things grow. At the same time, they learned how | to cook on fireplaces that they made with their own hands. Many of them slept in (3) beds that they designed and built themselves.

All of them were engaged in useful | work. They learned the fundamentals of first aid under the guidance of | a nurse. They took long overnight trips on which they learned how to read a | map.

All these activities mean hard work, both for the children and for the (4) directors of the camp. But they all enjoy it.

We are now beginning | to make plans for next summer, and we are confident that you will once | again co-operate with us. If you have any suggestions that | will make our camps even more valuable, please write us. Sincerely yours, (5) (1.29)

2

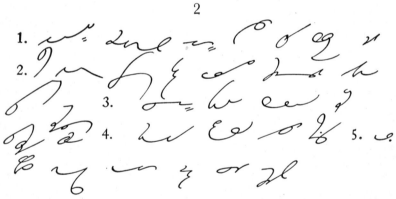

Key: (1) Toronto, first-class, New York, to make, I had, arrival, station. (2) However, trunk, baggage, possible, already, few minutes, departure, I did not have, investigation. (3) American, boarder, I learned, official, advised, wire. (4) Followed, explained, day or two, I have not had. (5) Regarding, I hope that, you will be able, locate, as soon as possible, another, in a few days.

Gentlemen: On May 16 I purchased from your agent at Toronto | a first-class ticket from Toronto to New York. On the day that I | was to make the trip I had the Smith Trucking Company call for my | trunk and deliver it to the station. On my arrival at the station (1) in the evening, however, I could not find the trunk.

The man in | charge of the baggage said that it was possible that the trunk had already | been put on the train; but, as it was only a few minutes before | the departure of the train, I did not have time to make an investigation. (2)

When the train reached the American border, I learned | definitely that the trunk was not on the train. An official advised me | to send a wire at our next stopping point, asking the Toronto agent | to send the trunk on the next train in case the trunk had arrived at (3) the station after my departure. I followed his advice.

When I reached | New York, I explained the case to your agent there. He advised me to | wait a day or two; then, if the trunk had not arrived, to take the matter | up with you.

As it is now May 25, and I have not had any (4) information regarding my trunk, I am writing you. I hope that | you will be able to locate the trunk. I must have the trunk as soon as | possible, as I am leaving for another city in a few | days and must use it, as well as the papers that it contains. Yours truly, (5) (1.30)

3

Key: (1) Possible, interested, invite, catalogue, shortage, wool. (2) Country, as a result, difference, hundreds, indication. (3) Enthusiasm, tribute, American, women, economy, counts, persons. (4) Thousands, letters, another, without, woman, Nashville. (5) Many times, beauty, don't, one of these, anywhere else, Very respectfully yours.

Dear Madam: There has never been a time, so far as I re-
member, when | it was possible to save so much on rugs as you can
save now. With the | thought that, as a homeowner, you are
interested in rugs, I invite | you to write for our new catalogue.

Because of the wool shortage in (1) this country, wool prices
have gone higher and higher. As a result, | the difference between
our prices and retail stock prices on rugs is | greater than ever. Our
Order Department is receiving hundreds | of orders from all parts
of the country—an indication of the (2) enthusiasm with which
our rugs are being received. These orders are | also a tribute to the
thrift of American women, who are | interested in economy in these
days when every dollar counts. |

I wish that you could talk to a few of the hundreds of persons
who visit (3) us and read some of the thousands of letters that come
to my desk. | I believe you would then not let another day go by
without giving | our rugs a trial.

Here is a paragraph from a letter I received | several weeks
ago from a woman in Nashville:

"Twenty years ago (4) I ordered five blue rugs from you.
During those twenty years they have been | cleaned many times.
They have lost very little of their beauty."

Don't you think | you owe it to yourself at least to try one of
these rugs in your own | home before you buy a rug anywhere
else? Very respectfully yours, (5) (1.35)

4

Key: (1) Afraid, beginner, assure, reason, today. (2) Enter the, aptitude, test, last year, five hundred, persons, successful, qualified. (3) Course, offered, writers, institute, America, thousands, ability, developing. (4) Copy, fascinating, progress, acquire, first. (5) Requires, few minutes, absolutely, coupon, immediately, to us.

Dear Miss Jones: Do you feel that you can write but are afraid that a | beginner does not have a chance? Let me assure you that there is no reason | for this feeling. There is more room for beginners in the field of writing | today than ever before.

You may make sure that you can write before (1) you enter the field by taking our Writing Aptitude Test.

Not all | persons who take the test pass it by any means. Last year, more than five hundred | persons tried the test, but only a fraction of them were successful | in passing it. Those persons who pass the test are then qualified to take (2) the Smith Course in Writing, offered by the Writers Institute of | America. This course has trained thousands of beginners to use their writing | ability to increase their earnings.

The Smith Course teaches you to | write by developing your individual style instead of having (3) you copy the styles of others. With this course, you work at home on your | own time.

It is fascinating work. Each week you can see the progress that | you are making. In a matter of months you can acquire the | "professional" touch. Then you are ready to sell what you write.

The first step, (4) however, is to take the Writing Aptitude Test. It requires only | a few minutes to take, and it costs you absolutely nothing. Mail | the enclosed coupon, and the test will be sent to you immediately. | Then return the test to us, and we will correct it. Sincerely yours, (5) (1.36)

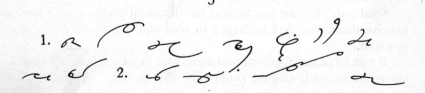

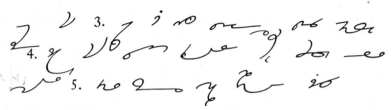

Key: (1) Young, to make, simple, conserving, perhaps, forever, first, course, certain. (2) Retain, mature, undoubtedly, single, investment, further. (3) To buy, house, otherwise, economically, unit, insurance. (4) Establish, fund, education, children, savings, financial, merely, country. (5) Surely, as many, copies, we hope you will not, hesitate.

Dear Mr. Young: Your family today has an important choice to | make.

The choice is a simple one. It is between conserving what you now | have or letting it get away from you, perhaps forever. If you | choose the first course, you will take certain steps in your own interest and in (1) that of your family. You will, first of all, retain all your bonds until | they mature, as they are undoubtedly the best single investment| you can make. Further, a glance at the interest you get from them will | show you that you get your best return the longer you own them.

Next, you will (2) certainly own your own home if it is possible to buy a house | at a fair price; otherwise, you will save regularly to buy one when | it can be bought economically.

Then, you will want to see that | your family as a unit is protected by enough insurance. (3) You will also want to establish a fund for the education | of your children.

Finally, you will want to maintain a growing savings | account.

As financial experts, we suggest these things to you. We do so, | not merely because they help our country, but because your family (4) will surely benefit by them.

Send today for our free booklet on | financial problems and how to solve them. We shall be happy to send you | as many copies as you wish.

If you have any financial problems, | we hope you will not hesitate to get in touch with us. Yours truly, (5) (1.37)

6

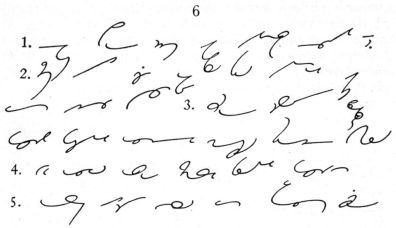

Key: (1) Improve, ability, successful, to prepare, describe, methods, interesting. (2) Effective, to do, whether, report, board, directors, to choose, organize, together, to make. (3) Facility, started, exercises, practice, procedures, recommends, you will find, volume, different. (4) Things, record, writer, assurance, pointers, practical. (5) Language, to understand, card, of course, obligation, while.

Dear Mr. Brown: Here is a book that will help you improve your writing | ability. The book is called "The Art of Successful Writing" and is | by John H. Gray.

We asked Mr. Gray to prepare for us a book in | which he would describe his methods for making his writing so interesting (1) and so effective.

No matter what type of writing you have to | do, whether it is a business letter or a report to a board of | directors, this book will help you. It will show you how to choose and | organize your material and put your thoughts together so as to make (2) your writing interesting and effective.

It will help you gain | facility in writing. Mr. Gray shows you how to get started and then sets | up many exercises that will give you practice in applying | the procedures that he recommends.

You will find this volume different (3) from any other book on writing that you have ever seen. Mr. | Gray is known for doing things and then writing about them. In this case his | great record as a writer is your assurance that the pointers he | gives you are practical. He knows what methods have been successful in his (4) work, and he tells about them in language that is easy to understand.

Just mail | the enclosed card, and we will send you "The Art of Successful | Writing" for ten days' trial. You will, of course, be under no obligation. | Send the card now, while you are thinking about it. Very truly yours, (5) (1.37)

7

Key: (1) Fact that, I have been, run, away, juicy, front. (2) Himself, desirable, follow, for a long time, human beings, ability, understanding. (3) To understand, prospective, indicating, becoming, heard, otherwise. (4) Literature, started, specialty, booklet, describes, naturally. (5) Fortune, overnight, sound, to make, tells, costs, Yours truly.

Dear Sir: Here is a fact that I have found to be true of our | organization in the forty years I have been selling through the mail. If you | throw an apple at a horse, he will run away, no matter how juicy | the apple may be. But if you hold it in front of his nose and let (1) him smell it and convince himself that it is desirable, he will | follow you for a long time to get that very same apple.

Horses and | human beings have much in common. The ability to handle | horses or human beings is largely a matter of understanding. (2) I am trying my best to understand you, as your name is before | me as a prospective agent. You wrote first, thus indicating your | interest in becoming an agent and increasing your income. I | should never have heard of you otherwise.

I need new agents now to mail out (3) our literature. I started in business in 1910 | as a printer. Printing advertising pieces was my specialty.

With | this letter I am sending you a booklet that describes in detail | the offer I have to make. Naturally, I cannot promise you a (4) fortune overnight; but I do offer you a sound chance to make extra | money.

My book, "How to Increase Your Income by Mail," tells in great detail | how you can get started in your own home. The book costs only $2—and | you can return it if you are not satisfied with it. Yours truly, (5) (1.38)

8

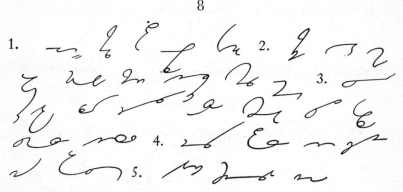

Key: (1) New York, agency, has been, major, because. (2) Adjust, themselves, kept, representatives, solicit, ask you, to give us, definite, information. (3) Amount, to spend, certain, studied, entire, develop, idea, prepare, outline, to carry. (4) Submitted, explain, conclude, we do not, you want, obligation. (5) Discuss, few minutes, one of our.

Dear Mr. Barnes: The New York Advertising Agency has been in | business for over thirty years. It has gone through two major depressions | and two wars. It has seen many changes take place in business. It has | seen many advertising agencies fail because they were not able (1) to adjust themselves to those changes. We have not only kept our business | going but have also increased it.

If you invite one of | our representatives to call, he will not solicit your business. He will | ask you to give us definite information about your plans for (2) advertising, the amount you wish to spend, and certain other facts. This │ material will then be studied by our entire staff. If we are able │ to develop a new sales idea for your products, we then prepare │ an outline of that idea, with suggestions on how to carry it (3) out. This will then be submitted to you by our representative, │ who will explain it to you in detail. If you conclude that our idea │ will not work or that we do not offer the kind of service you want, │ you are under no obligation. If our idea appeals to you, and (4) you want to give it a trial, our representative will then discuss │ with you the details of the plan.

    Would you like to have us make a study │ of your business on this basis? Will you give us a date when you will │ have a few minutes to talk to one of our men? Very sincerely yours, (5) (1.38)

9

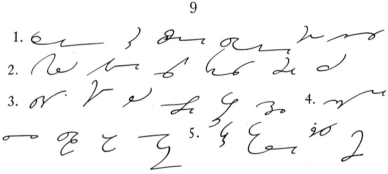

    Key: (1) Salesman, force, assignments, accomplishments, future, together. (2) Different, departments, in addition, bulletin, first, I want. (3) Outstanding, you have done, turned, machines, previous, consequently. (4) Customers, immediate, accept, represent, improvement. (5) Positions, problems, hesitate, convenient.

    To the Salesmen: Many months have passed since you left the sales force to take │ your assignments in the factory and in the office. I feel that now │ is the time to talk to you about your accomplishments and your future. │ It is difficult to get all of you together at one time for (1) a meeting, as you are assigned to different departments and work │ during different hours of the day. In addition, such a meeting would │ take you off your jobs and thus hold up your work. Therefore, this bulletin | will take the place of a regular meeting.

In the first place, I want to (2) thank you for the outstanding job you have done in the factory and | in the office.

Our Troy factory has turned out more machines so far this | year than in any previous year of its history. In addition, | it has turned out all the necessary repair parts. Consequently, (3) our customers may obtain the same high type of service that they have | always received.

In the immediate future, we will not accept orders | for any new machines. At present, we are working on designs | that will represent a big improvement over our present models. We (4) expect the new models to be good sellers.

If your new positions | offer any problems in which you would like help, please do not hesitate | to write me. Better still, come in to see me if it is convenient. | It would be nice to have a personal chat with you. Harry Edison (5) (1.39)

10

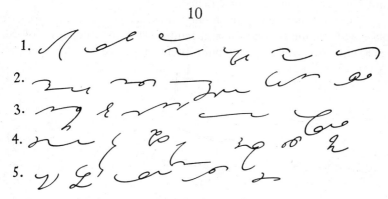

Key: (1) Automobile, radio, electrical, reports, quality, organization. (2) Consumers, connection, manufacturer, product, entirely. (3) To give you, tests, conducted, on the market, laboratory. (4) Circular, publication, we hope that, to become, subscriber, without, assure. (5) Refund, prefer, later, indicate, Sincerely yours.

Dear Sir: Are you planning to buy an automobile or a radio | or some other electrical equipment during the coming year? | If you are, we believe that our reports on the leading brands can help | you get high quality and save you money.

Our organization is (1) set up solely for the purpose of serving consumers. It has no | connection with any manufacturer and has no interest in | the sale of any product. It is financed entirely by consumers, | who pay $5 a year to receive the reports that we issue. (2)

The object of our service is to give you reports on products based | on tests conducted by our own staff. Our men buy the leading brands on the | market, take them to our laboratory, and test them. After the tests, | we issue a report that you can use as a guide for your own purchases. (3)

Please read the enclosed circular, which gives detailed information | about our publication. We hope that after going over this | material you will want to become a subscriber. If you feel you | cannot judge the value of our reports without seeing them, we assure (4) you that we shall be glad to refund the full price that you pay if you | are not satisfied.

You need not send any money now. If you prefer, | we will place your name on our list and send a bill later. Indicate | on the enclosed card which you would prefer to have us do. Sincerely yours, (5) (1.42)

11

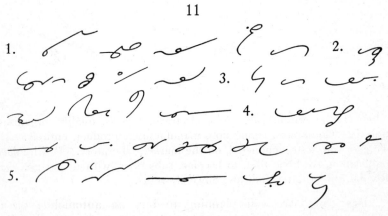

Key: (1) Editor, naturally, credit, has been, organization. (2) Occasions, practical, aside, include, current. (3) Punch, of course, learning, concerned, difference, however, recommend. (4) Lithography, minute, running, another, we might, sample, quickly, turn. (5) To make, self-contained, minimum, letting us know, representative.

Dear Sir: As an editor, you are naturally interested | in issuing a magazine that will be a credit to your organization. |

Every editor knows what it means to receive | important news after his copy has been written and everything is (1) ready for the press. You have probably been in such a situation | on many occasions. As a practical matter, you have probably | put the news aside for the next issue, much as you would have liked | to include it in the current issue. By the time the next issue comes (2) out, the news is old and has lost much of its punch.

Of course, we have no | way of learning how your magazine is printed. As far as we are concerned, | it makes little difference, as we handle all types of printing. | For a magazine such as yours, however, we would recommend the use (3) of lithography. With this method of printing, changes can be made | up to the very minute before the presses start running.

Another | suggestion we might offer is that you let us print a sample issue | for you to show you how quickly we can turn it out. Our plant is in (4) full operation day and night. It is never too late to make changes. | As our plant is self-contained, a minimum of time and expense is | required to make changes.

The enclosed card is for your convenience | in letting us know when our representative may call. Sincerely yours, (5) (1.44)

12

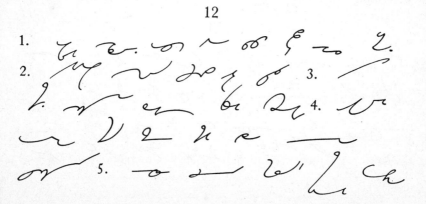

Key: (1) Reports, concerning, reaction, to our, without, exception, not only, offering. (2) Distribute, ground, fact that, to speak, attitude. (3) To do, everything, customer, years ago, buyers, developed. (4) Independence, longer, haven't, assume, efforts, they are, manner, accustomed. (5) Mind, cement, friendship, everybody else, pleasure.

To Our Salesmen: We are now beginning to receive the first reports | concerning the customers' reaction to our new fall styles.

These reports | are, without exception, favorable to us. They indicate that | customers are not only pleased with the type of goods we are offering (1) but that they are also pleased with the fair methods we are using to | distribute these goods. Many express their relief that we are keeping our feet | on the ground and not taking advantage of the fact that we are in | the driver's seat, so to speak. They tell us that they are pleased with the attitude (2) of our company in feeling that it is just as important | to do everything to satisfy a customer today as it | was two or three years ago.

For many years our customers enjoyed | a buyer's market and naturally developed a feeling of (3) independence. It is no longer a buyer's market, but our customers | haven't changed; they still feel that they can assume this independence. In their | efforts to buy the goods that they need at the present time, they are being | treated in a manner to which they are not accustomed.

Bearing this (4) in mind, we now have a fine opportunity to cement our friendship | with our customers. When everybody else is telling the | customer that he is lucky to get merchandise, let us tell him that | we still consider it a pleasure to sell to him. John S. Wilson (5) (1.44)

13

Key: (1) Sunny, emergency, educate, children, further. (2) Self-education, vacation, you want, welcome, United States, occasion. (3) Easily, conveniently, employer, provides, mind, why not. (4) Reserve, wonderful, security, worry, tomorrow. (5) Forget, afford, automatically, future.

Dear Mr. Burns: We all hear about saving for a rainy day but | how about saving for a sunny day? An emergency may mean good | luck and opportunities. It may be an opportunity to | educate children, buy a home or a farm, go into your own business, (1) or have further self-education or vacation and travel. | Opportunity knocks only once. When it comes, you want to be sure to welcome | it. One way you can welcome it is to have a nest egg of United | States Savings Bonds ready for just that occasion.

You can build up that (2) nest egg easily and conveniently by enrolling in the Pay | Roll Savings Plan. Your employer provides this plan for your protection, welfare, | and peace of mind. He is willing to spend the time to make this | available to you.

So why not take advantage of this opportunity? (3) The man who has saved a reserve has a wonderful sense of | security that the man who lives from hand to mouth can never know. He can | take today as it comes without having to worry too much about | tomorrow.

The Pay Roll Savings Plan knocks the if out of thrift because you (4) cannot forget to save. It is done for your automatically | and regularly payday after payday. Sign up for all you can afford | to take. United States Savings Bonds will build a future of ease | and security for you and your family. Yours very sincerely, (5) (1.45)

14

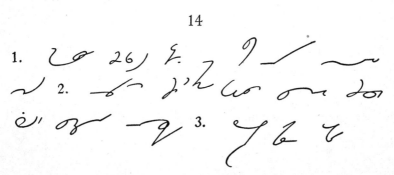

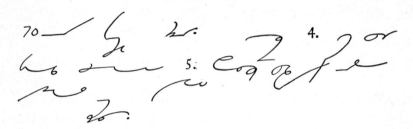

Key: (1) Flight, $2,600, such a thing, injure, however, indeed, glad to know, count. (2) Medical, few cents, protect, against, financial, hardship, accident, engaged. (3) Eligible, to join, report, $70,000,000, benefits, for one thing, given. (4) Coverage, another, policy, similar. (5) Application, accepted, until, do not let, investigating, tomorrow.

Dear Mr. Bailey: Would you fall down a flight of stairs for | $2,600? Of course, you would not do such a thing. If you did injure | yourself in falling down a flight of stairs, however, you would be indeed | glad to know that you could count on $2,600 to (1) take care of your doctor's bills and other medical expenses.

For | a few cents a day you can protect yourself against the financial hardship | that comes when you have an accident.

If you are a man between | eighteen and fifty-five and are engaged in some type of office work, you (2) are probably eligible to join this organization. As | you will see by the enclosed report, we have paid more than | $70,000,000 in benefits to our members.

A member of our | organization enjoys many advantages. For one thing, he is given (3) a wide coverage. He is protected against accidents | every minute of the day and night.

For another thing, the cost of a | policy is very small. A similar policy with other | insurance companies would cost 25 to 35 per cent more. (4)

You need send no money now. When your application is accepted, | you pay only $2. Your next payment is not due until July | 15.

Do not let another day go by without investigating | our policies. No one knows what tomorrow may bring forth. Yours truly, (5) (1.45)

15

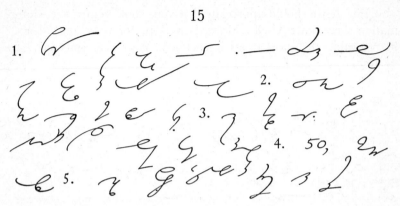

Key: (1) About this time, publications, represents, more than, a million, various, mailed, to be sure, properly, listed, will you please. (2) I am sure, advantage, give us, effort, exert, pushing. (3) Considerable, agencies, nothing, except, discount, to make, margin, profit, subscriptions. (4) 50 per cent, as a result, last year. (5) Copy, appreciate, self-addressed, for your convenience, to us, Yours very sincerely.

Dear Sir: Each year about this time, we revise our price list of | publications. This price list represents more than a million copies of | various magazines that are mailed each year.

To be sure that your | publication is properly listed, will you please fill out and send us the (1) enclosed information sheet.

As I am sure you realize, it is to | your advantage that you give us the very best rate you can. The better | the rate you give us, the more effort we can exert in pushing your | publication.

The listing of your publication in our price list has (2) considerable advertising value. In fact, a number of other | agencies make a charge for listing magazines in their price lists. | We ask nothing except a discount that will enable us to make | a fair margin of profit.

Most of the subscriptions we sell during our (3) regular fall and winter campaigns are upon the basis of a | 50 per cent discount from the regular rate.

As a result of our | successful efforts last year, we are making even greater plans for | selling subscriptions. Our staff of agents will be increased considerably. (4)

As the copy for our price list must be in the hands of the printer

| by July 1, we should appreciate it if you would return the | information sheet now. A self-addressed envelope for your convenience | in returning the sheet to us is enclosed. Your very sincerely, (5) (1.45)

16

Key: (1) Decided, effect, automobile, accidents, 50 per cent, last year, of course. (2) Against, insured, whether, they are, complete, policy, circumstances. (3) Difficulty, modest, one of the, economical. (4) Invest, membership, any one of the, until, weeks ago, lowered, feature. (5) Special, to our, foundation, personal, program, already, Very sincerely yours.

Dear Mr. Green: People are driving more these days. This increase in driving | has had a decided effect on the number of automobile | accidents, which have risen more than 50 per cent over last year. | Of course, automobiles are only one of the many causes of accidents (1) against which our members are insured. They are protected against | accidents from almost every cause whether they are at home, at | work, or at play. They are protected by a complete policy that | covers them under all circumstances.

You may wonder what a policy (2) that does so much for its members costs. The cost is very small; it | is so low that you will have no difficulty meeting payments, no matter | how modest your income. One of the reasons we are able to | keep the cost so low is our economical plan of operation. (3)

Now is a good time to invest in one of our policies. The small |

membership fee that you will pay on any one of the plans will cover you | until June of next year.

Just a few weeks ago we again lowered | the rates for the optional health insurance feature that we offer as (4) a special service to our members. You need this vital protection | as a foundation for your personal security program even | if you are already carrying some form of group insurance.

Apply | now, while the need for protection is so great. Very sincerely yours, (5) (1.46)

17

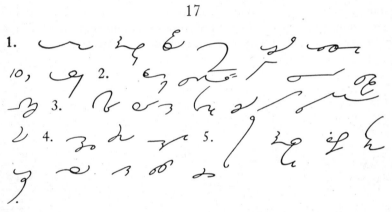

Key: (1) Longer, subscription, expired, Government, recently, requirements, 10 per cent, large. (2) Circulation, actually, down, amount, accept, in this way. (3) Devote, articles, because, we want, to do, editorial, further. (4) Consequently, fewer, newsstands. (5) Everybody, subscribers, hereafter, be sure, receiving, card, to us, without, Sincerely yours.

Dear Mr. Smith: I regret that we can no longer send you a copy | of the News Magazine. Your subscription expired last week.

As you may | know, the directors have recently ordered us to reduce our paper | requirements by 10 per cent. Because of the large increase in our (1) circulation, we shall actually have to use 30 per cent less | paper in each issue than we used last year.

Even before this reduction, | we had taken steps to save paper by cutting down the amount | of advertising we would accept. In this way we could continue to (2) devote the same amount of space to pictures and articles. We are | planning to accept even less advertising in the near future, because | the last thing we want to do is to reduce the number of | editorial pages. ✓

Even this further reduction of advertising (3) will not save as much paper as the directors' order requires. | Consequently, we shall have to print fewer copies of the News Magazine | each week.

That is why we cannot send you a copy of the News | Magazine this week. That is why the newsstands will not have enough copies (4) to satisfy everybody this year. That is why only | subscribers will hereafter be sure of receiving their copies. That is why | I am enclosing a stamped, addressed card for you to sign and return | to us and thus renew your subscription without delay. Sincerely yours, (5) (1.47)

18

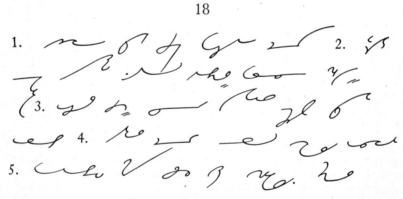

Key: (1) To call, attention, change, procedure, sometime. (2) Circumstances, impossible, to do so, handled, Treasury, premium, Washington. (3) Recently, Chicago, amount, temporarily, in a few days, items, releases. (4) Disregard, some of the, mailed, complete, records. (5) Please let us know, up to date, exactly, thank you for, co-operating, fully.

Gentlemen: The purpose of this letter is to call your attention | to a slight change in the usual procedure of sending you | material for promoting the sale of bonds. It was our hope that we could | send you several pieces of material sometime during the early (1) part of October. I regret to say that circumstances have | made it impossible for us to do so.

The actual work of sending | out all our releases is handled by the Treasury Mailing | Department. Because space is at a premium in Washington, this (2) Department was recently moved to Chicago. The great amount of | material and equipment that had to be moved has held up our mailing | operations temporarily.

We will send you, in a few days, | several items that you may regard as releases for your December (3) issue. Please disregard the fact that some of the items bear the | notation "For November magazines." The release for January | magazines will be mailed on or about December 1 so that it | will reach you in plenty of time.

So that we may complete our records, please (4) let us know what material you have used up to date and how much | you still have on hand. If you will let us know exactly what type of | material can best be used in your magazine, we will supply it. |

Thank you for co-operating with us so fully. Yours very truly, (5) (1.50)

19

Key: (1) Few minutes, prove, turning, point, we hope, industries, America, aviation. (2) To protect, country, especially, school, one of the, first. (3) Reputation, offer, advancement, correspondence, study, fundamentals. (4) Supervised, greatest, benefit, it is not, program. (5) Sending you, separate, booklet, entitled, in the future, post card, arrange, inspection.

Dear Mr. Brown: The few minutes it takes you to read this letter may | prove to be the turning point in your whole life. We hope, therefore, that you will | read it carefully from beginning to end.

Right now, one of the fastest-growing | industries in America is aviation. The demands (1) being placed on aviation are being increased every | day in order to protect our country. To meet these demands, aviation | needs men who are especially trained to fill the jobs now available. |

The School of Aviation was one of the first schools in the country (2) to offer a course in aviation. Its reputation is | known all over the country. The men it has trained are in well-paying jobs | that offer every opportunity for advancement.

Through the | use of our correspondence course, you may study the fundamentals of (3) aviation during your spare time. Your study is supervised so | that you may be sure to receive the greatest benefit from the time you | spend in study.

It is not possible to discuss fully in a | letter all the features of the program we offer. We are taking the (4) liberty of sending you under separate cover our booklet | entitled "Aviation in the Future." After you have read the booklet, | return the post card that is enclosed with it, and we will arrange | an inspection trip to our airport at your convenience. Yours truly, (5) (1.50)

20

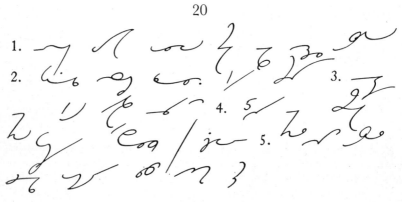

Key: (1) Encouraging, automobile, record, you have not been, in the past, consequently, entitled. (2) Policy, carefully, selecting, $1, victim. (3) Misfortune, injured, $100, disabled, medical. (4) $5,000, injury, available, provided, application, judge, whether or not. (5) Continue, entirely, simply, refunded, without, to keep, force.

Dear Friend: We are vitally interested in encouraging safe | automobile driving. If your record shows that you have not been in an | accident in the past twelve months, you are a careful automobile | driver. Consequently, you are entitled to apply for our new (1) accident policy.

Our experience has been that, by carefully | selecting those whom we insure, we can give the most protection at | a rate as low at $1 a month.

No matter how careful a driver | you are, you may be the victim of an accident. If such a (2) misfortune occurs and you are injured, your policy will do many | things for you.

It will give you $100 a month beginning on | the first day that you are disabled.

It will pay you $5 a | day for forty-two days for medical expenses.

It will pay (3) $5,000 to your family in case you suffer a fatal injury. |

This policy is available to you for $1 a | month provided your application reaches our office by September | 28. When your policy comes, judge for yourself whether or not (4) you wish to continue this type of protection. If you are not entirely | satisfied, simply return the policy and your money will | be refunded without question. I am confident though that, after you | have read the policy, you will want to keep it in force. Yours truly, (5) (1.50)

PART II

60 WORDS A MINUTE

21

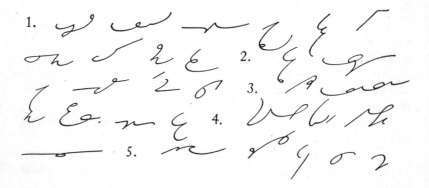

Key: (1) Recently, learned, mutual, to build, possible, down, I am sure, wanted, if you are, people. (2) Probably, lifetime, to be sure, modern, transform, attention. (3) Decision, literature, explaining, instruct, proper. (4) Ventilation, bothered, drafts, minimum. (5) To call, estimate, postage, act, comfort.

Dear Miss Jones: I recently learned from a mutual friend that you are planning to build | a new house in the near future in White Plains. I wish it were possible for me to | sit down and talk with you about it. I am sure I could make many suggestions that | would make your new house the "dream house" that you have always wanted.

If you are like most people, (1) this will probably be the only house you will build during your lifetime. Consequently, | you will want to be sure that it has all the modern features that transform an | ordinary house into a real home.

One of the matters to which you should give careful | attention is the type of windows you will install. Before you reach a final (2)

24

decision on that matter, I hope you will take time to read the litera-
ture that | I have enclosed explaining Johnson windows. After you
have read this literature, | I am confident that you will instruct your
builder to install Johnson windows in | your new home. These win-
dows will insure that your home will have plenty of light and proper
(3) ventilation. They are easy to open and close. When they are
closed, you can be sure | that no air will leak into the house. During
the winter you will not be bothered by | drafts caused by faulty
windows. This will help you keep your heating costs at a minimum. |

Johnson windows are reasonably priced. If you will let me know
what time would be (4) convenient for me to call, I shall be happy
to go over the plans of your house with | you and make an estimate
on the cost of installing our windows. A card is enclosed | for your
convenience in letting me know when I may call. It needs no postage.

Act | now and insure yourself of window comfort in your new
home. Very sincerely yours, (5) (1.32)

22

Key: (1) Itself, especially, proud, mother, daughter, quite, some
time, Europe, in spite. (2) Careful, somehow, to sail, disturbed, porter,
possibly, however. (3) Immediately, touch, officials, steamship, anything, earnestly, one of the, therefore, rush. (4) Down, farewell, aboard,
proceeded, started, years ago. (5) Adopted, confident, agree, we are
sure, anxious, to serve you.

Dear Mr. West: The Johnson Hotel has always prided itself on the service it | gives its guests. We are especially proud of the service we were able to render | to a mother and daughter who recently stayed with us.

For quite some time they had planned | a trip to Europe and finally were able to arrange it. But, in spite of (1) all their careful planning, they somehow forgot the hour on which their ship was to sail. | Consequently, both mother and daughter were greatly disturbed when the porter told them that | at that very moment their ship was pulling out and that they could not possibly catch | it before it left. The porter, however, decided to report the case to Mr. (2) Smith, the manager, who immediately got in touch with the officials | of the steamship company and asked if anything could be done. He talked so earnestly | that the officials relaxed their rules and agreed to supply a tug to take the mother | and daughter to the ship. One of the members of our staff was, therefore, called to rush (3) the mother and daughter to the tug. There he helped them down to the deck of the little | tug and waved them farewell as the boat rushed away. They caught the ship down the bay and went | aboard and proceeded on their journey, which would never have started without the help | of our staff.

Service is our business. When our first hotel was opened many years ago, (4) we adopted as our motto, "The guest must be served." We have tried to live up to | that motto ever since.

We are confident that you will agree that those guests were well | served. We are sure, too, that when you visit our hotel you will find our entire staff | as anxious to serve you as they served that mother and daughter. Very sincerely yours, (5) (1.34)

23

Let 5. ⸺ ⸺ ⸻ ⸻ ⸻ ⸻ ⸻

Key: (1) October, to turn, attention, Christmas, we want, special, offering. (2) Subscription, at this time, withdrawn, careful, world, alive, find. (3) Rushed, last-minute, season, for your convenience, listed, renewal. (4) Mailman, beautiful, announcement, we are sure, friends. (5) More and more, succeeding, pleasure, we hope, grand.

Dear Sir: Even though it is only October, we are going to ask you to turn | your attention for a moment to Christmas.

We want to tell you that, if you place your | Christmas gift order for the News Weekly early, you can take advantage of a special | rate we are offering our old subscribers.

This rate is $3.50 (1) a year—a saving of $1 on every new subscription you send us at | this time.

This special rate will be withdrawn three weeks before Christmas.

We want to give your | gift order—and every order—the most careful and exact attention. But world | events today make people so alive to the news that they find in the News Weekly (2) that we fear we may be rushed with last-minute orders if the special rate should still be | open at the height of the Christmas season.

For your convenience, we have listed | your last year's gift orders on the enclosed order form. You need make only a check mark | next to each subscription in order to enter its renewal. On the back of the (3) form is a space where you can enter additional gifts at the same $3.50 | rate.

Just before Christmas the mailman will deliver a beautiful announcement | card to your friends saying that you are sending him or her the next fifty-two issues | of the News Weekly as your Christmas gift.

We are sure your friends have valued your gifts (4) of the News Weekly more and more with each succeeding week. We know that they have received | much pleasure from having a gift that everyone has talked about and asked to borrow. |

We hope, too, that you will always be glad and perhaps a little proud that you were among | those who discovered what a grand Christmas present the News Weekly makes. Yours truly, (5) (1.34)

24

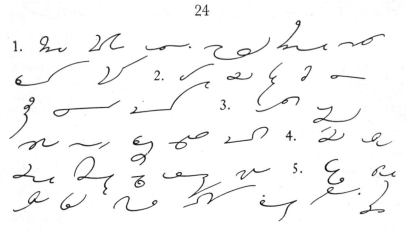

Key: (1) As you know, fountain pen, recurring, complaint, everyone else, contact, seldom, founded. (2) Ordinary, word, possible, usually, ink, excessive, amount, sometimes. (3) Indication, refilled, cure,
corrected, surface, naturally, some of this. (4) Transferred, writer, fin-
gers, develops, inside, removed, water. (5) Properly, users, entire,
point, this letter, at this time, helpful, dealing, Very sincerely yours.

Dear Mr. Brown: As you know, in the fountain-pen business
there is one constantly | recurring complaint from customers and
salesmen and everyone else coming in contact | with the sale or the
use of fountain pens. That complaint is that the pen leaks.

This complaint | is seldom well founded. I have never known
a fountain pen to leak in the (1) ordinary sense of the word. It is
no more possible for a pen to leak than it | is for a cork to sink
in water.

Usually, when the supply of ink inside | the pen gets low, the
ink will flow too fast and an excessive amount will gather on | the
point. This excess sometimes drops off the pen as it is being used.
This excess on the (2) point is an indication that the pen needs to
be refilled, not that it leaks. Refilling | will cure the trouble.

If this excess flow is not corrected quickly, the excess | ink may
flow into the cap of the pen when the pen is laid down. In this way,
the inside | surface of the cap will be covered with ink. Naturally,
some of this ink will (3) be transferred to the grip section of the

pen. When the writer grasps this section, his fingers | will be stained by this ink. When this condition develops, the ink from the inside | of the cap must be removed. This can easily be done by rinsing out the cap of | the pen with water.

Many complaints of leaking arise from the fact that the pen is (4) never properly filled. Pen users sometimes do not understand that, to fill the fountain | pen, the entire point must be placed in the ink.

I am writing this letter to | you at this time with the thought that it may be helpful to you both in the care and use | of your own fountain pen and in dealing with customers. Very sincerely yours, (5) (1.34)

(25)

Key: (1) Next year, interested, reasons, almost, according, apparently, alone. (2) Gone, 40 per cent, some time ago, very much, future, considerably, during the past year. (3) Turnover, rapid, guarantee. (4) Selecting, measurements, perfectly, it is not, to do. (5) Deposit, balance, completed, prefer, extra, Very cordially yours.

Dear Mrs. Adams: Have you been thinking about getting a new fur coat next year? If you | have, you will be interested in the following reasons why you should buy it | at once:

Almost every week the price of raw furs is increasing. According to | present trends, there is apparently no price limit in view. Within the past year alone (1) the prices of some types of furs have gone up more than 40 per cent.

We now have | on hand a supply of fine furs that were purchased some time ago, when prices of furs | were much lower than they are today. The furs that we will purchase in the future will | cost considerably more.

During the past year our sales have increased over 200 (2) per cent. Consequently, our turnover is very rapid; and therefore we cannot | guarantee the length of time that our present stock of furs will last. To take advantage | of our present prices, you will have to act quickly. This letter is going out | to our five thousand charge-account customers; and, unless you act soon, you may be (3) disappointed.

By selecting your furs now, while our staff of tailors is not so busy, | you can have a coat made to your individual measurements. Your coat will be given | painstaking care so that it will fit you perfectly.

It is not necessary | to pay in full for your coat at this time. All you have to do is pay a 20 per (4) cent deposit and the balance when the coat is completed. If you prefer, you may | take advantage of our easy-payment plan, which will give you ten months to complete payment. | After your fur coat is completed, we will put it in cold storage without any extra | charge and deliver it to you in the fall. Very cordially yours, (5) (1.37)

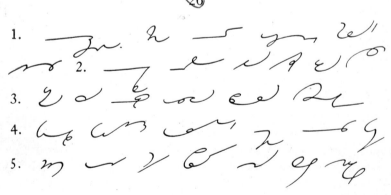

Key: (1) Manufacturing, assure, more than, resignation, friendship, together. (2) Manager, until, it is not, decision, was not, to make. (3) Offered, I want, myself, record, excellent, development. (4) Policies, products, leadership, in the future, many of the, proved. (5)

Successful, worked, forward, appointed, count, wherever, co-operation.

Dear Jack: This is my last day with the Smith Manufacturing Company. This does not | mean that you will not hear from me again. I assure you that you will hear from me often. | It would take more than a letter of resignation to end the friendship that has | grown between us during the years we have worked together. This is, however, the last (1) letter I shall write you as sales manager of the Smith Manufacturing Company. |

I have waited until my last day to write this letter because it is not an | easy letter to write. The decision to leave the Smith Manufacturing Company | was not an easy one to make. But I could not pass up the opportunity (2) that was offered me—a position as vice-president in charge of sales and advertising | of the Johnson Motor Company.

That is all I want to say about myself. | Now I want to talk about you. Your record of sales has been excellent. It has | matched the development of the company. We all agree that this development (3) can be traced to the policies of Mr. Smith. During the years of depression, Mr. | Smith brought out new products and opened up new markets to you. That new business helped | you and helped the company to come through the depression in good shape. You can rely | on that same type of leadership in the future.

Many of the sales plans that proved so (4) successful during the past few years were worked out by Fred Gray. Fred is taking a | well-deserved step forward—he has been appointed the new sales manager. You can count on | him to help wherever you feel that two heads are better than one. Fred deserves your full | co-operation. I know that I can count on you to give it to him. Yours truly, (5) (1.37)

27

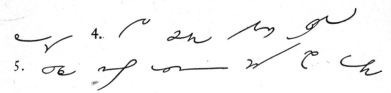

Key: (1) Thank you for your, concerning, automobile, figures, various, card, indicates, unjust. (2) Quotation, refused, regardless, absolutely, unless. (3) Interests, reports, capable, Springfield, include, district, liberty, he will understand. (4) To know, we are sure, discuss, entitled. (5) Answer, you may have, recommend, suited, we hope, pleasure.

Dear Mr. Adams: Thank you for your inquiry of August 15 concerning | automobile insurance and asking for figures on the various types of policies | we offer.

Your card indicates that you do not want an agent to call on you. | We are sorry, but we cannot be so unjust either to you or to our agent. (1) There is more to the purchase of insurance than the mere quotation of a price. We | have always refused to sell insurance blindly; and, frankly, we do not think you would | buy it, regardless of the price quoted.

An insurance policy is absolutely | no good unless you need it; and, if you need it, you also need the agent. He (2) is the person who looks after your interests and helps make out your reports in case | of loss.

We have some very capable men located in Springfield, including our | district manager, John Shields. We are taking the liberty of sending your card to | him. If you do not want to see him when he calls, just tell him so. He will understand. (3) I want you to know, however, Mr. Adams, that our agents are not high-pressure | salesmen. Mr. Shields is such a fine fellow that we are sure you will be glad to know | him, whether you discuss insurance with him or not. He is a regular fellow | and we think you are, too.

Just ask him to show you the sheet entitled "You and Your (4) Automobile." That tells the whole story. He will be glad to answer any questions you | may have about our insurance and also to recommend the policy that he | feels will be best suited to your needs.

Again, thank you for your interest, Mr. | Adams; we hope that we may have the pleasure of serving you in the near future. Yours truly, (5) (1.38)

28

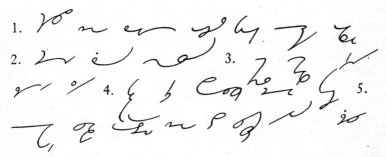

Key: (1) Fortunately, one of our, years ago, recently, porch, moved, repairs. (2) Forgot, healed, climbed. (3) Injury, compensation, $1,000, extended, include. (4) Possibility, choose, application, sums, benefit. (5) Membership, accept, let us know, one of our, assist, advice, don't, hesitate.

Dear Mr. Stone: This is a tale about two toes and how Mr. Smith received | $1,000.

Mr. Smith, who fortunately purchased one of our policies several | years ago, recently broke a toe in a fall from his porch. The porch steps had been | moved while some repairs were being made; and, in his haste one day to catch a train, Mr. (1) Smith forgot. The broken toe laid him up for four weeks, and he received $200 | because he carried a policy calling for $50 weekly benefits | in case of accident.

One day, before Mr. Smith's broken toe was completely | healed, he climbed on a chair to open a window. His foot slipped and he fell again, breaking (2) another toe. It took four months for this injury to heal; and he was paid | $800, bringing his total compensation to $1,000.

Since Mr. | Smith took out his policy, the protection has been extended to include many | other benefits, as shown in the list enclosed with this letter. Perhaps you will (3) not have the same trouble that Mr. Smith had, but there is always the possibility | that you will be the victim of some other type of accident.

Play safe; choose the | insurance plan that best fits your needs, and return your application today. You do | not have to invest large sums of money in order to benefit by this plan. All (4) you do is pay the membership fee of $3 when we accept your application. |

If you are not sure of the plan that would be most satisfactory for you, let | us know and we shall be happy to send one of our representatives to assist | you and give you any advice he can.

Don't hesitate; act now. Very truly yours, (5) (1.40)

29

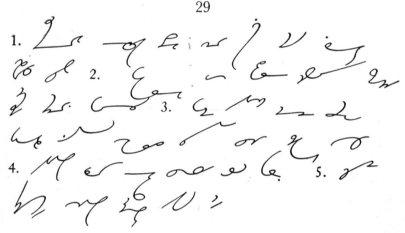

Key: (1) Several months, might be, assistance, one of the, who have been, found, helpful, we hope that the, ideas. (2) Problems, of course, experiment, started, as a result, sufficient, for one thing, permanent. (3) Person, discuss, someone, finger, policies, handled, completely, editor, another, establish, gather. (4) Distribute, certain, must be able, accurate, third, bringing. (5) We do not, justified, contribute, subscription, depend, support.

Dear Friend: For several months this magazine has been placed on your desk free of charge, with the | hope that it might be of some assistance to you in your work.

You may be one of the | many businessmen who have been good enough to write us, telling us that they have found | it helpful. In any case, we hope that the magazine has given you some ideas (1) and helped you solve some of your business problems.

The Business Monthly is, of course, an | experiment. We have kept close watch on this experiment since it started, and as a | result we are convinced of this: We are not rendering sufficient service to meet | the needs of our readers.

For one thing, we need a permanent reporter who can meet (2) you and talk to you in person, who can discuss with you your everyday business | problems. We need someone who can keep his finger on the policies of the mail-order | business. This is a full-time job that cannot be handled completely by your | editor.

For another thing, we must establish a number of departments to gather (3) and distribute information on certain problems that are common to all of us. | These departments must be able to give you accurate answers to questions that grow | out of your everyday business transactions.

In the third place, we need some method of | bringing before our readers each month samples of the most effective mailing pieces (4) issued during the month.

All these things cost money, money that we do not feel | justified in asking our advertisers to contribute.

Therefore, from now on The Business | Monthly will be sold on a subscription basis of $2 for twelve issues. We | know we can depend on you to support us in our new policy. Yours very truly, (5) (1.40)

30

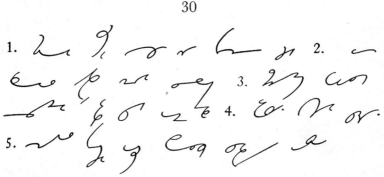

Key: (1) False, savings, gather, other, become, situation. (2) Of course, salary, disabled, one of those, emergencies. (3) If you do not have, protection, medicines, special, attention, reason. (4) Operating, dividends, outstanding. (5) Country, benefits, receive, application, accepted, entire.

Dear Mr. Lynch: Do you realize that by one false step you can use up all the savings | it took you years to gather? If you fall and break an arm, for example, you may | have heavy medical expenses as well as other expenses that always go | hand in hand with an accident. If you become sick, the same situation is, of (1) course, true.

Even if you work for a salary and your income does not stop when you | are disabled, you will find that you will have to dip into your savings. If you are | one of those who must use almost their entire income to live from day to day, with | no opportunity to save for emergencies, you are the one who needs insurance (2) protection most. If you do not have insurance protection, you may run into | debt or you may have to have poor medical care when you need the best. Very often | the cost of medicines will be high, or you may need special attention for one reason | or another—and all this costs money.

By dealing direct with our members, we (3) are able to give them more insurance for their money than any other leading | insurance company can. Operating in this way, we have no heavy sales costs | and we have no dividends to pay. Our organization, which has been in business | for more than fifty-five years and is, at the present time, one of the outstanding (4) insurance companies in the country, provides insurance at cost. Read the list of | benefits that you will receive on the enclosed application blank. Fill out the blank and | send it in today.

If your application is accepted now, the membership fee | will cover the entire cost of your protection until September. Cordially yours, (5) (1.41)

31

1. [shorthand outline]
2. [shorthand outline]

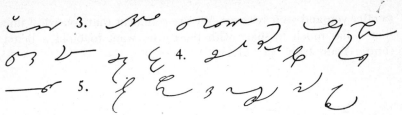

Key: (1) Florida, message, already, appeared, some of the, in the future, wonderful. (2) Sunshine, rest, troubles, thousands, people, week or two, sometimes, overlooked. (3) Industry, agriculture, investors, large, capital, attractions, furthermore, sensible, property. (4) Exempts, taxation, valuation, many other. (5) It has been, I hope you will, yourself, you will find, who want, to build.

Dear Friend: Florida has so much it can share with you that the state has decided to | publish messages from time to time to tell you the good news. Several of these | messages have already appeared in some of the country's leading magazines, and more | will appear in the future.

Most people think of Florida as a wonderful (1) vacation spot, where they can take advantage of the sunshine and enjoy a rest from their | business troubles. True, Florida is a wonderful vacation spot, where each year thousands | upon thousands of people spend a week or two or more. But a fact that sometimes | is overlooked is that Florida is also a land of great opportunity (2) for industry, for agriculture, and for business. It provides many opportunities | for investors, both large and small, to put their capital to work.

Florida | has many attractions as a place to live in and to work in. Furthermore, it has | enacted sensible laws that protect your interests and your property. You see, (3) Florida has no state income tax, no state sales tax, and no state tax on land or houses. | Florida also exempts from taxation the first $5,000 of the | valuation of your home.

I could mention many other tax laws that have attracted | people from all parts of the country, but it would take too much time to go into (4) them all.

It has been said that to live in Florida is to enjoy fifty-two | vacations a year—one for every week.

I hope you will come soon and see for yourself | what Florida has to offer you and your business. We are confident that you will | find that it has much to share with those who want to build a better future. Yours truly, (5) (1.41)

32

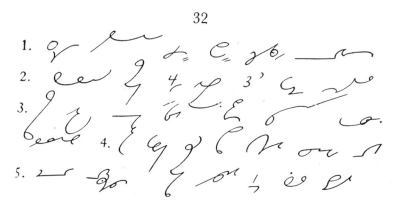

Key: (1) I understand, dealer, Chicago, April, we decided, months ago. (2) I learned, average, 4,000, traveling, three cents, person, country. (3) I have been able, to spend, impossible, transportation, expect, attempted, lining, territories. (4) Prestige, favorably, I believe, dividends, announced, intention. (5) Some of the, enthusiastic, doubts, 100 per cent, hardly, assistants.

Dear Mr. Gates: Our purchasing agent has today sent you our order No. | 3165 for six Johnson airplanes, which I understand you will deliver through your | dealer here in Chicago by the first of April. All six are to have the special | motors that we decided upon when I spoke to you some months ago when we first (1) considered airplanes for our men.

Since I learned to fly last June, I have covered an | average of almost 4,000 miles a month, traveling alone and with other men | of our organization at a cost of about three cents a mile a person. This | flying was done all over the country in several different airplanes. In those (2) 4,000 miles I have been able to spend considerable time in twenty-two | different states, which would have been impossible with any other means of transportation. |

With our fleet of Johnsons we expect to do a lot of the things we have never | before attempted in the way of lining up dealers in new territories. (3) I have found that the added prestige of making our calls in an airplane has had some | influence in getting dealers to consider our line favorably. If this | continues to be true, and I believe it will, our organization will reap rich | dividends from the airplanes that we are purchasing.

When I announced our intention to (4) use airplanes, some of the men were not too enthusiastic. They did not think they could | learn to fly and had some doubts about the success of this plan. Our men are now 100 | per cent sold on your airplanes and can hardly wait for us to get them here.

I am | grateful for your assistance in getting this program started for us. Yours sincerely, (5) (1.41)

33

Key: (1) Woods, entered, mind, biggest, seldom, person, to know. (2) Others, almost, he must understand, he must be able, co-operation, friendship, years ago. (3) Determined, to find, people, qualities, investigated, world's, men and women, results. (4) Pamphlets, why not, everything, let us, approval. (5) Profit, wealth, description, comments.

Dear Mr. Woods: What makes people successful? That question has probably entered the | mind of every human being who is interested in getting ahead.

Dealing | with people is probably the biggest problem that we all have to face. There seldom | has been a time when it was more important for a person to know how to get (1) along with others than the present time.

If a person is to be successful in almost | any business, he must know how to get along with people. He must be understanding | and be able to adapt his thinking to their thinking. He must be able | to win their co-operation and their friendship.

Six years ago our organization (2) determined to find out what makes people successful. We decided to find out | why one person is more successful than another, what qualities he has that others | have not. Our staff has investigated the lives of more than five hundred of the | world's most famous men and women. The results of this investigation were written (3) up in a series of fifty-two pamphlets. In these pamphlets, everything that played a | part in the success of those five hundred people is taken up. The cost of the | fifty-two pamphlets is $3.

Why not let us send you these pamphlets at once so that | you can examine them on approval? After you have received them, keep them for fifteen (4) days. If you feel that you will profit by them, mail us your check for $3. If | you feel that they do not contain a wealth of information that you need, just return | them.

A complete description of these pamphlets is given in the enclosed folder. In | it you will also find comments of people who have profited by them. Yours truly, (5) (1.42)

34

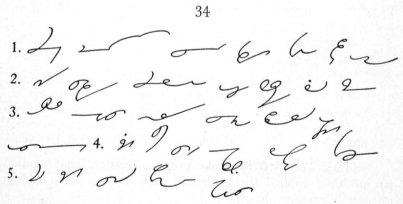

Key: (1) Very much, some time ago, amount, past due, better, exception, rule. (2) Your order, accepted, familiar, receipt, arrived, heard, assume. (3) Entirely, mistake, credit, I am sure, excellent, reputation, recommendation. (4) Hesitation, however, acknowledged, embarrassing, elapsed, became. (5) Further, extension, account, I hope you will not, to protect.

Dear Mr. Pace: You pleased us very much some time ago when you sent us your order| for $142 worth of our goods. You can please us again by sending | us a remittance for that amount, which is now long past due. Everybody | feels better when bills are paid, and I know that you are not an exception to the rule. (1)

When your order came, it was accepted on the basis of our regular terms, with | which we know you are familiar. The goods were shipped the day that the order was received, | and we have a receipt showing that they arrived at your factory on January | 16. As we have not heard from you since that time, we naturally assume that (2) the goods arrived in first-class condition and that you found them entirely | satisfactory.

There could be no mistake in granting you credit, I am sure, because you | have an excellent reputation in every way. The people to whom we wrote | when you first asked for credit gave you such a fine recommendation that we had no (3) hesitation in granting you almost unlimited credit.

The fact, | however, that you have not paid this long-overdue bill or even acknowledged any of our | letters asking for payment places us in a very embarrassing situation. |

Because of the time that has elapsed since your bill became due, we cannot permit (4) a further extension; and, unless we have a prompt payment or a reply explaining | your delay in paying, we shall have to place your account with our Legal Department. |

I hope you will not force us to take this action. A check for $142 | is all that is necessary to protect your credit standing. Yours truly, (5) (1.42)

35

[shorthand outlines: 3. 4. 5.]

Key: (1) Interested, mailed, Christmas, went, years ago, amount. (2) Toward, critical, period, earnings, occasion, to profit, policy, previous. (3) Twice, extra, become, economical. (4) To share, two hundred thousand, carry, anybody, eligible, thousands, businessmen. (5) Further, representative, indicate.

Dear Mr. White: You will be interested in the story of Mr. Smith, who mailed | his Christmas cards and received $5,450. /0,460

There was ice by | the mailbox where Mr. Smith went to post his cards for his friends more than two years ago. | He fell and broke his leg. At $50 a week the amount he received from us (1) was $5,200. He also received $250 | toward the cost of his doctor's fees. This money helped tide Mr. Smith over a very | critical period of reduced earnings and added expenses

Mr. Smith has had | occasion to profit by his policy with us on seven previous occasions. (2) Five times he was the victim of accidents in his own home. Twice he needed operations | that kept him from work for a considerable period.

If an extra | income would be a help to you, should you meet with an accident or become ill, play | safe and provide for that income now. The most economical way to insure that (3) extra income is to share your risk with more than two hundred thousand members who carry | our insurance policies.

A new member's first regular payment is due ten | weeks after the time he joins. Anybody from eighteen to fifty-five is eligible | for this policy. Thousands of businessmen who have occasion to travel (4) are on our lists.

Fill out the enclosed application blank, and we will see to it that | you receive further information. If you would care to have our representative | call to see you, just indicate the time and place that would be most satisfactory | and he will be there. There will, of course, be no obligation on your part. Yours truly, (5) (1.44)

36

Key: (1) Recently, application, enable you, to us, wondering, whether. (2) During the last, thousands, small, arrangements, privacy, without, necessity. (3) Organization, assured, absolute, knowledge, transaction, obligation. (4) Inquiries, courteous, if you wish, privilege, one time, actual. (5) $300, assistance, you will have, booklet, complete, 12/10 charges.

Dear Mr. Brown: We recently sent you information about our vacation loan | plan. We also sent you an application blank that would enable you to take | advantage of this service.

As you have not returned the application blank to us, we | are wondering whether there is some additional information we can give you (1) about this plan.

During the last forty years our organization has financed thousands | of people like you during the summer months, at which time their income is small. Our | plan enables you to make all the necessary arrangements for a loan in the | privacy of your own home. All the details can be made by mail without the necessity (2) of your making a trip to our office.

When you borrow from our organization, | you are assured of absolute confidence as no one outside our office | will have any knowledge of your transaction with us. By filling out our application | blank, you are placed under no obligation unless the loan is completed and (3) you receive the money. We make no inquiries that may be embarrassing to you. |

Our service is quick and courteous. You may arrange to take as long as twenty payments | to retire your loan if you wish. On the other hand, you have the privilege of repaying | the entire loan at one time. Our charges are based on the actual time (4) that you use the money.

If a loan of $50 to $300 will | be of assistance to you for the summer months, fill out the application blank and | return it to us. In a matter of days you will have the cash.

We are enclosing | a booklet that gives complete information about our service and charges. Yours truly, (5) (1.45)

(37)

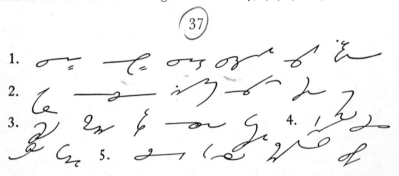

Key: (1) American, Minneapolis, announces, accidents, in addition, hospital. (2) To bring, men and women, who do not have, medical, feature, injured. (3) Confined, as a result, special, minor, provides. (4) $1,000, family, entire, persons. (5) Examination, post card, if you would like, attached.

Dear Mr. Blair: The American Insurance Company of Minneapolis | announces a new plan of insurance that pays $25 a week for ten | weeks for both accidents and illness. In addition, it will pay $25 | a week for four weeks for accidents that confine you to the hospital. The purpose (1) of this new policy is to bring protection within the reach of men and women | who do not have large savings with which to meet sudden medical expenses.

This new | plan also has a feature that covers accidents that occur while you are traveling. | You receive $50 a week if you are injured while riding in a bus (2) or a train and $75 a week if you are confined to the hospital | as a result of that accident. There is another special clause that pays | up to $25 for doctors' bills, even for a minor accident such | as a cut finger. The plan provides for all types of accidents.

In case of your death (3) as a result of an accident, the policy pays $1,000 to | your family. It pays $2,000 if your death occurs as a result | of an accident while you are traveling.

The entire cost is only $12 | a year for men and women from sixteen to sixty-nine. For persons between the (4) ages of sixty-nine and seventy-five, the cost is only $15 a | year. No medical examination is required.

If you would like to have details on | this new plan, write us a letter or a post card, asking for our special booklet. | The booklet is free; and no obligation is attached to it. Very truly yours, (5) (1.45)

38

Key: (1) Looking, who can be, represent, at least, industrial, forced, employment, beyond. (2) Curtail, however, finds, becoming, more and more, demand, assumption, position. (3) Judge, standards, to select, considerable, workshops, we want, to understand. (4) Thoroughly, they will be able, effectively, desirable, to build, profitable, $7,000. (5) Personality, acquired, interview.

Dear Mr. Trees: We are looking for a man who can be trained to represent our | organization in New York City. We prefer a man who has had at least four years of | experience in selling to industrial plants.

Today many fine salesmen are | being forced to look for other employment because of conditions beyond their control. (1) Many business organizations are being forced to curtail their sales efforts | because, due to shortages, they cannot obtain materials. Our organization, | however, finds that its services are becoming more and more in demand.

We | are writing to you on the assumption that a man in your position is a good (2) judge of the type of man who would meet our high standards and that you would probably know | of some man who is looking for a better opportunity. We try to select | our men carefully. Once they have been employed, we go to considerable expense | in training them at our workshops and in the field. We want our men to understand our (3) business thoroughly so that they will be able to serve our customers | effectively.

The position we now have open is a desirable one. It offers | an opportunity for a hard-working man to build up a profitable | business paying $4,000 to $7,000 a year net.

In general, (4) we find that the type of man who makes the best success in our business is | married, has a pleasing personality, and has acquired good work habits. If you know | of such a man, please call his attention to this letter if you care to do so. Send | us his name, and we will arrange an interview with our sales manager. Yours truly, (5) (1.48)

39

Key: (1) Young, friend, quotation, spoken, anywhere, obviously, possible, collect, two thousand. (2) They are, furthermore, represent, gathered, to provide, editors, a thousand, foreign, selected, arranged, subject matter. (3) Edited, especially, people, called, various, preparation, ideas. (4) Speeches, discussions, easily, judge, nothing else, on the market. (5) It has been, kind, acquaint, attached.

Dear Mr. Young: A friend recently wrote us that he thought the Magazine of Quotations | must bring him every good story that is printed or spoken anywhere. |

Obviously, that is not possible. This year, however, the Magazine of Quotations | will collect more than two thousand such items. They will be brought to you each week while (1) they are new and fresh. Furthermore, those items will represent the best stories that are | gathered each month.

To provide this service, our editors look into every new | book that is published. They read more than a thousand American and foreign newspapers | and magazines. All the best items are selected and arranged by subject matter (2) so that you can find a story to fit almost any situation.

The | Magazine of Quotations is edited especially for people who are called upon | to make speeches before various groups but whose time for the preparation of | their speeches is limited. The Magazine of Quotations supplies you with ideas (3) for speeches or discussions that you can easily apply to the particular | occasion, when you are called upon to speak.

You cannot judge the Magazine of | Quotations by any other magazine. There is nothing else like it on the market. | The Magazine of Quotations was first published in 1929, and since that (4) time it has been the only magazine of its kind.

The Magazine of Quotations | costs $5 a year. To acquaint you with the magazine, however, we are making | a special offer of twenty-six issues for only $2. Use the attached | form in taking advantage of this special offer. Very sincerely yours, (5) (1.56)

40

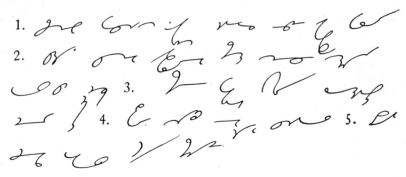

Key: (1) Exactness, practical, handbook, strongly, anyone, to pre-pare, printed. (2) Outstanding, against, disappointments, effects, command, consultant, layout, sketch. (3) Advertisement, proportion, devoted, illustrations, some of the, suggestions. (4) Expert, continuously, misunderstandings, actually. (5) Assistants, simply, reply, forwarded, if you do not.

Dear Mr. Clark: In the advertising and publishing business there is a need for | exactness in detail that will save time, labor, and materials. That is why a | practical book like the "Advertising Handbook" is more strongly a "must" than ever | before for anyone who is called upon to prepare printed material.

This (1) outstanding book is real insurance against disappointments in getting the effects | you desire with the money at your command. The author, who is an experienced | art consultant, offers simple, effective ways to build a finished layout from a | small sketch. His book shows how to arrange units so that every detail in the (2) advertisement is in proper proportion. There is a section especially | devoted to how to indicate type and how to place illustrations.

Some of the most | successful advertising men today are using the suggestions given in the | "Advertising Handbook." In following the author's suggestions, you do not have to (3) be an expert advertising man in order to get the effects you have in mind. |

The ideas he sets forth will continuously save time and money, prevent | misunderstandings in preparing printed material, and help make plain to others how | you wish it prepared.

But you must actually see the "Advertising Handbook" to (4) judge how helpful it can be to you and to your assistants. Once you have seen the book, | we know that you will not wish to be without it. Simply fill out and mail the reply | card that is enclosed, and the book will be forwarded at once. Look it over; then | send us $3, or return the book if you do not care to keep it. Yours truly, (5) (1.56)

PART III

70 WORDS A MINUTE

41

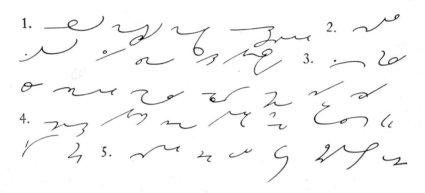

Key: (1) Mailed, you will find, you will be able, manufacturers. (2) Country, handled, include, useless, to us, described. (3) A gallon, freight, why not, colors, complete, uncertain, in the future, your order, c.o.d. (4) Instructions, discuss, one of our, drop, under no, obligation, P.S., short time, furnish. (5) Containers, as soon as, although, prove, if you would like to have, reason.

Dear Mr. James: The paint book that you asked us to send you was mailed yesterday.

If you will follow | the suggestions in that paint book, you will find that you will be able to save a good deal of money | on your paint bills.

As you look through the pages of the book, you will notice that you will not have to | pay high prices to get the best paint.

Our paint is made for us by one of the best-known paint manufacturers (1) in the country. The paint you buy is handled only once in its journey from the | manufacturer to you. Selling expense is very low. The price you pay does not include any useless | handling costs. The saving that is brought about by this method of handling paint is passed on to you. |

For your house, it occurs to us that you would be interested in the paint described on page 16 (2) of the paint book. This paint costs $3 a gallon, and we pay the freight charges.

Why not select the paint | you need and order it today while our stock of all colors is still complete? Because of | uncertain conditions, we cannot be sure that we shall be able to get all colors in the | future. You do not have to send money with your order. We shall be glad to ship your paint c.o.d. You (3) will find complete instructions for ordering on page 2.

If you feel that you would like to discuss | your paint problems with one of our men and have him estimate how much paint you will need, just drop us a | card telling on what date he should call. There is no charge for this service, and it places you under | no obligation. Cordially yours,

P.S. For a short time we can still furnish your paint in metal (4) containers. These metal containers will not be available as soon as our present supply is | gone. A new type container will then be placed in use; and, although it will prove satisfactory, we | are afraid it may not stand up so well as the metal one. If you would like to have your paint in | metal containers, that is another reason why you should hurry in sending us your order. (5) (1.28)

42

Key: (1) I hope you will not, indifferent, your letter, I should like to have, has not yet, replied, hardly. (2) Neglected, studies, except, apparently, personally, in a few days. (3) Advise, I want, develop, utmost. (4) Surprised, courage, to know, bitterness, toward, refused, admit, schoolwork, progress, rapidly. (5) Ability, fullest, extent, wisest, to do, assist, locating, any time, in the future, hesitate.

Dear Mrs. Post: I hope you will not think that I have been indifferent to your letter in | regard to your son John. The main reason for my delay in answering your letter is that I wrote to | Mr. Smith and Mr. Green. I told them that I should like to have their opinions in this matter. |

Mr. Smith has not yet replied to my letter. Mr. Green said he hardly knew what to write about (1) John. His opinion is that John has been interested in art but has neglected his other | studies. He said that John has failed in all subjects except art during the past two years. He said that John | apparently cannot see the importance of anything outside of art. Mr. Green said that | he liked John personally and would be glad to help him in any way that he can. In a few days, (2) Mr. Green will write to John giving him advice in regard to his studies.

I hardly know how | to advise you about John. I am fond of the boy, and I want to give him the right kind of advice | at this time. I think that, if he were my boy, I should put him in an art school where he could | develop that fine talent of his to the utmost.

I deeply regret that Davis College would not receive (3) him, but I am not at all surprised. I shall write John today telling him to keep up his courage. | I believe that he will, and it gives me real pleasure to know that he has not shown any bitterness | toward the college authorities that have refused to admit him. I am sure the authorities | did what they believed to be right.

I am confident that John's schoolwork will progress rapidly once he (4) is placed in a special school where his ability for art can be utilized to the fullest | extent. If you and Mr. Post decide this would be the wisest thing to do, I shall be happy to | assist you in locating the best school for John.

If there is any help that you think I can give | your son at any time in the future, I hope you will not hestitate to write me. Sincerely yours, (5) (1.29)

43

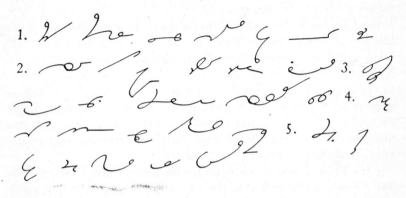

Key: (1) If you order, evergreen, immediately, country, probably, month, season. (2) Garden, to do, to be done, start, strong, healthy. (3) Advise, quality, anything, familiar, guaranteed, without. (4) Costs, continue, to come, next year, dislike, given. (5) Finishing, touches, property, as soon as, this letter, return, promptly.

Dear Friend: If you order now, I can give you extra value on your fall order for evergreen | trees. You see, if you order your evergreen trees this fall and plant them immediately, they will be | ready to start growing the first day that spring comes to your part of the country. If you do not order | until spring, I cannot get your trees to you until probably a month of your growing season (1) has gone by.

Most people feel that this extra month's growth is important, and they send me their orders | in the fall. Then, too, if you have a garden, you know how busy you are in the spring. It is much more | satisfactory to do your tree planting in the fall, when there is far less to be done in your | garden.

Therefore, to be sure that your evergreens get a good start next spring and are strong and healthy, I (2) advise you to order your trees now.

I am sure I do not need to say very much about the | quality of my evergreen trees. Your own experience with them tells the story better than anything | I could write. You are familiar with the strong, beautiful trees that I raise. You know that each | tree that

I ship you is guaranteed to live. If it doesn't, I replace it immediately without (3) charge.

But I must tell you this: I do not know how much longer I can keep my prices as low as they | are at the present time. Costs are rising and will probably continue to rise for some time to come. | Next year it may be necessary to raise the prices of the trees, much as I should dislike to | do this. So here's my offer. Take advantage right now of the low prices given in the enclosed (4) folder. Invest at once in those evergreens that you need to put the finishing touches to the | beauty of your property. Don't risk having to pay more by waiting until next year to order.

As | soon as you finish reading this letter, fill out the enclosed order blank. Then mail it in the return | envelope, with your check or money order.

You will receive your trees promptly for fall planting. Yours truly, (5) (1.30)

44

Key: (1) Engineer, operates, cooling, system, hard, worse, as soon as possible, recognizes, shortages. (2) Various, idea, we want, without, obligation, given. (3) Found, investment, installed, many times, to do, trouble, more than. (4) Specification, card, cure, prefer, one of our, recommendations. (5) Compliments, practical, prolong, you want, handy, receive, Very sincerely yours.

Dear Mr. Wilson: The other day I was talking to an engineer who operates a | cooling system like yours. He told me that the past summer was a hard one on the cooling system and that | next summer would probably be worse. He is, therefore, going to overhaul it as soon as | possible. He recognizes the fact that this will not be an easy job because of shortages of (1) various kinds, but he feels that now is the time to get the job out of the way when there is no | immediate hurry. It is my feeling that this man had the right idea.

In any plans for | overhauling that you may have, be sure you give consideration to our piston rings. We want | you to try them without the slightest risk or obligation. After you have given them a trial, we (2) are confident that you will join the thousands of other people who have tried them, found them to be | a good investment, and installed them. You, too, will find that these piston rings will pay back their cost many | times over. Our piston rings enable you to get more ice at a low cost.

May we ask you to | do us this favor: Pick out the engine that is causing you trouble, that is costing more than it should (3) to run. Then fill out the enclosed specification card on that engine, and send it to me. On | the basis of these specifications, we will tell you how our piston rings will help you cure the trouble | you are having; or, if you prefer, we should be glad to send one of our men to examine | the engine and make definite recommendations on the spot.

In return for doing this for us, we (4) will send you, with our compliments, a copy of our "Handbook for Engineers." It is full of | practical information that may help you prolong the life of many of your engines. This book contains | information that you want to have handy for quick reference. A copy of the "Handbook for | Engineers" will be on its way to you the same day that we receive your card. Very sincerely yours, (5) (1.34)

45

1.

2.

Key: (1) Worried, reason, apartment, destroyed, personal, drawer, special, bankbook. (2) Kept, burned, everything else, separate, compartment, unless. (3) It is not, local, handsome, colors, offering, general. (4) Mind, built, strong, asking you, indicating, you have been. (5) Your remittance, aside, small, special, they will, rapidly, card.

Dear Mr. Lane: Bill Smith is worried, and he has good reason to be. It seems that there was a small | fire in his apartment. Before the fire was finally put out, it had destroyed most of his personal | papers. Bill Smith made the mistake of keeping his personal papers in one drawer of his desk, | with no special protection. Consequently, his bankbooks, insurance policies, and other important (1) papers will now have to be replaced.

If Bill Smith had kept his valuable papers in a | King safe, the papers would not have been destroyed even though fire had burned everything else in his apartment. |

The King safe has two separate compartments. Each will hold almost five hundred ordinary | letters. In addition, it has a secret compartment with a special lock. Unless you know where to (2) look for this compartment, it is not easy to locate.

The safe is handsome enough to blend in | easily with your furniture either at home or at the office. It comes in several colors, | from which you may choose.

How much does a King safe cost? For the next month only, we are offering a | King safe for the low price of $12. In the general market the safe sells for $15. (3)

For only $12, you can set your mind at ease regarding the personal papers that you | must keep at home. The safe is so well built and strong that it will last you a lifetime.

We are not asking | you to send any money at this time. Just tell us on the enclosed card that we may send you a | King safe on trial, indicating the color you prefer. File your papers in it, and use it for (4) a few weeks. Then, if you are convinced that it is just the thing you have been looking for, send us your | remittance for $12. If not, just return it to us at our expense.

But do not delay. We | have set aside only a small number for this special offer, and we are confident that they | will go rapidly. So be sure that you get yours by sending the free trial card at once. Yours truly, (5) (1.34)

46

Key: (1) Many times, overlooked, edition, classic, you would not have, amount, to purchase, at least. (2) Outstanding, selected, editorial, board, mailed, together, you would like, without, obligation, one of the, dividends. (3) $10,000,000, average, actually, among the, available. (4) Some of the, anyway, why not, twice, system, if you decide. (5) Offered, postage, we are sure, wise, choice, becoming, to say, quotations, prominent.

Dear Mr. Baker: Perhaps many times you have given some thought to joining the Book Club but have | simply overlooked doing so. Now is a good time for you to join. By joining now, you will receive | free of charge a beautiful edition of a famous old classic.

When you join the Club, you do | not have to pay any fixed amount each year. All you have to do is agree to purchase at least four (1) books a year from the Club. Each month an outstanding book is selected by our editorial | board. The book is mailed to you, together with a bill. Then you decide whether you would like to keep the | book. If not, you simply return it without any obligation on your part. For every | two books that you buy, you will receive one of the Club's beautiful book dividends. In the past year the (2) retail value of the books given to members was over $10,000,000.

When the book | dividends are taken into consideration, the average amount members pay for all the | books they receive is actually less than $1.75 each, which is far below | the average retail price of the same books. Among the books the Club makes available to you are (3) some of the very books you would like to read and would probably buy anyway. As that is the | case, why not get such books as a Club member? You thus make sure you do get and read them; and, with the money | you pay out for books, you get about twice as many books through our dividend system.

If you decide | to join, all that is necessary is to sign and mail the enclosed card. The beautiful edition (4) of a famous classic that is offered to new members will be sent to you at once. No postage | is necessary on the card. We are sure that you will find that you have made a wise choice by | becoming a member of the Book Club.

Read in the enclosed folder what others have to say about | the Book Club. You will find quotations from the letters we have received from prominent people. Yours truly, (5) (1.34)

47

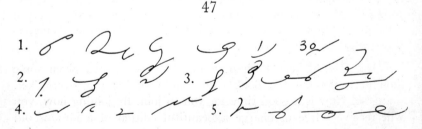

Key: (1) Idea, developed, provide, life, $100, $30,000, investments. (2) Touching, let us say, you want. (3) Thereafter, wife, limited, amount. (4) Worked, things, son, daughter. (5) Future, in addition, mind, mailed.

Dear Mr. Brown: A new idea has been developed to help you provide for an income for | life. In the old days, there was only one way in which you could retire; you had to be rich. To get a | life income of $100 a month, you had to have about $30,000 in | good investments.

Today, however, you can provide an income for yourself when you retire without (1) touching your present savings. You can do this by taking advantage of the Mutual income | plan.

This is the way the plan works. Let us say that you are now forty years old and that you want to | retire at fifty-five on an income of $150 a month. By using our plan | this is what you will get:

1. A check for $150 when you reach fifty-five and a (2) check for $150 every month thereafter as long as you live.

2. A life | income for your wife in case you die before you reach fifty-five.

This plan is not limited to men | of forty. You may be older or younger. The income is not limited to $150 | a month. It can be any amount from $10 to $200 a month or (3) more. You can retire at fifty-five, sixty, or at any age that you decide you have worked long | enough.

This plan gives you an opportunity to get the things you need. You can get them without touching | your present savings. If you need money to send your son or daughter to college, this plan will | enable you to obtain that money.

Return the enclosed coupon, and you will receive without charge (4) a free booklet entitled "Your Future." This booklet will give you the full details of the plan that | we offer you. It will also suggest ways in which a plan can be worked out to meet your own needs. In | addition, the booklet will answer for you many questions that have no doubt been in your mind. Your | copy will be mailed without cost. Do not delay. Fill out the coupon and mail it now. Sincerely yours, (5) (1.35)

48

Key: (1) Successfully, operate, customers, question of time, policy, touch. (2) Recently, heard, for some time, inquire, whether, trouble, something, appreciate. (3) Very much, displease, personal, attention, friendly, thousands, simply. (4) Unhappy, statement, amount, explained, to do so, happier. (5) If you would like to have, sum, otherwise, become, rather, you will be able.

Dear Mr. Drews: It goes without saying that a business organization can successfully | operate only as long as its customers remain satisfied and happy. Once customers lose | faith in an organization, it is only a question of time before that organization | will go out of business.

It has always been our policy to keep in close touch with all our (1) customers to see that they are satisfied with our services and our goods. In going through our books | recently, we noticed that we have not heard from you for some time. The purpose of this letter, therefore, | is to inquire whether there has been any trouble about an order that has been keeping you | from dealing with us. If we have done something to lose favor with you, I should appreciate it (2) very much if you would drop me a line or two letting me know what we have done to displease you. I | will give the matter my personal attention, I assure you.

Our company will never get so | big that it will lose friendly interest in its customers. Although we have thousands of customers, | we look on each one as a real friend and not simply as a name and address in our files. It makes (3) us very unhappy not to hear from our old customers.

About a month ago we sent you | a statement showing a small amount that you owed us. If there is anything that you would like explained | regarding this charge, I shall be glad to do so. There may be a good reason why you have not paid | this little bill. If so, please

let me know and we shall feel happier about the matter. If you would
(4) like to have a little more time to pay your bill, we shall be happy
to let you have as much time | as you will need to raise the sum.
Otherwise, I shall appreciate receiving a check from you for | this
charge, which has now become rather old.

I also hope that you will be able to favor us | with another order.
We can serve you well, and we can save you a good deal of money.
Yours truly, (5) (1.36)

49

Key: (1) Women, vacation, because, bothered, learn, parties, determine, spend. (2) Successful, spoil, short trip, one week, Milwaukee,
Sunday. (3) Western, country, slightly, include, railroad, mind, assistance, gone. (4) Contains, suggestions, interesting, helpful, friends.
(5) Post card, send you, regardless, preference, connect, arrangements,
to us, forward, information.

Dear Miss King: Are you like so many other women who have
put off planning a spring vacation | because you do not like to be
bothered with the details? If you are, you will be happy to learn
about | the vacation parties we plan for this spring.

All you will have to do is decide which trip you | would like to
take and determine how much you can spend on the trip—our Travel
Department will take care (1) of the rest. It will insure you a suc-
cessful vacation without any of the details that | often spoil a vaca-
tion.

Each of the parties will be under the guidance of a man who has had | many years' experience in this type of work.

If you are interested in a short trip, the | Travel Department is planning a one-week tour of the Black Hills. Parties will leave Milwaukee on Sunday (2) night and return on the following Sunday. You will have seven days of pleasure in our western | country. The cost will be slightly less than $100. This figure will include your railroad | fare, your hotel, and all other expenses.

Perhaps you are the type that does not mind details; you | may prefer to do things your way, with just a little assistance now and then from those who have gone over (3) the road before. If so, we have just the thing for you—our twenty-four-page booklet entitled | "How to Plan a Vacation." This booklet contains many suggestions that will help you plan a vacation. | We are confident that you will find the booklet both interesting and helpful in planning | a vacation. We shall be happy to send a copy to you and to any of your friends who are (4) planning to take a vacation. Just drop a post card to us today, and we will send you as many | booklets as you can use.

Regardless of your preference, we believe we can be of help to you | in connection with your hotel arrangements. Just fill in the attached blank and return it to us | in the attached envelope. We shall be glad to forward the desired information. Yours truly, (5) (1.36)

50

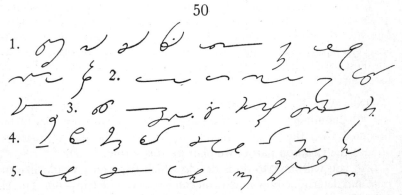

Key: (1) Attractively, you want, went, behind, recommend, to choose, reliable, contractor, specify. (2) On the market, of course, color, combinations, proud, furthermore. (3) Without, manufacturing, whether, photographs, actual, furnishing. (4) Several hundred, appear, effects, certain, simplest, intend, in the future, be sure. (5) Leisure, examine, pleasure, wonderful, if you would like, Cordially yours.

Dear Sir: When you see a well-painted house, a house painted so attractively that you want to move | right in, you can be sure that a good deal of thought went into the painting. Behind every satisfactory | paint job, there is a lot more than meets the eye. That is why we always recommend to | homeowners who are about to paint that they choose a reliable contractor and specify the (1) best paint on the market. Of course, there is another factor to be considered, and that is color. | Unless your color combinations are just what you want them to be, you may not be satisfied.

We | can help you with all three of these problems. To begin with, we can recommend to you a contractor | who will give you a job of which you will be proud. Furthermore, we can assure you that his price will (2) be reasonable. We can recommend Johnson paints to you without reserve. We have been | manufacturing paints for more than thirty years, paints that are attractive and will stand up in all kinds of | weather.

To help you solve the color problem, we have prepared a large book of color photographs of | actual homes and rooms that are complete in every detail of furnishing and color. There are (3) several hundred of these photographs.

Here you can see how colors are actually going | to appear in your home. You do not guess; you know what effects certain colors will produce in each room. | Reference to these photos is the simplest way to select the color scheme for your home, both | inside and outside.

Whether you intend to paint now or in the future, be sure to see the Johnson (4) Color Guide. We shall be glad to have you borrow one to take home. Look it over at your leisure, and | let the other members of your family examine it. We are sure you will all find it a real | pleasure to see what wonderful effects Johnson paints can produce.

If you would like to borrow the | Johnson Color Guide, drop in at our store at 464 Second Avenue. Cordially yours, (5) (1.37)

51

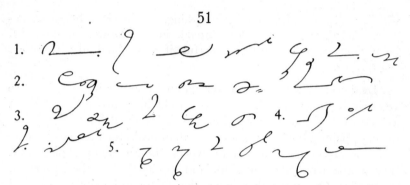

Key: (1) This morning, I have been, mailed, students, previous, forming, reasons. (2) Applications, almost, Union, Canada, several months ago. (3) Assumed, we are sure, you have not, pressure, act. (4) Intensive, includes, everything, hundreds. (5) In the past, one of the best, fun, ideas, you will be able, remember.

Dear Friend: I still have your name on my desk this morning because I have been hoping that your enrollment | in our course in selling would arrive. Perhaps you have mailed it, and it has not yet reached me. I thought | it best to write you about it, as we can take only a few more students.

In my previous | letters about the class that is now forming, I gave you many reasons why I was sure you would (1) greatly benefit from your study. May I suggest that you glance over those letters now and also | read the booklet that is enclosed.

Applications for the class are pouring in every day, and it | looks as if we shall have a full class soon. These applications are from almost every state of | the Union, and many are from Canada.

When you wrote for our booklet several months ago, we (2) assumed that you were interested in the courses we had to offer. We are sure that you have | not lost interest since writing us and that your delay in sending in your application is due | to pressure of work or some other important reason. To get into this present class, you will | have to act soon. Why not take a few minutes today and fill in the necessary information (3) on the application blank that I am enclosing.

As you may remember, the fee is only | $10—a special offer for this class. Up to this time, the fee has been $40 for | the complete course and $20 for the intensive course. This fee of $10 includes | everything.

You will never regret the money spent on this course. We are confident that you, like hundreds (4) of others who have taken the course in the past, will think of it as one of the best investments | you have ever made. The course will bring you interest and fun and ideas that you will be able | to use immediately. It will help you increase your income and will open the door to | promotions.

Remember, your application must be on my desk by May 15. Yours very truly, (5) (1.38)

52

Key: (1) Recently, writers, compose, friends, during the last year, I wanted, none of the, letters, mistakes. (2) Perfect, improved, of course, occasionally, perhaps, dissatisfied, won't, complaint. (3) Improvements, became, years ago, effect, to be sure, leather, testing. (4) Designer, combines, sometimes, offset, personally. (5) Wherever, family, suitable, to buy.

Dear Miss Scott: Recently I asked one of our letter writers to compose a letter that I could | send to our friends who have not purchased any shoes from us during the last year. I wanted him to write | the letter as if he were making a personal call on you. He tried five times but none of the | letters seemed to hit the mark. Each one gave the impression that our organization could make no mistakes, (1) that our shoes were perfect, and that our service could not be improved on.

I realize, of course, that | we are only human and that mistakes will happen occasionally. I realize that perhaps | the reason you have not visited us recently is that you were dissatisfied with your last | pair of shoes. If that is so, won't you please present your complaint before the manager of the store from (2) which you purchased the shoes. You may be sure that he will do his best to see that you are satisfied. |

We have made many improvements since I became general manager about two years ago. Still | other improvements are being put into effect. For example, to be sure that the leather | in our shoes will give long wear, we have just installed a special testing machine. We have also just employed (3) an experienced designer to be sure that our shoes possess the style that combines beauty | and comfort,

Our organization has been in the shoe business for more than seventy years. | Unfortunately, however, a little slip on the part of a clerk may sometimes offset the good | features of our shoes and turn a customer away. I personally have made it a policy to (4) seek and adjust these human errors wherever they have been made.

Just recently we received a | new stock of shoes for the spring season, and we are confident that you and every member of your | family will find a pair suitable to his or her needs. The shoes are reasonably priced; | and, once you see them, you will want to buy several pairs. Won't you visit our store again? Yours truly, (5) (1.40)

53

5.

Key: (1) President, merchandise, results, organization, interested, easily, field. (2) We may be able, requirements, customers, become, permanent. (3) Awards, contests, in our opinion, concerned, kind, to build, banks. (4) Why not, sample, reasoning, businesses, some of our, 400 per cent, supermarkets. (5) Formerly, less than, earned, increases, problem, solve.

Dear Mr. Lee: If you are president of a company that sells its merchandise in packages, | you are interested in net results. If you are sales manager of such an organization, | you are interested in increased sales. If you are an advertising manager, you are | interested in results that you can easily check.

Because of our experience in this field, (1) we may be able to satisfy all three of these basic requirements.

Our theory is that the | purpose of advertising packaged merchandise is to get people to try the articles. If people | who try your products at home are won over, they will become permanent customers; and | you will build a big business. If not, your product has failed, and not your advertising.

The advertising (2) ideas we use have never won any awards in contests, but they have made money for the | dealer. That is the test of good advertising.

In our opinion, too much advertising today | is concerned with keeping the company name before the public and building good will. The kind of | good will we like to build is the kind that banks will lend money on, good will that is based on the sale of (3) the product.

Therefore, why not sample your products now in millions of homes at a small cost?

This simple | line of reasoning has done a great deal to the businesses of some of our clients. In one case, | our methods increased the sale of a product more than 400 per cent in one year. In another | case, one product that had an average sale of one package a week in supermarkets increased its (4) sale to five cases a week, in spite of the fact that it used less advertising than formerly. |

Our organization is less than two years old. Our orders are up over 300 per cent | since March. More than 60 per cent of these orders are based on the earned increases of our clients. |

If you have an advertising problem, let us help you solve it. We are at your service. Yours truly, (5) (1.41)

54

Key: (1) Records, during the past, we thank you for the, country, promptly, independent, thousands, people. (2) Endeavors, anxious, because, purpose, one hundred, years ago, depositors, one of our. (3) Popular, accounts, explained, circular, one of them, handles. (4) Neighborhood, employees, various, Government, current, earnings, past. (5) Deposited, turned, merely, useful.

Dear Friend: Our records show that during the past three months you have purchased through us over $500 | worth of bonds. We thank you for the opportunity you have given us to work with you.

You | are helping your country when you save so that you can pay your income taxes promptly. You are | also helping your country when you save in order to keep yourself independent.

Thousands of the people (1) in New York look to the Mutual Savings Bank to assist them in each of these endeavors. They | are saving regularly and buying bonds every payday. We are anxious to help in this way, | because the very purpose for which we were organized more than one hundred years ago is to | serve those who save.

If you are not one of our depositors, you may be interested in knowing (2) that we offer three popular types of savings accounts, each one designed to serve a particular | purpose. These three accounts are completely explained in the circular that is enclosed. We are | confident that one of them will meet your needs exactly.

Many of our friends take advantage of our | department that handles deposits by mail. You may find that this department may also be a (3) convenience in taking care of your present banking matters.

If you should be in our neighborhood, stop | in and let one of our employees explain to you the benefits of our various accounts and | services.

Please remember that this bank also buys Government bonds with your savings. Remember | that you help your Government most by buying bonds from current earnings rather than from past savings. Most (4) of the money now deposited in banks is being turned into bonds. By purchasing bonds with | past savings rather than current earnings, you merely supplement what your bank is doing.

Remember, | too, that now is the time to plan for the future. Money in the bank will prove useful to you in | the future. It may be the means of tiding you over an emergency. Yours very truly, (5) (1.43)

55

Key: (1) You might be, attached, improvement, entirely, different, courses, method. (2) Accomplish, heard, lectures, outstanding, authority, formerly, personally. (3) Ordinary, correspondence, lessons, self-instruction, learner, interesting, women. (4) Themselves, progress, everything, inspect, if you wish. (5) Obligation, I am sure, arrangement, examined, surprised, easily, self-confidence.

Dear Mr. Smith: A friend of yours has suggested that you might be interested in seeing the | attached proofs of a new course that we are issuing.

The course is written by Miss Mary Brown, who has | devoted many years of her life to speech improvement. She has devised a method of teaching | speech that is entirely different from other courses. In thirty days this new method will do for (1) you what it takes other methods as long as a year to accomplish.

Perhaps you have heard Miss Brown's | lectures on the radio. Her work in speech has been outstanding, and today she is considered an | authority in her field.

Formerly, only those living in a few large cities could benefit | through the classes she personally conducted. Now, this same type of training is available (2) by mail. This course, however, is not like the ordinary correspondence course. There are no | examinations to take. The lessons are planned for self-instruction. As the learner goes from lesson to | lesson, he will quickly notice the improvement in his speech. The lessons are always interesting | and exciting.

The course is designed to meet the needs of business men and women who have little (3) time for themselves. It is planned so that the learner can devote as little as fifteen minutes a | day to the lessons and still make progress.

Our present plan provides for a seven-day free trial. We will | gladly send you everything that you need and prepay the charges. You may inspect the course | yourself at no cost whatever. You need send no money.

After seven days, if you wish to return the (4) material, you may do so with no obligation on your part. I am sure you will consider | this arrangement very fair.

If, after you have examined the materials we send you, you | wish to take the course, send us your check for $15.

I know you will be surprised to see how | quickly and easily Miss Brown's course will develop your speech and increase your self-confidence. Yours truly, (5) (1.43)

56

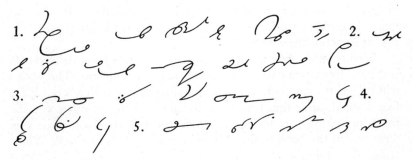

Key: (1) Vocabulary, likely, thousands, tests, definitely, interested. (2) Results, test, whether, regardless, engaged, words, factory, ability. (3) Command, ahead, found, announcement, wonderful, process. (4) Besides, behind, postage. (5) Examination, with the understanding, you do not, to us, otherwise.

Dear Mr. Smith: Do you know that the greater your vocabulary, the more likely you are to | succeed? The truth of this statement has been proved time and time again by thousands of tests that have been | given. These tests definitely show that men who are the leaders in business can use a large number | of words.

Both the Army and the Navy are interested in the vocabulary of their men. (1) Every man who enters the Army and the Navy takes a vocabulary test, and very | often the results of this test are considered in deciding whether he should be given a | rating.

Regardless of the field in which you are engaged, the number of words you know and can use | correctly is an important factor by which others judge your ability. Therefore, a better (2) command of words will help you get ahead in business.

The chances are that you always wanted to | increase your vocabulary; but up to now, you have never found a method that would work. That is | why you will welcome this announcement of a wonderful new book called "Building a Useful | Vocabulary." This book really makes the process of learning new words an interesting game. It is (3) divided into thirty daily chapters. Each day you spend fifteen minutes with this book. You will enjoy | your work with this book.

"Building a Useful Vocabularly" does many things besides adding words | to your speaking and writing vocabulary. It tells you many interesting stories behind | our words, stories that will help you understand them better.

It costs only a postage stamp to have (4) this book delivered to you for a free examination. No money need be sent now. The book | will be sent to you with the understanding that you may keep it for five days. If, after that time, you do | not feel that it offers you the most interesting way to increase your vocabularly | you have ever seen, return the book to us. Otherwise it is yours for only $2. Yours truly, (5) (1.45)

57

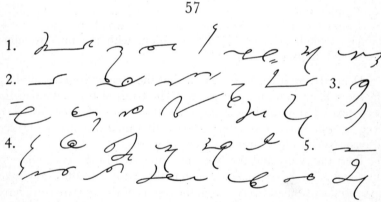

Key: (1) Few months, considerably, themes, subject, Christmas, suitable, restrictions. (2) More than, create, conducted, in the past, each month. (3) That have, international, circulation, otherwise, devoted, features, valuable, individual. (4) Publication, prior, advance, reasonable, subscribe, entire. (5) Number, together, indication, familiar, last year, immediately, available.

Dear Mr. Young: In the next few months our cover designs will be changed considerably.

Starting | with the enclosed series of designs, we are releasing covers based on general monthly themes. The | enclosed series, as you will notice, deals with the subject of Christmas. With this change in design we | believe that our covers will prove even more suitable for magazines such as yours. Restrictions on (1) paper have been lifted, and in the near future we shall release more than one cover design each | month. This will give you an opportunity to select the most suitable design.

Cover designs | like the one enclosed create added interest in your magazine. Tests that we have conducted | in the past have proved this again and again. By using our cover designs each month, you will put your (2) magazine on a par with magazines that have an international circulation. By | using our designs, you save a good deal of time that you would otherwise have to spend planning your monthly | cover. This time that you save can be devoted to planning other features that will make your | magazine more valuable to your readers.

Cover designs may be ordered in individual (3) lots for each issue of your publication. New designs are issued monthly prior to the | publication month so that you can make your selection well in advance.

The cost of this service is | very reasonable. We will send you each design for $20. If you subscribe for an | entire year, the cost of the twelve designs will be $200.

When ordering the designs you wish, (4) please be sure to list the number of the cover, together with an indication of the date | on which you must have it.

If you are not familiar with the service we offer to editors like | yourself, or if you have not seen the designs that we released last year, write us today and we will | immediately send you a set of the covers that are still available. Very truly yours, (5) (1.46)

58

1. *[shorthand symbols]*

2. *[shorthand symbols]*

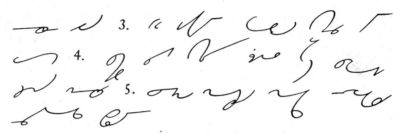

Key: (1) Separate, handbook, latest, called, already, out of date.
(2) Considerably, consequently, rewritten, last year, lessons, learned,
points, mind, it is not. (3) Things, should be done, pleasant, definite,
down, organization. (4) Activities, edition, devoted, history, objective,
accomplished, second, you might. (5) I am sure, you will find, you
will be able, incorporate, needless to say, appointment.

Dear Mr. Strong: Under separate cover we have sent you today
all the material that | we have available on how to prepare an em-
ployee's handbook.

You will be interested in | our experience in helping the Miller
Manufacturing Company prepare its latest | handbook. When we
were called in, that company already had a handbook; but it was
out of date. The (1) organization had grown considerably since that
handbook was prepared; consequently, the | book had to be com-
pletely rewritten. The new handbook was ready at the end of last
year. The new | handbook benefited by many lessons that had been
learned during the work on the first handbook. |

The following points were kept in mind in the preparation of
the new handbook:

1. It is not a (2) rule book that lists things that should be done
and should not be done by the employee.

2. The handbook should | take advantage of the pleasant feeling
of satisfaction with which an employee takes a new job. | The hand-
book should play a definite part in maintaining that feeling of satis-
faction.

3. It | should set down facts that will make the employee feel
that he is a part of the organization. It should (3) give him information on every phase of the organization's activities.

In the | first edition of the handbook a good deal of space was devoted to the history of the | company. This objective was largely accomplished by the time the second edition was published. |

These are just a few thoughts that come to me at this time. It occurs to me that you might care to write to (4) the Miller Manufacturing Company and ask them for a copy of their latest handbook. | I am sure you will find many suggestions that you will be able to incorporate in your own | handbook.

Needless to say, we are at your service. If you think that you will profit from a visit | with one of our men, call us on the telephone and we will arrange an appointment. Yours truly, (5) (1.47)

59

Key: (1) Following, thinking, you want, to purchase, economically, unnecessary, prospective, up-to-date. (2) Modern, hidden, costs, simply, arrange. (3) Investigation, confidential, application, completed, broker, agent. (4) Included, outlay, liability, damage, in addition, insured, amount, unpaid, assembly. (5) Toward, reply, postage, welcome, Very sincerely yours.

Dear Mr. Smith: We believe that you will be interested in the following information | if you are thinking of purchasing a new car. It goes without saying that you want to purchase that | car as economically as possible and without paying unnecessary financing | charges. In order to give you and other prospective car purchasers an up-to-date financing (1) service at a reasonable cost, the American Bank offers you a modern, | economical plan. The plan enables you to buy your car from any dealer you may select and to | save money on its total cost.

The plan we offer does away with hidden charges and | unnecessary costs. You simply come to our bank first to arrange for the money you need at the low bank (2) rate and then purchase your car when you want to and from whom you want to. There is no delay and no | long investigation. Your business with us is confidential. When you finance your car with us, your | money will be ready for you within twenty-four hours after your application is completed. |

Under this plan you may place the necessary insurance with your broker or agent. This cost (3) may be included in the monthly payments, thus saving you a larger cash outlay. You may | also include the cost of public liability and property damage if you wish. In addition, | your life is insured for the amount of the unpaid balance on your automobile loan | without cost to you.

With more cars constantly coming off the assembly lines, now is the time to take the (4) first step toward getting your car at the low bank rate. In order to arrange for financing your car, | simply mail the enclosed reply envelope, on which no postage is required, or bring it to one of our | conveniently located offices, where you will be welcome. Once your credit is established, you | will be able to finance your car through this modern, extremely convenient plan. Very sincerely yours, (5) (1.49)

60

Key: (1) Morning, confidential, developments, executives, provides, ideas, you will find. (2) Weekly, report, prepares, critical, up-to-the-minute, procedure, information. (3) Anywhere else, gathered, thousands, nowhere else, exclusive, appears. (4) Firsthand, actually. (5) Effective, card, subscribing, today.

Dear Sir: Now you can have on your desk every Monday morning a confidential letter | giving you the latest developments in the public relations field. This letter gives you the plans of | other public relations executives. It provides you with new ideas and methods for | selling your company to its employees and to the public.

You will find this information in the (1) Public Relations News, the only weekly letter in this field. This confidential letter is | a personal report to you. It prepares you today for the critical months ahead by giving | you up-to-the-minute news and guidance on good public relations methods of procedure. | Every week you will receive this letter full of ideas and information that is not (2) available anywhere else at any price.

If this vital information had to be gathered | by you or your organization, it would cost you thousands of dollars. Nowhere else can you get the | exclusive information that appears weekly in this valuable letter.

Although the country's | leading public relations men have many sources of information at their command, they use (3) Public Relations News to get firsthand information in the field. Every day public relations | men tell us how they find the Public Relations News a valuable aid. It gives them all | the information they need and want in one report each week.

You, too, can actually save hours | of reading time and yet have the information you need to plan your public relations program. Public (4) Relations News is important to you. It gives you the information you must have to do | an effective job.

The enclosed card brings Public Relations News to you for only 34 cents | a week on a yearly basis. Surely this is a small sum compared to the benefits that will | come to you by subscribing to Public Relations News. Mail the enclosed card today. Yours truly, (5) (1.56)

PART IV

80 WORDS A MINUTE

61

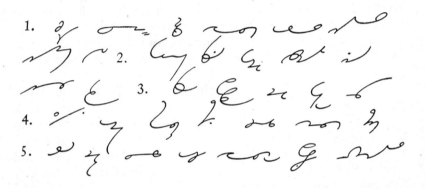

Key: (1) We understand, American, society, collection, really, you would like, you do not have, to know. (2) Brokerage, behind, persons, thousands, who want, together, people. (3) Buyer, appraisal, as soon as, purchaser, any time. (4) Including, reasonable, valuations, everything, secrecy, connection, if you wish. (5) Third, as soon as possible, immediately, receipt, collector, appreciate, in this country.

Dear Mr. Drake: We understand that you are a member of the American Gun Society and that you | have a large collection of guns. Perhaps you have often wondered how much your guns are really worth at today's | prices. Perhaps there are times when you would like to sell a few of your guns because you do not have the space to store | them or because you need cash to meet your immediate needs.

You will be interested to know that this store is (1) now organizing a gun brokerage service, the first and only one of its kind. What is behind this new service? | It is all very simple. Many persons, like yourself, have guns or rifles that they never use and would like | to sell them. Then there are thousands of persons who want to buy good guns. For the first time, there will be a service that | will bring these people together. We will see to it that the seller gets a good price for his gun. For this service, (2) we will charge just a small fee. We will also see to it that the buyer gets good value for the money that he | pays.

This service will enable you to get a fair appraisal of your guns based on today's prices. Acting as | your agent, we put your guns on sale. As soon as a gun is sold, you will receive a check. If you should change your mind | about selling your guns before we have obtained a purchaser, you can call for them at any time you want them (3) and no fee will be charged.

The fees that you pay will cover all expenses, including advertising, insurance, | and selling. The fees are reasonable and are based on the valuations of the guns.

Everything is an | open book in this new service. There is no secrecy in connection with the sale or the purchase of guns. The | seller knows how much the buyer pays; the buyer knows how much the seller gets.

If you wish to take advantage of (4) this service, bring your guns to the third floor of our store as soon as possible. A member of our staff will | immediately give you the retail value at which we believe we can sell your guns. If you agree, we will give you | a receipt and place your guns on sale.

As a gun collector, you can appreciate the value of this service. | We believe this service will meet with the approval of every gun collector in this country. Yours truly, (5) (1.32)

62

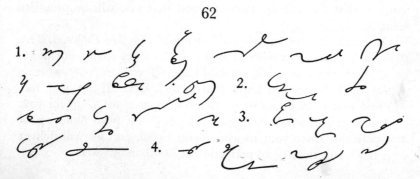

Key: (1) Successful, street, positions, observing, good deal, clothes, dividends, social, knowledge, appearance, attractive. (2) Personalities, generally, to select, perfectly, standards, cost. (3) Expect, respect, completely, proud, examine. (4) Any other, establishment, you will find, you want, hundreds, patterns, measurements. (5) If you wish, deferred, let us, satisfied.

Dear Mr. Barry: To be successful, you must look successful. As you walk down the street, you can, nine out of ten | times, pick out men who hold important positions simply by observing the way they are dressed. Successful men give | a good deal of thought to their clothes. They know that it pays big dividends in both business and social life to look well. | Furthermore, they take great satisfaction in the knowledge that their appearance is attractive. Their clothes fit their (1) personalities as well as their bodies.

How do most of these successful men choose their clothes? They generally have | them made to order by a tailor who takes pains to select the best materials and to make the clothes fit | perfectly. Our tailors have for years been making suits for successful men. Every suit our tailors make must meet our | high standards before it is released to the customer.

What is the cost of a suit made to order? The cost is (2) much less than you might expect. We will make a suit cut in any style that you like, in a fit that will please you in | every respect, for as little as $50. You do not pay us a penny until you are completely | satisfied that the suit fits perfectly and that you will be proud to wear it.

Just examine the samples of | material that are enclosed. This material will give you more value for your money than you can get in (3) any other tailoring establishment. If you are now wearing clothes made by us, you know that to be a fact. | If not, you, too, will find that to be a fact soon after you let us make a suit for you.

Come in and select the | material you want from hundreds of new patterns. Have your measurements taken, and we will deliver your new | suit tailored to perfection in less than one week.

As I said, our prices are very reasonable. If you do (4) not feel that you can pay in full for a new suit, we shall be glad to have you take advantage of our deferred-payment | plan. This will give you five months in which to pay. If you wish to take advantage of this plan, why not come in | to see us soon and let us explain how the plan works.

Come in today and select the material for your new | suit. We are confident that you will be completely satisfied with any suit you buy from us. Sincerely yours, (5) (1.34)

63

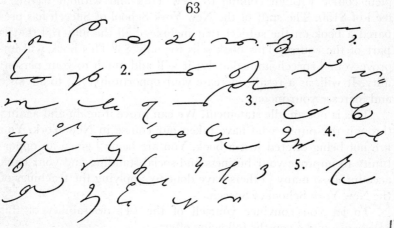

Key: (1) Young, to make, careful, words, connecting, enthusiasm, uninteresting, businessman, unfortunate. (2) Many of them, advancement, country, New York, school, lessons, enabled, many times. (3) Complete, prepared, on the subject, includes, improve, immediately, personality, as a result. (4) Increase, idle, statement, pupils, social, teachings, yourself. (5) Desirability, entitled, effective, expense, rushed, Cordially yours.

Dear Mr. Day: No man is too young or too old to make a careful study of the words he uses. Words are the | main connecting link between him and other people. They can reflect enthusiasm or be flat and uninteresting. |

In our dealings with people every day, our voices play a part. A good voice is one of the most | important assets a businessman can 'have. Most men do not get the most out of their voices. The unfortunate (1) thing is that many of them do not realize that they are losing opportunities for advancement because | of their voices. Many famous men all over the country who have realized the importance of their voices | have come to New York to study in the New York School of Speech. They have paid as much as $150 | for ten lessons and paid it gladly. The lessons have enabled them to earn many times the cost.

Now, for the first (2) time, it is possible for you to get this complete course without coming to New York and without paying a fee | of $150. The staff of the New York School of Speech has prepared a book on the subject that includes | all the material that is part of the course. This book sells for only $3. This book will improve your | speech immediately; it will add much to your personality. It will, as a result, increase your opportunity (3) to advance and increase your income.

This is not an idle statement. We can prove it again and again | through the pupils who have taken our course in New York. You are not being offered just a book. You are being | given an opportunity to improve your business and social standing and your bank account as so many | others have done by applying the teachings of the New York School of Speech.

To let you convince yourself of the (4) desirability of this course, we make you the following offer:

We will send you a copy of this book, | entitled "Effective Speech." Keep it for two weeks. At the end of that time, send us your check for $3 if you believe | the book is worth the price; or return the book at our expense if you feel that it has not helped you.

Send us your | name and address on the enclosed card. Your copy of "Effective Speech" will be rushed to you at once. Cordially yours, (5) (1.36)

64

1. [shorthand outlines]

2. [shorthand outlines]

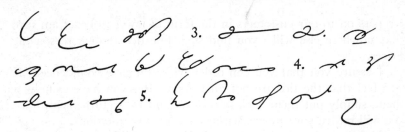

Key: (1) Recently, proud, transaction, industry, worst, definitely, another, for one thing. (2) Selection, pictures, idea, variety, thousands, brown, popular, executives. (3) Examine, wearing, quite, occasions, colors, point, operate, economy. (4) Quantities, substantial, nowhere else, simply. (5) Be sure, difficulty, attach, accounts, envelope.

Dear Mr. Fay: At one time you bought from us a box of ties. While those ties were made of the best material that | was available at that time, we were never proud of that transaction. It came at a time when conditions in | our industry were at their worst and materials of any kind were difficult to get. Now conditions are | definitely very much better. Will you give us another chance to show you what we can do?

For one thing, we (1) can offer you a far wider selection of ties today. In the enclosed folder you will find thirteen pictures | that will give you an idea of the range and variety from which you may choose. Style No. 5 is our best seller | this season. We have sold thousands of this style in recent months. It goes well with either a grey or a brown suit. | It is a popular tie with executives all over the country.

While you have the pictures in front of you, (2) examine style No. 8. While men are not wearing quite so many plain colors as in years gone by, yet they like | to have one or more such ties for special occasions. We have given you eight colors from which to choose.

At this point, | may I discuss briefly the matter of prices. To operate with the greatest of economy, we have | established a one-price policy. Each of our ties sells for $1.10. If you order ten ties at one time, (3) each tie will cost only $1. We buy our materials in large quantities, thus making substantial savings. | These savings we pass on to our customers in the form of lower prices. I am sure that nowhere else will | you find such fine ties at such reasonable prices.

I assure you that you can order with complete confidence. | If you feel that the ties are not all we say after you have examined them, simply put them back in the box and (4) return them to us. We will return your money without asking any questions.

Use the order blank enclosed. Be | sure to fill in all the necessary information so that there will be no difficulty in shipping. Also, | be sure to attach your check, as we do not carry accounts. Your order will be shipped the day it reaches us. | An envelope that requires no postage is enclosed for your convenience in sending your order. Sincerely yours, (5) (1.37)

65

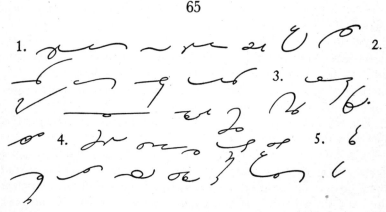

Key: (1) Catalogue, correct, strong, worse, opened, to make. (2) Medium, organization, message, well written. (3) Remove, up to date, minimum, inserts, conveniently, definite, binding, tightly. (4) Factor, economically, let us, initial. (5) Experience, give you, indicate, card, answer, suggestions, obligation, part.

Dear Mr. White: No doubt you spend a good deal of time and money on the preparation of your catalogue. You | take great pains to see that it is correct in every detail and that it is nicely printed on strong paper. | But, when you send it out to your customers, does it help to sell your goods or does it simply lie on the customer's |

shelf or, even worse, is it thrown away without even being opened?

It is easy to make your catalogue (1) a good selling medium by placing on it a Smith loose-leaf cover on which the name of your organization | is stamped in gold. When a customer receives a catalogue in a cover of that type, you can be sure that | he will open it. Once he has opened it, he will read your sales message if it is well written and printed.

A | Smith loose-leaf cover for your catalogue has many advantages. Here are a few of them:

It is easy to (2) add and to remove pages. This feature will enable you to keep your customer's catalogues up to date at | a minimum of expense by sending them inserts from time to time.

The catalogue opens very conveniently. | The pages lie flat and are easy to read. A catalogue in which the pages lie flat has a definite | advantage over one that has the regular binding, which snaps shut unless it is held tightly.

A loose-leaf (3) catalogue saves paper, which is an important factor at the present time. Whenever changes have to be made, the | whole catalogue does not have to be reprinted. The page on which a change is to be made can be replaced quickly | and economically.

When you are ready to put out your next catalogue, let us help you plan it. We will show | you how the Smith loose-leaf cover can be used without adding too greatly to your initial cost. We have had a (4) great deal of experience in catalogue planning and preparation, and we are confident that we can give | you some ideas that you will find useful. If you will indicate on the enclosed card the most convenient time, we | will send a representative to see you. He will be happy to answer your questions and to offer any | suggestions he can. There will be no obligation on your part to use the suggestions that he will make. Yours truly, (5) (1.38)

66

1.
2.

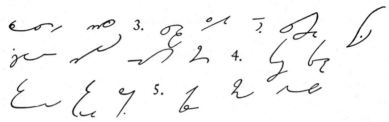

Key: (1) $100,000, it has been, club, exclusive, become, romance, without. (2) Membership, application, America's, unlike, similar, selected, worth while. (3) Accept, includes, interesting, advance, beforehand, whether or not, you don't, notify, effect. (4) Benefit, bonuses, popular, publishers, urging. (5) To join, assure, at least.

Dear Friend: How would you like to receive, free of charge, a gift copy of a new book that has been sold to the movies | for more than $100,000 even before it has been published?

The Book Club has received an exclusive | printing of this new book that we are confident will soon become a best seller. The name of the book is "The | Romance of the West." A copy of this book will be sent to you at once, without charge, if you will sign and return (1) the enclosed membership application to America's best-known book club.

A membership in the Book Club | will definitely save you money on your book purchases. Unlike other similar organizations, the Book | Club never charges its members more than $2 for the books that are selected. The same books are always on | sale in the regular edition for as much as $5. You can judge for yourself how worth while membership (2) in the Book Club will be.

Furthermore, you need accept only four books a year—not one every month, as many | people think. Membership includes a monthly copy of the Book Club's interesting magazine. This magazine tells | you, in advance, about the books that are to be offered by the club. Thus, you may decide beforehand whether or | not you think the book will appeal to you. If you feel you don't want the book, simply notify us to this effect, (3) and the book will not be sent.

There is still another way in which the members of the Book Club benefit. After | each four books that you purchase, you will receive, free of charge, a book bonus. Like the regular monthly books, these book | bonuses are also popular books that you will enjoy reading. These books often sell at $5 or more | in the original publisher's edition.

We have a special reason for urging you to accept our (4) invitation to join at once. If you join now, we can definitely assure you, that there will be no increase in | the book bonus selections for at least one year. Furthermore, there will be no membership fee or extra charges | of any kind. You will pay for only the selections you decide to purchase, and these purchases will cost you | no more than $2 plus postage charges.

Fill in the form that is enclosed, and mail it to us at once. Yours truly, (5) (1.38)

67

Key: (1) To know, $100,000, community, fund, ourselves, contributions, reasonable, expect, collected. (2) Directly, carry, amount, district, last year. (3) Recognized, residents, we hope that, next year, pleasure, personal, success. (4) Splendid, assistance, favor, campaign, will you please, whether, unusual, officers, you will be able. (5) To serve, criticisms, very much, co-operation, in the past.

Dear Mr. Smith: You will be glad to know that up to the present time we have raised the sum of $100,000 | for our community fund. This amount represents an increase of about 25 per cent over | the goal of $80,000 we set for ourselves when the drive was organized. Contributions are still coming | in, and it is reasonable to expect that the final sum collected will be nearer (1) $120,000. This fine showing can be traced directly to the job done by you and the other men who helped | to organize and carry out the drive.

The enclosed sheet gives the figures as they stood on November 6 and shows | the exact amount that each district contributed, along with the figures for last year. You will notice that a | number of new districts are represented. These new districts are a source of great satisfaction to us. It (2) is an indication that the value of the work we are doing is being recognized by more and more of the | residents of our village. We hope that next year these new districts will continue to work with us and that we shall | have the pleasure of adding a great many others.

No doubt you derive a great deal of personal satisfaction | from your part in making this drive a success. The director and the president have both asked me to express (3) to you their thanks for your splendid assistance.

We are asking the men who have worked with us one final favor before | closing the books for this campaign. Will you please indicate on the enclosed card whether you are willing to assist | in next year's drive. We realize that it is unusual to ask you about next year's drive when this year's is | not yet over, but it will give next year's officers a list to start with. We hope that you will be able to serve; (4) but, if for some reason you cannot, will you please suggest the names of others who you believe will be willing to | serve in your place.

We should also appreciate any suggestions or criticisms you may have to offer | in regard to the way this campaign was carried on. You may be sure that they will be given every | consideration.

Again, thank you very much for your splendid co-operation in the past. Very sincerely yours, (5) (1.40)

68

1. *[shorthand outlines]*

2. *[shorthand outlines]*

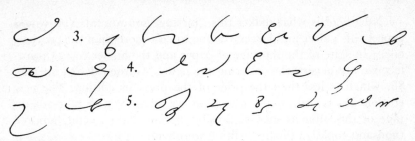

Key: (1) Unusual, accept, special, immediate, garden, extraordinary, lifelong, a million. (2) Amateur, one of the, columns, thousands, promptly. (3) To pay, bigger, better, experts, up to date, likely, answered, language. (4) Index, you want, expect, newer, previous, nevertheless, less than. (5) Advise, as soon as possible, eight hundred thousand, first, thoroughly, worth.

Dear Mr. Vance: This message is so unusual, and the time so short for you to accept the special offer | we are making, that we are enclosing a stamped envelope for your convenience in making an immediate | reply.

When we first published the "Garden Book," we knew at once from the extraordinary reception it received | that a lifelong ambition of ours had finally been realized. Here at last was the book that a million (1) amateur gardeners had hoped some day to see.

We have received many fine comments about the book. One of the | largest newspapers in the nation wrote in its columns that the "Garden Book" was almost too good to be true. | Another large newspaper wrote that the book was all that most gardeners would ever need.

After such fine reviews, thousands | of people wanted to see the book. After they looked through its pages, they promptly bought all available copies (2) of the first four printings. They were so happy with the book that many said they would be willing to pay as high | as $15 for a copy.

The new edition is even bigger and better. Forty experts have had | a hand in making it as complete and up to date as possible. It brings you a million words on gardening | help.

Every question about gardening that you are likely to ask is answered in simple language. There is (3) a convenient index that enables you to turn quickly to just the facts you want.

Now here is what makes this | message so unusual. You would expect this newer and larger volume to cost more than the previous one. | In spite of the shortage of paper and the higher cost of printing, we are nevertheless offering the new | "Garden Book" for only $3, which is less than the price of the previous edition. The new edition (4) is just off the press, but we advise you to take advantage of this offer as soon as possible because over | eight hundred thousand copies of the first edition were sold.

You may have the "Garden Book" to examine free | for five days. Test it thoroughly with your own garden questions. If you are not surprised and delighted with its | completeness, send it back. Keep it only if you are convinced that it is worth many times its cost. Very truly yours, (5) (1.42)

69

Key: (1) To our, employees, attention, proper, airport, to find, passengers, kindly. (2) To formulate, standard, provided, pleasant, easier, you want, system. (3) Benefit, longer, counter, cancellation, transferred, to make, however. (4) Effort, be sure, identify, immediately, telephone, mention, hold. (5) Promptly, observe, rules, pleasure, occasions, confirmation, initiative.

To Our Employees: It has come to my attention that employees traveling on our planes on passes have not | been receiving proper treatment. Very often an employee would go to the airport and wait for many hours | for a seat, only to find that all seats had been assigned to paying passengers. Often the employee has left | the airport feeling not too kindly about his company. This situation, now that it has come to my (1) attention, will be corrected in the near future. I have asked the Travel Department to formulate a plan by | which our employees will be given the same standard of service as that provided for paying passengers. This | new plan will make traveling on a pass more pleasant and a whole lot easier.

Under the new plan you simply | call the regular ticket office and tell them what space you want. They will handle your travel plans.

This new system (2) will benefit both you and the company. No longer will you have to waste time and money riding to and from | airports, hoping to get a seat on a plane. Nor will you have to stand in front of the ticket counter at the airport, | waiting for a flight on which somebody has made a cancellation. All this work is now transferred to the | regular ticket office, which is in a far better position to take care of it. To make this plan work, however, (3) requires the co-operation of every employee who uses his pass. Very little effort on | your part is necessary.

Here are some of the things you can do:

1. Be sure you know the flight number and date on | which you plan to travel.

2. When you call, identify yourself immediately, giving your name, address, | telephone number, and your pass number. Be sure to mention the type of pass you hold.

3. Call the regular ticket (4) office promptly if you change your plans.

If you will observe these rules, I am sure you will find your pass valuable | when you make trips on personal business or for pleasure.

There may be occasions when, without confirmation, you | may obtain a space on your own initiative by appearing at the airport around flight time. Seats often open | up at the very last minute. But circumstances such as these are beyond the company's control. John Brown (5) (1.43)

70

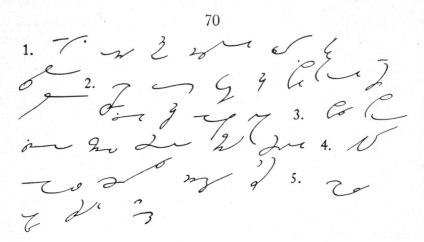

Key: (1) Entertaining, result, suffer, schedules, certain, possibilities, ideal. (2) Combine, organization, profit, social, habits, interview, determine, himself, socially, knowledge, trouble. (3) Aptitude, ability, humor, as you know, failure, if you want, factors. (4) Depended, employ, candidate, succeed, supervision. (5) Complete, report, findings, under consideration.

Dear Mr. Morris: All work and no play will make Jack a dull salesman. On the other hand, if he gives too much | consideration to entertaining his customers, he may be wasting a good deal of his time, with the result | that his sales suffer. Some salesmen have been known to plan their schedules so as to be in certain cities, not because | of the sales possibilities in that city, but because they know that they will have a good time there. The ideal (1) salesman will know how to combine business and entertaining so that his organization will profit most.

A | man's social habits are not always revealed in an interview. In an interview you can learn a good deal about | a man, but you cannot determine whether he knows how to handle himself socially. Yet this knowledge would | be of great value to you before you hire him as a salesman and go to the expense and trouble of training (2) him.

The Smith Aptitude Test not only reveals a man's ability to mix with other people but also | tells a good deal about his sense of humor.

These factors, as you know, play a great part in the success or failure |
of an individual as a salesman. If you want to be sure to hire only
the men who will produce for | you, it is vital for you to have first-
hand information on these factors.

For many years leading organizations (3) throughout the country have depended upon the Smith Aptitude Test to supply them
with desirable | information about men they were about to employ.

Very often the test shows that the candidate is not | suited for
the job for which he is being considered, but that he has great ability
in some other line. | Thus the organization can make the best use of
his service in the job in which he will succeed.

No supervision (4) is necessary in giving the Smith Test. All
you do is give the man the necessary papers, which | we supply.
After he fills them out, you send them to us. We rate the papers and
make out a complete report of | our findings. This report is mailed
only to you. The report will contain a recommendation whether you
should | or should not hire the candidate under consideration.

Write us for more information. Very truly yours, (5) (1.43)

71

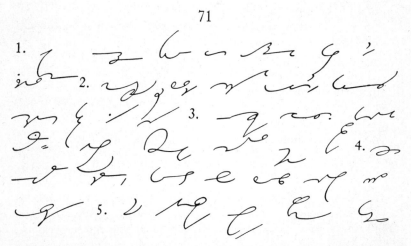

Key: (1) To become, museum, born, of course, inducements, privileges, support, history. (2) You will find, earliest, customs, located,
prominent, construction, possible, a dollar, several thousand dollars.
(3) Engaged, collecting, pictures, Indian, traveled, developed, country,
in the future, exhibit. (4) Canoe, modern, steamship, promises, any-

where, earnestly, contribute, worthy, lifetime. (5) Further, described, neighborhood, I hope you will, personally.

Dear Friend: This is an invitation for you to become a member of the City Museum, the museum | of the city in which you were born. I cannot, of course, offer you any special inducements or privileges | that you will receive when you pay your dues, as other organizations can. All I can say is that this is an | appeal to you to help support this museum, which tells the history of our great city.

In the City Museum (1) you will find the story of this city from its earliest days. You will see how its customs changed and how | it grew into one of the most important cities in the world.

The museum is now located in the | beautiful building that was given to the city by a prominent citizen. Its construction was made possible | by gifts from about two hundred fifty citizens, who gave from a dollar to as much as several thousand (2) dollars.

The museum is now actively engaged in collecting a series of pictures showing the city | from the days that it was an Indian village up to the present time. It will show how people lived in their | homes and the types of lighting and heating that they used. It will also show how they traveled and how they developed | the city into one of the largest cities in the country.

In the future we plan an exhibit of the (3) part that shipping played in the development of our city, from the Indian canoe to the modern steamship | of today. This exhibit promises to be the most interesting of its kind ever presented anywhere. | It is one that everyone will want to see and study.

We earnestly hope that you will find it possible | to become a member and that you will contribute to this worthy cause. Your membership will last a lifetime, (4) and you will not be asked to pay any further dues.

The different types of membership are described on the enclosed | folder. Select the type that you prefer; and send in your application for it, together with your fee. We | will then send you a membership card.

When you are in this neighborhood, I hope you will come in to see me. I shall | be glad to tell you more about the museum and to show you around personally. Very cordially yours, (5) (1.43)

72

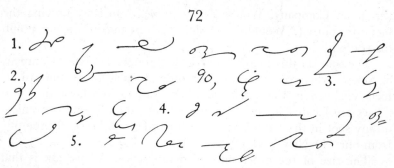

Key: (1) Fact that, to believe, mailed, weeks ago, collection, achievement, merchant. (2) To choose, furthermore, complete, 90 per cent, perhaps, reason. (3) Profit, several hundred, greatest, proportion. (4) Easily, your order, manner, convenient, United States, promptly. (5) Turn, difference, misplaced, duplicate.

Dear Friend: Here is a fact that some people may find difficult to believe. The Jones Company catalogue that we | mailed to you two weeks ago contains more than 45,000 items. Considering present times, a collection | of 45,000 items represents a real achievement. It is an interesting bit of information | for all of us in this line of business. Especially is it important for you as a successful merchant. (1) It means that when you open your Jones Company catalogue you have a complete stock of merchandise from which | to choose. Furthermore, you can be sure that, after you have ordered it, you will receive it.

Just how complete our stock | is is indicated by the fact that many merchants buy as much as 90 per cent of all their goods from the | Jones Company. Perhaps the most important reason why they do this is that our goods sell quickly and give the merchant (2) a good profit.

Records of several hundred stores show that the ones that make the best profits are the ones that | buy the greatest proportion of their stock from the Jones Company. The smaller this proportion is, the smaller are | the profits; the greater the proportion is, the greater are the profits.

These merchants have proved to their complete | satisfaction that it pays them to buy the greatest proportion of their stock from the Jones Company. Wouldn't you like (3) to start proving this fact for yourself? Wouldn't you like to start making bigger profits for yourself?

You can do this | easily. Just look through the Jones Company catalogue when you have another order to place. Use the order | form enclosed in the catalogue when sending in your order. Our offices are located in such a manner | that there is one convenient to any spot in the United States. Your order will be filled promptly from our (4) New York office.

The size of the order makes no difference. All we ask is that your orders average $15 | or more through the year. This will enable us to keep our handling costs in line, which, in turn, will enable | us to continue to offer you lower prices that mean better profits for you.

If in some way your Jones | Company catalogue has been misplaced, do not hesitate to write us for a duplicate copy. Sincerely yours, (5) (1.43)

73

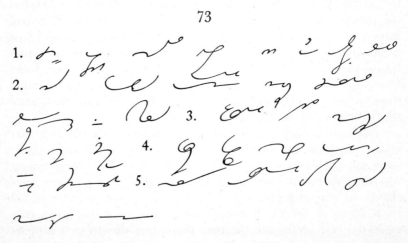

Key: (1) Chicago, reputation, country, travelers, world, superior, anticipating, thoroughly. (2) You want, pleasant, welcome, unofficial, secretary, telegrams, a hundred, different. (3) Operators, duty, you will find, everything, comfort, housekeeper. (4) Private, prepare, garage, located, entrance, few minutes. (5) Credit, entitles, automobile, account, you will understand, more and more.

Dear Mr. Green: There are many reasons why the Chicago Hotel has the reputation of being one of | the finest hotels in the country.

For more than seventy years, the Chicago Hotel has been serving travelers | from all parts of the world.

From the very moment that you step from your cab or car, you will find the superior | service of the Chicago Hotel anticipating your every desire.

A thoroughly trained clerk will (1) assign you the type of room you desire at the price you want to pay. A pleasant floor clerk will welcome you to your | floor, where she will be your "unofficial secretary" during your stay. She will take your telephone messages | when you are out of your room. She will handle your incoming mail and your telegrams and supply you with information | of every type. She will be happy to perform for you any one of a hundred different (2) services that will make your stay more pleasant. For the convenience of our guests, we have a staff of telephone | operators constantly on duty.

On each floor of the Chicago Hotel you will find twenty maids to keep your | room clean and equipped with everything necessary for your comfort. So thorough is the service that the | housekeeper must inspect 107 different items every time that your room is made ready for use. (3)

The Chicago Hotel has been famous for its food since 1871. Today, there are six public | dining rooms and thirty-five private dining rooms. Nine kitchens prepare the food for these rooms.

When you come to the Chicago | Hotel, our doorman takes care of your car. He drives it for you to our garage, which is located just one block | from the main entrance of the hotel. The car will be delivered to the front entrance a few minutes after you (4) call for it. Your credit card entitles you to charge all your automobile bills. Or, if you prefer, they may be | placed on your room account.

From the moment you arrive until the time you leave, you will understand more and more how | the Chicago Hotel has earned its fine reputation.

The next time you plan to be in Chicago, be sure to | write us in advance so that we may reserve for you the exact accommodations that you wish. Cordially yours, (5) (1.44)

74

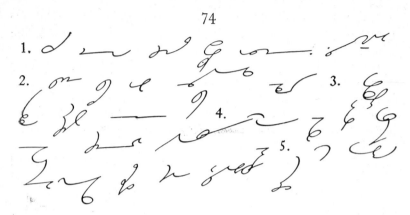

Key: (1) I want, summer, secondly, appreciation, recommending, headquarters. (2) I wonder, actively, rest, needless to say, uncertain. (3) Preparations, busier, for a few days, more and more, however. (4) Quality, in the past, special, private, improvements, few months, delighted, in spite. (5) Confident, pleasant, you will be able, efficiently, future, self-addressed, Very sincerely yours.

Dear Mrs. Jones: This letter has two purposes. First, I want to thank you for visiting us at the South Beach Hotel | this summer. Secondly, I want to express to you my appreciation and that of the owners of the | hotel for recommending it to Mrs. Davis and her party of five people. As you probably know, the | party made the hotel its headquarters during the entire summer and plans to come back again next summer. (1)

I wonder whether you know that our organization also manages the West Shore Hotel in Palm Beach during | the winter months. The season actively begins in November and runs through till March. If you are planning a rest | this winter, needless to say we shall be happy to have you with us.

Perhaps you are uncertain about the | activities of a hotel like ours during these trying times. If you are, let me assure you that we have made (2) preparations to operate the West Shore Hotel as usual. Present indications are that we shall be | busier than ever before. More than ever, people want to relax, even if it is only for a few | days, from the strain of the times.

These are difficult times. The price of food has risen more than 20 per cent, and some | items are becoming more and more difficult to get at all. You may rest assured, however, that we will use (3) every effort to maintain the high quality of all meals that we have maintained in the past.

As at the South | Beach Hotel in the summer, our guests will enjoy many special advantages at the West Shore in the winter. | We shall continue to maintain our private bathing beach, on which many improvements have been made during the past | few months.

What's more, you will be delighted with our rates, which are lower this year than ever before, in spite of the (4) rise in the cost of living.

We are confident that your stay in Florida will be a pleasant one and that it | will refresh you so that you will be able to perform your regular duties more efficiently.

We are looking | forward to receiving a reservation from you in the very near future. To be sure that your reservation | comes direct to me, please use the stamped and self-addressed envelope that is enclosed. Very sincerely yours, (5) (1.44)

75

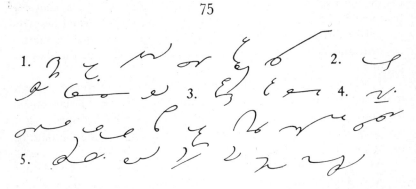

Key: (1) Thank you for your, representing, discount, another, observe, that did not. (2) Let us, entire, premium, third. (3) Expects, suppose, terms. (4) Quoting, actually, regardless, I believe, respect, definite, customers, I doubt. (5) Violating, earned, forward, further, in the future, you will find.

Dear Mr. Henry: Thank you for your check for $17.34, representing the 5 per cent | discount taken in error in your settlement of our March 12 invoice.

You write that you were allowed the 5 per cent | discount on two other lots of material that you bought from another company. You will observe that | we were the only manufacturers that did not allow the 5 per cent discount after 30 days. Let us (1) examine this situation, Mr. Henry.

The terms of sale provide that the entire amount be paid in 30 | days. If payment is made within 15 days of the invoice, a discount of 5 per cent is allowed. The discount | is a premium for prompt payment.

Let us say that there are three dealers in your town buying from one manufacturer. | Two of those dealers pay promptly in 15 days and earn their discounts. The third dealer pays in 30 (2) days and expects the same premium. Suppose you were one of the two who paid in 15 days. Would you consider | that the manufacturer had been fair to allow the third buyer a discount when he paid in 30 days? | I do not believe you would.

Let us consider the case of the manufacturer who sells to you on the terms | of 30 days net, with a discount of 5 per cent for payment in 15 days. Is the manufacturer (3) serious when he gives you those terms? Or is he merely quoting these terms as a matter of form and actually | giving the discount regardless of the date of payment?

I believe, Mr. Henry, that you really have more respect | for a manufacturer who has definite terms and expects all customers to keep within them. I doubt | that you would have respect for a manufacturer who allows a cash discount regardless of the date of payment. (4)

As a matter of fact, a manufacturer who does this is violating the law. The law says that a | manufacturer must not allow a discount unless that discount is earned.

We appreciate the order you | have placed with us and hope we may look forward to further orders in the future.

You will find us always willing | to give you every reasonable accommodation. Write us whenever you feel we can help you. Yours truly, (5) (1.45)

76

Key: (1) I want, gave me, discuss, furnace, on the market, some years ago, points, occurred, I hope that, articles, bring, profit. (2) At least, another, efforts, secondly, capital. (3) Prepared, territory, someone, harvest, attention, wherever, has been. (4) Comparatively, period, radical, possibilities, typical, example, accomplish. (5) 200, expects, greater, engineering, departments, almost, assured, won't, reconsider.

Dear Mr. Quinn: I want to thank you for the opportunity you gave me to discuss with you the Smith Furnace | that we placed on the market some years ago. Since that talk a number of points that we did not discuss have occurred | to me, and I hope that you will find an opportunity to consider them.

First, let me ask you a question. | How many articles are you handling at the present time that will bring you a gross profit of at least (1) $100? The chances are that there are not many.

Well, the Smith Furnace will bring in at least $100 | and, with proper handling, may bring in even more. There is not another article that will repay your selling | efforts so fully as the Smith Furnace. To begin with, it is easy to sell. Secondly, it brings in a large | enough profit to pay a dealer for giving a good share of his time and capital to it.

Our national (2) advertising has prepared the territory. All that is needed now is someone to harvest the crop. For | seven years the

Smith Furnace has been well advertised in over twenty magazines that are widely read. We have | spent more than $250,000 bringing the features of the Smith Furnace to the attention of | the public. Wherever newspapers and national magazines are read, the story of the Smith Furnace has been (3) told and retold.

More than 125,000 furnaces have been installed in a comparatively | short period, considering that the idea represented a radical change in heating methods. But the | sales possibilities have hardly been touched. The success of the dealers who handled the early models is | typical of what those who follow their example can hope to accomplish.

In Dallas, one dealer has been selling (4) 150 to 200 units a year; and he just wrote us that he expects an even greater sale | this year.

Our engineering, advertising, and selling departments are so complete that your store would be almost | like a branch of our company; and with such co-operation your success would be assured.

In view of these facts, | won't you reconsider your decision to wait until next year to handle the Smith Furnace? Very truly yours, (5) (1.46)

77

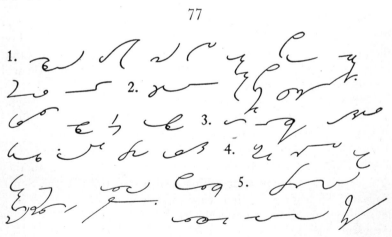

Key: (1) Concerned, automobile, you want, to know, responsible, ability, no such thing, formerly, more than. (2) Settlement, above those, accustomed, predict, next year, 100 per cent, last year. (3) Of course, engaged, industry, policyholders, power, reduce. (4) Officers, utmost, represent, prospect, investigated, record, application. (5) Background, sound, determining, requirements, normal, adjusted.

Dear Friend: No doubt you are concerned about the increased rate for your automobile insurance, and you want to know | what is responsible for it. I shall try to answer this to the best of my ability.

As you know, today | there is no such thing as a low-priced car. The car that formerly sold for $800 costs now | $1,500 to $2,000. Used cars now often sell for more than the former price of a new (1) automobile of the same make and model. These facts have been responsible for the raising of values to such an | extent that the settlement of claims would be very difficult under the old rates.

All costs today are so far | above those that we have been accustomed to paying that we cannot even predict that we can maintain the present | rates next year. Repair costs on automobiles for this year are more than 100 per cent above those of last (2) year. These increases must, of course, be included in the cost of insurance.

The companies engaged in the | automobile insurance industry last year lost more than $150,000,000; and we, of course, | lost our share.

It is my feeling that all automobile insurance rates could be much lower if we would all be | more careful. We, as policyholders in this great organization, have it within our power to reduce the (3) rate of insurance by reducing accidents to a minimum. Your officers are doing their utmost | to accept only persons who represent good risks. A new prospect is thoroughly investigated before | a policy is issued. His past driving record is checked, and we can usually tell by this means whether | he is a safe risk. On our new application forms we also ask for a number of character witnesses (4) so that we can have some background information with which to judge the person. This has helped us a great deal in | determining whether we should or should not issue a policy. I am happy to say, however, that our | organization is sound and is always ready to meet any requirements in the way of service or payments. |

When the day arrives that normal conditions are again with us, our rates will quickly be adjusted. Yours truly, (5) (1.46)

78

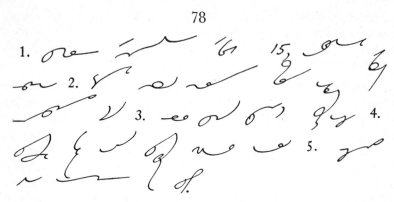

Key: (1) Agreement, transcontinental, transportation, 15 per cent, entitles, to charge, any one of our. (2) Systems, card, credit, avoid, reservations, undoubtedly, found. (3) Merely, account, identification, receipt. (4) Advance, possible, round, advisable, wallet, leather. (5) Incidentally, to our, welcome, attaching.

Dear Sir: Your company has entered into an agreement with the Transcontinental Air Lines for the purchase | of air transportation on an open-account basis at a 15 per cent discount. Under this agreement | your company has given you an air-travel card, which we have issued. This card entitles you to charge air | transportation to your company's account with us at a 15 per cent discount.

Any one of our offices (1) will honor your card in payment for transportation over the systems of eighteen leading air lines. The card will | be honored by our line as well as by any of the other seventeen air lines.

By using this credit card, | you can (*a*) obtain a discount of 15 per cent, (*b*) avoid carrying cash to purchase tickets, and (*c*) obtain | reservations more conveniently and quickly.

As you have undoubtedly found, your card is easy to use. (2) Merely telephone any office of our air lines about a reservation. Give your name, your company's name, | and the account number shown on your card. After the reservation is made, you can obtain your ticket at one | of the many conveniently located city ticket offices. You need only present your card as | identification and sign a travel receipt that authorizes us to bill your company.

Always make (3) reservations for air trips as far in advance as possible. If you are planning a round trip and know the schedule | on which you wish to return, it is advisable to request a round-trip ticket and a return reservation. |

For the convenience of our customers, we have made up a special wallet in which credit cards can be | carried. The wallet is made of a fine leather and is just the right size for holding the card. You can get one of (4) these handy cardholders from any one of our offices. There is no charge for it.

Incidentally, if you | should misplace your credit card, please report the loss at once to our main office. The card will be made void, and a new | one will be issued to you.

We welcome you as a new credit-card holder. To save you time when telephoning | for reservations, we are attaching two handy telephone stickers that give our New York number. Yours truly, (5) (1.48)

79

Key: (1) Concerned, complete, production, turn, certain, to do, circumstances. (2) Of course, schedule, facilities, unable, because, enthusiastic. (3) Emergency, whether, permanent, temporary, we have been, contract, adjust. (4) Some of the, resort, expected, pleasantly, surprised, slightly. (5) Why not, dividends, prepared, describing.

Dear Mr. Sims: Perhaps you, like many other manufacturers, are concerned that you cannot get your complete | line of goods ready for your dealers. Your production lines, however, can turn out only a certain number of | units and no more. Furthermore, your labor can do only so much and no more.

The best thing to do under such | circumstances is to face the facts and turn out as much as you can and let the rest wait until you have more time. (1)

Of course, it is only natural to feel that your own plant can do the best job of turning out your goods. But, if | there are some items that you must produce, but just cannot work into your manufacturing schedule, why not take | advantage of our manufacturing facilities? We suggested this to a number of other manufacturers | who were unable to do all their work because of heavy schedules; and they were not enthusiastic (2) about the suggestion at first. But, because the emergency was so great, they finally tried us to see whether | we could live up to our claims. Today we are turning out products for twenty manufacturers, and it begins | to look as though it were going to be a permanent rather than a temporary affair.

We have been | doing this type of contract manufacturing for more than fifty years. We know what it is to adjust our machines (3) to those of the other fellow.

Some of the manufacturers who came to us as a last resort naturally | expected us to do a good job, but they also were expecting higher costs for our work. They were pleasantly | surprised when they found that our charges were so reasonable. In most cases, we were able to do the job | at a cost only slightly higher than it would have been if the manufacturer had handled the job in his (4) own plant.

Why not give some thought to trying our service? Why not see exactly what we have to offer your company? | Why not find out how it may pay big dividends for you to look into contract manufacturing?

We have | prepared a handy 48-page booklet describing our service and our facilities in detail. It is | yours without charge or obligation if you will return the enclosed card immediately. Very truly yours, (5) (1.48)

80

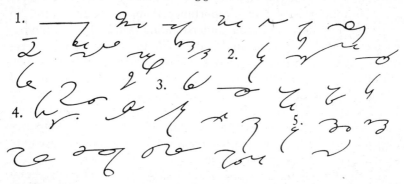

Key: (1) Managers, as you know, notebooks, source, to our, to push, careful, interfere, country, co-operation, to us. (2) Possible, customers, might, bring, conflict, effort. (3) Point, mind, represents, report position. (4) Better understanding, entire, desirable, quantities, considerable. (5) Consequently, you can see, complain, we may not be able, agreement, competitors, object, count.

To Our Office Managers and Salesmen: As you know, our line of school notebooks is a fine source of profit to our | organization; and we should continue to push the sale of these notebooks wherever we can. We must be careful, | however, not to interfere with the sales of the large number of dealers all over the country who also | handle our line. The co-operation of these dealers is very important to us, and we must do (1) everything possible to keep their good will by not selling direct to their customers.

Whenever you meet a | situation that might bring about a conflict between us and one of the dealers, be sure that you do all you | can to protect the interests of the dealer. Above all, be careful that you do not offer a customer | a price lower than that of the dealer and do not make any effort to take the business away from the dealer. (2) The point you should keep in mind is that every notebook that the dealer sells represents a profit for our | company.

If you have reason to believe that the dealer is treating the customers unfairly by overcharging | for our goods, report the situation to us so that we may take care of it from this office. We have | had a great deal of experience in matters of this kind and are in a better position to handle it (3) than are the men in the field.

This matter is of more importance than you may realize. So that you may have | a better understanding of the entire situation, let me say that we have found it desirable to | enter into an agreement with the Smith Notebook Company to handle our line. Through its dealer system, that | company sells great quantities of our goods, on which we realize a considerable profit without any (4) special selling effort on our part. Consequently, you can see that, if many of those dealers complain to | the Smith Notebook Company that we are trying to take away their customers, we may not be able to renew | the agreement.

If you find a consumer using a competitor's line of goods, however, by all means | make him an object of your best selling efforts.

I am sure we can count on your co-operation. James Austin (5) (1.48)

PART V

90 WORDS A MINUTE

81

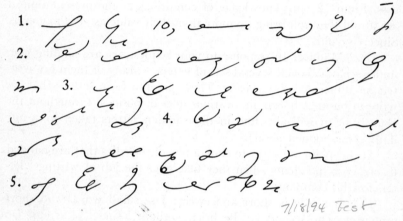

7/18/94 Test

Key: (1) Majority, purchasers, 10 per cent, remains, unsold, offered, interview. (2) Turned, reduction, removed, accounts, auction, private, success. (3) Response, separate, letters, illustrated, letterheads, various. (4) Point, we want, rules, correspondents, sentences, clearness, recipient, words, conversation, signal. (5) Whenever, expressed, effective, length, essence.

Dear Sir: You will be glad to know that most of the lots at the north end of the estate have now been sold at fairly good prices. | In the majority of cases, the purchasers have made a down payment of 10 per cent.

That part of the property facing | on Main Street that was reserved for stores still remains unsold. Although there have been some inquiries about these lots, the prices we | asked have been far too high. We are offered much less. You will remember that at our interview I expressed the opinion that the (1) prices we asked would be considered too high, and this has turned out to be the case. I suggest that they be revised. My own impression | is that a reduction of perhaps 25 per cent will have to be made before they can be sold.

The trees on the property | have been removed and sold. We managed to get $500 for them, as will be seen in the accounts.

The row of | houses along the river has been put up for auction. I have tried to sell them by private arrangements, but without success. From (2) my knowledge of conditions at the present time, I am afraid they will bring no more than their value as | old materials. Sincerely yours, *omit*

Dear Madam: In response to your request, we are sending you, under separate cover, several sets of letters. | Many of them are written on illustrated letterheads. These are the form letters that we write to business houses in | various lines of business throughout the country. You will also find in these folders letters taken from our daily correspondence. (3)

At this point we want to state a few of the rules that are handed to our correspondents when they take over the job of writing | letters for this company.

The first rule is short and sweet: Use small words and short sentences. The second is: Be brief, without losing | clearness. Do not go into too many details that the recipient has not enough time to read. As far as possible, | you should use only words and phrases that would be used in personal conversation. Confine the letter to a single page (4) whenever possible.

From your own experience, you know that many of the letters you receive fill two pages and could | as well be expressed in one page. There would be no loss in clearness, and perhaps the letters would be more effective. Most of the form | letters that we use are two pages in length when they first come to the vice-president for approval. They are revised many | times so as to get the essence of the letter in the fewest number of words.

Please return the letters. Very sincerely yours, (5) (1.31)

82

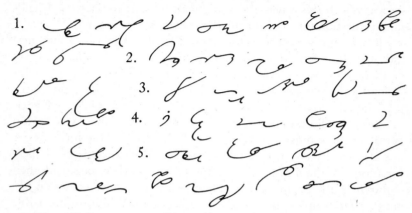

Key: (1) Last year, contribute, fund, I am sure, worthy, operate, to us, happiness, fortunate, admit. (2) Difficulties, contracts, complete, anxious, some of those, children, publicity. (3) Paid, workers, industry, beyond, many of the, families, poorer. (4) Whose, prosperity, summer, applications, fun, streets, pleasant. (5) Answers, supplied, thousands, $1,000, in addition, clerical, we hope that, you will find, to make, we enclose, already.

Dear Mr. Smith: Last year you were kind enough to contribute to our Fresh Air Fund. We know that there are many calls for contributions | during the year, but I am sure you will agree that none are more worthy than this one.

Some people seem to have taken it | for granted that the Fresh Air Fund would not operate this year. But why should that be so? In these trying times, it seems to us that | everything we can do to add a little happiness to the lives of the less fortunate should be done.

I must admit that (1) we have had our difficulties. For many months it looked as if we could not get the necessary help to operate the camps, | but I now have on my desk the contracts of a complete staff. In a few weeks they will be moving in to get the camps ready for | the boys and girls who will soon follow.

There is still one point about which we are anxious. Will some of those people who contributed | last year think that there can be no poor children left in New York this year? So much publicity has been given to the wages (2) being paid to workers that our friends might question the need for these free camps.

But we must remember that New York has had very | little new industry. It is true that wages have gone up; but so has the cost of living. For many families, the cost of | living has increased far beyond any increase in income. Because of these facts, many of the poor families that we helped | last year are even poorer this year.

Leaving all that out of consideration, however, there will always be many thousands (3) of homes in New York whose fortunes are not affected by any rise or fall in prosperity. The one hope of these families | is the Fresh Air Camps to which they can send their children in the summer. Year after year, as summer comes on, we get thousands upon | thousands of applications. Will it be impossible to take care of all these children this summer? Must we leave them to | get what fun they can from the hot streets? Or shall we send them to the camps, where they will have two pleasant and profitable months in the (4) fresh air?

The answers to these questions must be supplied by you and thousands of other friends.

This year we are once again making | our personal contribution of $1,000. In addition, we are assigning two of our employees to take care | of all the clerical work without charge.

We hope that you will find it possible to contribute again. To make it | as easy as possible for you to send us your check, we enclose an envelope that is already addressed and needs no postage.

Yours truly, (5) (1.31)

83

Key: (1) During the past, to know, grateful, possible, card, amount, indicated, as soon as. (2) Cleaner, you will find, complete, submit, volume. (3) Listed, number, floor, wax, in spite. (4) Firms, obliged, nearly, current, in the past, convenience, to us, minimum, clerical. (5) Established, less than, regulation, to be sure, as soon as possible.

Dear Mr. Brand: The sole purpose of this letter is to thank you for the orders you have been giving us during the past six | months. We wish you to know that we value your business very much and are grateful for the opportunity to be of service | to you. This increased business makes it possible for us to send you the enclosed bonus card.

Each time you place an order | with us, attach the card to the order, and the amount of your purchases will be indicated on it. As soon as your card (1) shows purchases of $25, we will send you, free of charge, a dozen bottles of our rug cleaner. You will find complete | details of this plan on the back of the bonus card.

You will receive a dozen bottles on each card that you submit. The more | cards you submit, the better we shall like it. We issue cards on the basis of volume of business. This offer will hold until | October. I know that, as soon as your customers learn about the things that this rug cleaner will do, you will have a great many (2) calls for it.

This seems a good opportunity to send you a copy of our new price list, which has just come off the press. I | am enclosing a copy. In it you will find listed many new products for which we have great expectations. You will also | find a number of price changes on our older products. The increase in price on our special floor wax, which you have been selling | so successfully, is only slight, in spite of the large increase in our costs. Because of the fine orders that you and many other (3) firms have been sending us, we are not obliged to increase prices nearly so much as current trends would indicate. Please notice | that your profits on our wax products are still at the same high level. In fact, you will make slightly more money on each case than you have | in the past.

The new check list that is given on the back cover of the price list is for the convenience of our customers, | so that they can check the items they need and return the list to us with the minimum of clerical work.

Of course (4) these new prices are established under laws governing our type of business; and no products may be sold for less than the prices | listed. This regulation protects your full profit.

To be sure that you get the products that you want, let us fill your fall orders | as soon as possible. The farther ahead you can determine your needs, the better are your chances of getting exactly | what you want and when you want it. If you wait until the last minute before ordering, you | risk disappointment.

Yours very truly, (5) (1.32)

84

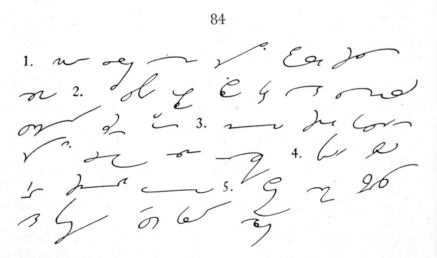

Key: (1) Worn, energy, gone, studying, explains, fatigue, cure. (2) Adapt, richer, happier, possess, themselves, ignorant, accustomed, physical, overwork. (3) One of the most, features, practical, stimulating, simple, anyone, engaged. (4) Bothered, tired, one hundred thousand, few months, on the market. (5) Approval, coupon, after that time, to us, benefited, transaction, pointed, conserve.

Dear Mr. Lee: Do you feel worn out every evening after putting in a day at the office? Is your energy competely | gone at the end of the day, so that you cannot enjoy your family or your friends in the evening? If that is the | case, you will be interested in our new book, "How to Save Energy."

This book was written by a doctor who has spent many | years in studying people and why they tire quickly. In this book he explains the cause of fatigue and how to cúre it. The plan (1) suggested in the book is easy to adapt to your own life. The book has hundreds of suggestions that will enable you | to make your life richer and happier.

Only those who know how to release the energies they possess can live a really | full life and reach the goals they have set for themselves. Most persons who lack energy are ignorant of the real causes of | their fatigue. They have been accustomed to thinking that it was brought about by physical and mental overwork. In nine cases (2) out of ten this is not so, and the book shows why.

Probably one of the most valuable features of the book is the practical | five-point plan it gives for stimulating energy. This plan is so simple that anyone can easily follow it. | In addition, the book shows you how to organize your life so that it is well balanced. The plan is so flexible that it | can be followed by almost any person regardless of the type of work in which he is engaged. Once you start using the plan, (3) you will no longer be bothered by that tired feeling. New energy, enabling you to tackle difficult tasks with ease and | confidence, will start to flow through you. What is more, you will really start to enjoy life.

More than one hundred thousand copies of | the first edition of "How to Save Energy" were sold in the first few months that the book was on the market. The book has now | gone into its fourth printing.

We are so confident that you will want to own a copy that we are willing to send you one on (4) approval. If you will fill out the enclosed coupon and return it to us, we will send you a copy, which you may examine | for ten days. If after that time you do not feel that the book has benefited you, simply return it and the transaction | will be closed.

If you find that the book has pointed out to you ways to conserve energy, then send us your check for $2.50. | This offer is open for a limited time only; so be sure to take advantage of it soon. Sincerely yours, (5) (1.35)

85

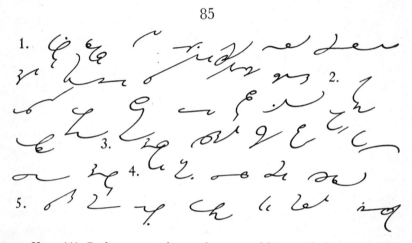

Key: (1) Perhaps, surprise, to know, nothing, to find, current, familiar, substance, volumes, editors, discussed, extracts. (2) To be sure, retained, original, approval, almost, exception, handled, represented, last year. (3) Subscribers, thousands, afford, expert, program, annual, subscription. (4) Offering, immediately, first, canceled. (5) Editions, form, enriching, pleasure, P.S., friends, who might be.

Dear Friend: Perhaps it will be a surprise to you to know that you can be well read for $4 a year—and it will cost you nothing | to find out how.

You can enjoy current best-selling books in condensed form at a great saving of time and money. You can become | familiar with the substance of new books in all fields, even though you do not have time to read the complete volumes.

Each month | our editors study the new books that are being widely discussed and then select four of the best. They make extracts of each book, (1) using the author's own words. Each book is cut down to about one hundred pages.

To be sure that the style and content of each | book are retained, each of our versions is sent to the original publisher and author for their approval. Almost without | exception authors have been delighted with the way their books were handled.

By actual count the forty-eight best-selling books | that were represented in the Reader's Monthly last year cost $140 in the regular editions. Yet our (2) readers obtained the vital content of these books for only $4.

As a subscriber to the Reader's Monthly, you will | join thousands who are making great savings in time and money on new books that no well-informed persons can afford to miss. You will | be assured of receiving each month an expert selection of the world's finest books in all fields.

Start to enjoy our planned reading | program, and make a saving over the regular annual subscription price of $4 by accepting this special (3) offer at the reduced rate we are offering to our new subscribers only. Send the enclosed form to us with no money. | The current magazine will be sent to you immediately. If you are not delighted with the very first issue you receive, | tell us so within ten days and your subscription will be canceled without question. If you are completely satisfied, pay | only $2 for a seven months' subscription. In those seven months you will receive the vital contents of twenty-eight books (4) that would cost you more than $70 in the regular editions.

Send no money now. After we receive your | subscription, we will send you a bill each month along with your copy of the Reader's Monthy. Just mail the enclosed form, to start cutting | your reading bills and enriching your reading pleasure. Very truly yours,

P.S. After you have read this letter, please pass it | on to any of your friends who might be interested in joining our club. You will be doing them a genuine service. (5) (1.40)

86

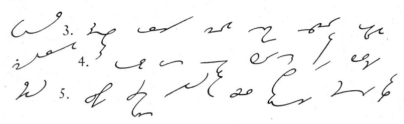

Key: (1) Recently, one of the most, birthday, accepted, accompany, there wasn't, word, explanation, policies. (2) We understand, difficulties, common sense, requirements, promptly. (3) Subscriptions, renewed, one of those, coupon, any one of the, reports, hundreds. (4) Letters, of course, impossible, articles, subjected, earliest, if it is not. (5) Attached, checkbook, don't, worry, absolute, forgot, special.

Dear Friend: I received quite a shock recently. For years, I have ordered one of the most important fashion magazines for a | friend as a birthday present. This year I placed the order as usual. Two weeks ago I received word that only two-year orders | were being accepted and that cash should accompany the order. There wasn't a word of regret or explanation. |

This has led me to review our own policies on the Business Monthly. Have we made the same error that the fashion magazine (1) has made? I can assure you we have not. We understand all too well the difficulties under which publishers must work with | the paper shortage. This paper shortage means that we cannot fill all the orders we receive. Common sense tells us, however, that | we should make every effort to take care of the requirements of those friends who have been getting our magazine through the years. |

That is why this letter is going to you. The last copy of the June issue of Business Monthly was sold on June 1. Experience (2) indicates, however, that about 20 per cent of the subscriptions ending with June will not be renewed. Do you | wish to speak for one of those places? If you return the enclosed coupon at once, we have reason to hope that we can begin the | order with July.

I think you will agree from reading any one of the past year's issues that Edward Davis is turning | out a wonderful magazine. Take, for example, his reports on world business conditions today. We have in our files hundreds (3) of letters from readers saying that this is a feature they would not miss. It is, of course, impossible to tell you about | all the important articles that are to appear this fall. I can tell you, however, that each article is subjected to | this test: Is the article vitally important? If it is, it appears in the earliest possible issue. If it | is not, there is no place for it in the Business Monthly.

If you wish to enjoy the Business Monthly in the days ahead, let me (4) urge you to return the attached coupon at once.

If your checkbook is not handy, don't worry about it. We will send you a | bill later. But be sure to send that order along promptly. We cannot give you an absolute promise, but we will do our best | to begin your subscription with the July issue. Cordially yours,

P.S. I forgot to mention that there is a special | price of $2.50 for one year to servicemen. Orders for servicemen will be given preference over all others. (5) (1.41)

87

Key: (1) Sample, some time ago, we hoped, worth while, co-operate, up to date, speakers. (2) First, good enough, receipt, behind, during the past year, hundreds, volumes, I am sure, effort, dividends. (3) Description, together, discounts, developments, moment, earliest, another. (4) Department, forthcoming, approximate, on the market, we want. (5) Maximum, constant, succeed, assured, criticisms, courtesy.

Dear Mr. Brown: Enclosed is a sample of the first issue of Book News, the first printing of this magazine. You will remember | that I wrote you some time ago regarding our plans for this new magazine and how we hoped to make it worth while for all publishers | to co-operate with us in its publication.

In order that the information that we supply in that magazine | shall be complete and up to date, we need your co-operation as well as that of all other publishers. How can you (1) co-operate? Here are a number of ways:

First, please be good enough to acknowledge receipt of this sample issue. While you | are writing, tell us what you think of the magazine and the idea behind it.

We should also like to have a list of all | the books you published during the past year. I realize that some publishers have issued hundreds of volumes during that time, | but I am sure that the time and effort spent in making this list for us will pay real dividends. If it is possible, I (2) should also like to have a brief description of each book, together with information on the number of pages it contains, | how much it sells for, and what discounts are allowed to dealers.

Book News can be of most value to book dealers if it contains | the latest developments in the book field. Consequently, would you arrange to send me a copy of each new book the moment | it comes off the press? This will enable me to list the book in the earliest possible issue of the magazine.

Another (3) important feature of Book News will be a department in which we give very important information about | forthcoming books. Would you, therefore, let me know the names of the books on which you are now working and the approximate date on which | they will be on the market? I am enclosing a special form that will make it easy for you to give me this information. | You may obtain more of these forms from our office if you should need them.

We want to make Book News a magazine that will be of (4) maximum help to you and others in the publishing business. Without your constant help, we cannot hope to succeed in this | goal. We shall appreciate any information you supply us, and you may

rest assured that your suggestions and criticisms | will always re-
ceive our utmost consideration. I am sure that we can count on
your co-operation in this matter. |

If there is ever any way in which we can return your courtesy,
we shall be more than happy to do so. Yours truly, (5) (1.41)

88

Key: (1) Few months, occurred, to us, relative, you would like to
know, one of our, county, familiar, hundreds. (2) Already, positions,
many of them, graduated, profitable, whether, employment, period,
runs, December, why not, someone. (3) Christmas, millions, upon our,
throughout this, workers, accurate, without. (4) Distribution, previous,
different, modern, transportation, 10 cents, almost, performing. (5)
Assured, interviews, accept, neighborly, P.S., selected, community, however, against.

Dear Neighbor: During the next few months we shall need
a good deal of help, and the thought occurred to us that you might
know of some friend | or relative in this town who might be willing
to help us.

We thought you would like to know about our problem and
as one of our | good neighbors in this county you would help us.

You may have seen our advertisements in local newspapers. A sample is enclosed | just in case you are not familiar with our company and with our magazine. In the neighboring towns hundreds of fine people, (1) from sixteen years of age to sixty-five, have already obtained interesting and well-paying positions with us. Many | of them had just graduated from high school and had never worked before. A number of interesting and profitable jobs | for others, whether they have had office experience or not, are still available. The employment period begins | in October and runs through to the end of December.

Why not suggest the idea of working for us to someone you know. (2) You will not only help him or her to earn hundreds of dollars before Christmas, but in addition you will be doing a | real service in these times to millions of our readers. Your help will send Christmas copies of the News Weekly to them on time. That | is why we are calling upon our neighbors throughout this county to help us get workers who will give these readers the prompt and | accurate service that will make their Christmas a happy one. Without this help we shall not be able to get the News Weekly out (3) on time for distribution to our many readers. *Stop*

People who have worked with us in previous seasons know how delightfully | different the work is. Working conditions are pleasant, the hours are short, and the salary is good. Meals are served in our own | modern lunchroom, where the best of food is served. Transportation to and from work is only 10 cents each way from almost any | part of town.

You will be performing a helpful service by asking anyone who might be interested in a position (4) of this kind to visit us. All who come are assured of prompt interviews and the chance to earn hundreds of dollars before Christmas. |

Please accept our thanks for your neighborly help. Sincerely yours,

P. S. This letter is being addressed to a carefully selected | list of names in this community. We have not had an opportunity, however, to check the names against our | list of employees. If by some chance you are already an employee of the News Weekly, please pass this letter along to a friend. (5) (1.41)

89

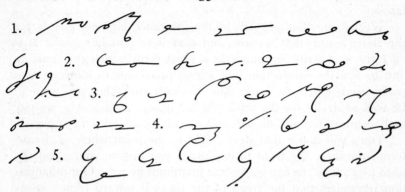

Key: (1) Do you know, they do not believe, term, some of them, really, policy, provides. (2) Premium, pure, nothing, assume, carry, first, everything else. (3) To pay, reason, to make, all right, describe, contribution, humanity, someone. (4) Commissions, including, point, we want, recognizes, toward. (5) Problem, person, ability, proving, drop, prospect, who want.

Dear Mr. Mills: Do you know that there are life insurance salesmen who will tell you that they do not believe in term insurance? | It does not seem possible; but there are some of them who are out in the field selling insurance every day, and there are some | of them in the home offices of life insurance companies, too.

Of course, they do not really mean that they do not believe | in term insurance. They must realize that every insurance policy that provides for cash values in later years has (1) a charge for term insurance in the premium payments.

Term insurance is pure protection—nothing more, nothing less. It is | term insurance that enables the insurance company to assume the risks of death. Without it, no insurance company | could carry on.

We believe in selling protection first so that, when a man dies, there will be money for food and clothing and | everything else that a family needs.

Have you noticed that, when a man dies, nobody seems to care about the kind of (2) insurance policy he owned? Everybody is interested, however, in how much the policy is going to | pay the family.

We assume that you are in the insurance business mainly for the same reason that we are, and that is to | make money. It is all right to describe insurance as a great contribution to humanity and to feel the satisfaction | of selling protection to someone who really needs it. At the same time, however, we think you want to be well paid (3) for the work you are doing. That is why we pay high commissions on all our policies, including term insurance.

You | will notice that we go right to the point when we discuss term insurance. We want to encourage you to give your client the most protection | he can get for the premiums he pays. Our organization recognizes that the trend of the times is toward term | insurance at low rates. That means that you can make quick sales that will bring more profit to you.

You realize, of course, that the insurance (4) problem of one person may not be the same as that of another person. Our job should be to sell each man the best type | of insurance, considering his ability to buy.

If you are working on a case that is proving difficult to close, | drop in to see us. We shall be glad to give you some new ideas on how to convince the prospect. We are always ready | to help you.

The client you can insure today is worth a dozen prospects who want the time to think over their problems! Yours truly, (5) (1.42)

90

Key: (1) Report, attendance, records, any other, find, another, Detroit, pointing. (2) Personal, usually, attitude, to make, absent, personnel. (3) Several times, telegram, reminded, immediately, second, removed, department. (4) Permitted, co-operation, foremen, absences, efficient, support, better, perhaps. (5) Expect, farther, against, replaced, similar, arrangements.

Dear Mr. Jones: I was sorry to see from your latest report that many employees in your factory have poor attendance | records.

I realize that you have a real problem to solve. If a worker does not want to work on Monday or on any | other day, there seems to be little that we can do about it. In many cases, the employee can easily find | another job if we fire him.

In our factory in Detroit, we have tried to solve this problem with posters pointing out the need (1) for steady work. The posters helped a little, but they were not personal enough. The worker usually took the attitude | that the posters were meant for the other fellow.

Our first device was planned to make it difficult for the employee who was | absent or late to get into the plant. An employee who is absent or late must give a good reason to the man in charge | of personnel. If he has no good reason for being away, a mark is put on his record. If he is absent or late several (2) times, he is replaced.

When an employee is absent, a telegram is sent to his home. In the telegram he is | reminded that our production is being held up by his absence; that, unless he has a good reason, he should report to work | immediately.

On the second day that an employee is absent without a good reason, his time card is removed from | the rack. In its place we put another card on which the employee is told to report to the Personnel Department when he (3) finally returns. He is not permitted to start work again until he satisfies the personnel manager that his | reason for absence is a good one.

Of course, we have the co-operation of our foremen. Each foreman realizes that, if | there are too many absences in his department, the work of that department is not very efficient. Naturally, | the foremen will support any plan that will make their records look better.

Does our plan work? Perhaps I can answer this best by telling (4) you that we have reduced absences by 50 per cent in the last two or three months. As time goes on, we expect to reduce | absences even further.

The workers seem to like the plan. Those who at first were against it were soon brought to see the advantages | of it. Only two or three who were not willing to co-operate were replaced.

If you should care to install a | similar plan in your factory, let me know, and I will make arrangements to talk with you and give you all the details. Yours truly, (5) (1.42)

91

Key: (1) Bargain, we have been able, nature, renewals, inducement, subscribers, entered, rush, pressure, involved. (2) Prevented, one year, under this, arrangement. (3) Additional, fewer, one of the, almost, somebody. (4) Convenient, I hope you will, to us, as you know, expire. (5) By the way, bring, armed, thoughtful, stationed, United States.

Dear Mr. Brown: Everybody loves a bargain. In years gone by, we have been able to offer our friends a bargain in | the nature of a Christmas present—a special one-year rate on renewals. This rate was an inducement to our subscribers to send | in their renewals so that they could be entered before the Christmas rush began. This arrangement enabled us to give | our friends a bargain and at the same time to relieve pressure on our office force.

This year the increased cost involved in printing the (1) News Magazine has prevented us from making this offer again. So we are doing the next best thing. We are offering to | pass along to subscribers the savings that come when a subscription is renewed for more than one year. This offer is good only until | November 10.

But there is still a way for you to save money on a one-year renewal. You can give the News Magazine | as a Christmas gift to one of your friends and mail the subscription in with your own renewal. Under this arrangement, the (2) first subscription will cost $4.50; the second subscription will cost only $3.50.

We are able | to offer you this lower rate on each additional subscription because fewer operations are involved in handling an | order of that type.

One of the nicest things about this special rate is the fact that almost everybody knows somebody | who would like to have the News Magazine for Christmas.

By ordering one subscription with your own renewal, the average (3) cost of these subscriptions will be only $4. By ordering four subscriptions along with your own renewal, the | average cost of each subscription will be only $3.70.

You will find the enclosed form convenient in entering | your own renewal and the gift subscriptions. I hope you will fill out the form and return it to us today. As you know, your | own subscription will soon expire also. Remember that this special rate is good only until November 10. Cordially yours, (4)

P. S. By the way, the News Magazine is one of the nicest presents you can give to men who are overseas. They will appreciate | its wide, complete coverage of the news. It will bring them back home again. You may enter gifts of the News Magazine to men | in our armed forces with the assurance that a card will be sent air mail, at our expense, telling them of your thoughtful gift.

The | subscriptions to men in the armed forces stationed in the United States will start with the December 29 issue. (5) (1.43)

92

1.

2.

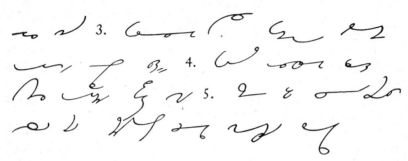

Key: (1) Automobile, on the market, of course, went, accidents, consequently, insurance. (2) Policies, fortunate, you will be able, offset, dividend, reputation, $6,000,000, not only, you want. (3) Premiums, demand, personal, telephone, located, major, United States. (4) Promptly, requirements, serious, difficulty, lawsuit, expensive, court. (5) Assume, also, amount, verdict, card, further, if you would like to have, simply, you will find, he will be able.

Dear Mr. Franklin: As a car owner, you will be interested in the new automobile insurance policy that | we are placing on the market.

You know, of course, that insurance rates went down during the war. There were not so many cars on the | road, and the number of accidents was consequently greatly decreased. But now that the war is over and there are many | more cars on the road, the number of accidents is increasing. This, of course, has meant that automobile insurance rates must go (1) up.

If you own one of our policies, you are fortunate because you will be able to offset most of this increase by | the dividend you will receive at the end of the year.

When you buy automobile insurance, you demand a company that | has a good reputation. The National Insurance Company is backed by more than $6,000,000. You cannot buy | safer insurance from any other company.

You not only want safety, but you want it at the lowest possible cost. (2) You will be interested to know that for many years the National Insurance Company has returned 25 per | cent of the premiums to its members as a dividend. Wouldn't you like to make a saving of this kind on your car insurance? |

But that is not all you demand. You also want personal service. When you are at home, our service is as close as your | telephone. When you are away from home, you can call on our agents, who are located in all the major cities of the United (3) States. They will answer your calls and will cover each accident promptly. Our policies meet every requirement of | the insurance laws.

A serious accident might cause you a great deal of financial difficulty. A lawsuit is expensive | even if you win it. On the other hand, if you lose, you may face ruin. When you hold one of our policies, we take | care of all legal matters for you. If the matter can be settled out of court, we settle it. If it cannot, we fight it for (4) you in court. If you should lose, we not only assume all the costs of the trial, but we also pay the amount of the verdict. |

Use the enclosed card to get further information. If you would like to have one of our trained representatives call to discuss | your automobile insurance with you, simply check the proper box on the card and indicate when he should call. You will find | that he will be able to tell you many things about your insurance that will be useful to you. Very cordially yours, (5) (1.43)

93

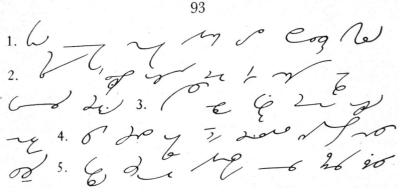

Key: (1) Board, membership, club, discussion, ordinarily, applications, different. (2) Voted, initiation, resident, as soon as, one thousand, custom, in the past, permanent, firsthand. (3) To make, next year, perhaps, former, resigned, in our opinion. (4) Attention, fact that, rejoin, interested, secretary, you would like to have, contact, acquaint. (5) Prepared, facilities, described, many of the, if you need, hesitate.

Dear Friend: The board of directors once again has decided to offer a winter membership in our club. Membership will | run from November 1 to April 1. After considerable discussion it was decided to offer this membership | for $75, to which the Federal tax is to be added.

Ordinarily, at this season of the year | we receive a number of applications for winter membership. The situation this year, however, is somewhat different. (1) The board of directors has voted to charge an initiation fee of $250 for all resident | members as soon as the quota of one thousand has been reached. We are now working on the last hundred to reach that goal.

The custom | in the past has been to establish this winter membership in order to give those who are thinking of permanent membership | an opportunity to see the many advantages of the club at firsthand. We shall take in winter members this year; (2) but I wish to stress that, if any of your friends are planning to join the club, now is the time to make the decision. In that | way they will save the cost of the initiation fee. I think you will agree that this is a considerable saving and should be | given consideration.

We know that you have many friends who might be interested in membership in the club next year. | You perhaps know of many former members of the club who have resigned in order to join clubs nearer their homes. In our opinion, (3) you will be doing your friends a real service by calling their attention to the fact that they can now rejoin without | paying an extra fee.

If you have any friends who are interested in joining, we suggest that you call our membership secretary, | Mr. Brown, giving him the names of any friends with whom you would like to have him get in contact. Mr. Brown will | then take care of acquainting your friends with our club and its many advantages.

I am enclosing a few copies of a new (4) booklet that we have recently prepared, showing the many facilities available to members. In it are described | many of the plans that we have in mind for the immediate future. Our club is planning many new improvements for the | convenience of our members, and I know you will want to read about them. You may also wish to show this booklet to your friends who | are interested in joining the country club. If you need more copies, do not hesitate to write me for them. Yours truly, (5) (1.45)

94

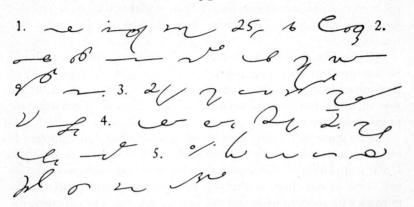

Key: (1) Career, who might be, school, 25,000, to see, applications. (2) Immediately, without, more and more, country, likely, comfortable, warm, estimates, coming. (3) $2,000,000,000, kept, almost, students, completed, found, machines. (4) Learn, earnings, developed, interfering, completion, lessons, modern. (5) Including, board, railroad, of course, card, few days, act, sooner, industry.

Dear Mr. James: At the present time we are looking for men whom we can train for a career in air conditioning. Your name | has been suggested as one who might be interested in this type of work. Our school has been chosen by the Smith Air Conditioning | Company to train 25,000 new dealers.

It is plain to see that there are many opportunities in air | conditioning in the immediate future. Every day newspapers and magazines are referring to new applications (1) of air conditioning. A visit on a hot day to a store or office that has air conditioning immediately | shows the advantage that that store or office has over one that is without it.

More and more stores throughout the country are realizing | the value of air conditioning. They know that the public is more likely to deal in a store where they can be comfortable, | no matter how warm the weather outside may be. An important authority estimates that in the coming year (2) more than $2,000,000,000 worth of air-conditioning equipment will be purchased. This equipment will have to be installed | and kept in repair; and that is why trained men will be needed in the immediate future, more than ever before. Almost every | day we receive letters from students who have recently completed our course, telling us how valuable they found | our training.

If you like to work with tools and machines, then you should be interested in obtaining full information about (3) the vast opportunities in air conditioning. You will be eager to learn of the way in which hundreds of men of all | ages have used our training to increase their earnings.

Our course of training is so developed that you can complete it in your spare | time without interfering with your present position. Upon completion of the lessons we will send you every week, | you will come to our shop, where you will be given ample opportunity to work with modern tools and machinery. All your (4) expenses, including your board and room, during your stay in the shop will be paid by the school. Your railroad fare to and from the | shop will also be paid, of course.

It would take too long to tell you all about our many plans at this time; but, if you will fill out | the enclosed card, we will see to it that complete information reaches you within the next few days.

Act now. The sooner you | become a part of the air-conditioning industry, the quicker you will be able to share in its profits. Sincerely yours, (5) (1.45)

95

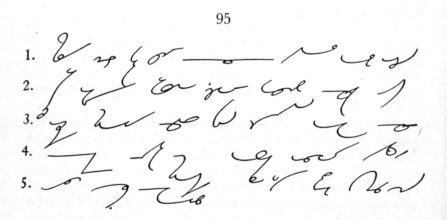

Key: (1) Avoid, unnecessary, possible, out-of-town, minimum, delivery, letters, recent. (2) Obviously, reported, operator, whether or not, practice, might be, individual. (3) Received, followed, naturally, beyond, standard, will you please, mind. (4) Management, undesirable, involved, larger, recorded, decided. (5) Indicate, giving, employee, overtime, expense, definite, count.

To the Staff: We have been asked by the telephone company to avoid unnecessary use of the telephone as far as | possible. This applies, of course, to both business calls and personal calls.

The use of the telephone for out-of-town calls for business | purposes should be kept at a minimum. In many cases where the telephone has been used for out-of-town calls, | air-mail or special-delivery letters would have done just as well.

In checking recent bills, I find a large number of calls that were (1) obviously personal calls but that were not reported as personal calls to the operator. This means that they were paid | for by the company instead of by the employees making the calls. The operator cannot, of course, always know whether | or not an out-of-town call is for business or personal purposes unless she is told by the person calling. Our practice | has been to inform the operator when we make an out-of-town call so that the call might be charged to the individual (2) at the end of the month when the bill is received. I am sorry to report that this practice has not always been followed. | Naturally, this is not fair to those employees who have reported their personal calls and paid for them.

We are also charged | with a number of local calls far beyond the needs of the business. Every local call over seventy-five calls is | charged to the company at standard rates. Will you please also keep in mind that an extra charge is made for all calls of more than three (3) minutes. The management wishes to show every consideration to the members of the staff, but the use of the office | telephone for personal purposes has been too great. This is undesirable because of the expense involved.

It is | obvious that one person might run up a larger bill with a great many local calls than another person might through a | few recorded toll calls. In order, therefore, that everybody will be treated fairly, it has been decided that each of (4) us will be charged for every out-going personal telephone call. From now on, will you please indicate to the operator | before giving your number whether the call is a business call or a personal call. Of course, if the employee is | asked by the management to work overtime, his call home is a business expense.

It is necessary that there be a | very definite improvement in the telephone situation. May we count on your help in the future? John Macauley (5) (1.45)

96

Key: (1) Years ago, rapidly, bigger, improved, quarters, larger, location, dictated. (2) Modern, better, directors, to provide, expansion, in the future, furthermore, efficient. (3) Investigation, selected, New Jersey, ideal, opposite, railroad, center, constant, touch. (4) Messenger, deliveries, trucks, daily, disturbed, contrary, machinery. (5) Transferred, rest, equipment, interruption, gradual, moving, certain, in the past.

Dear Mr. Harris: The Smith Printing Company was organized more than thirty years ago. In those thirty years, our business | has grown so rapidly that we have found it necessary to move three times, each time to bigger and more improved quarters. Our present | printing plant at 400 Fulton Street has served us well during the last fifteen years, but once again we find it necessary | to move to a larger location. This latest move of ours is dictated by our policy of constantly obtaining (1) the most modern printing presses, so that we may give even better and faster service to our customers.

When our board of | directors finally reached the decision to move, it decided that we must keep the plant where it would be within easy reach | of our many customers in New York. The location had to provide ample space for expansion in the future. Furthermore, | it had to be in a section where we could get the labor necessary to do an efficient job.

After a thorough (2) investigation, our board of directors selected a site in Clifton, New Jersey. There we found a group of buildings with | about four acres of floor space that is ideal for efficient production at present and will allow for further expansion | in the future. Our new plant is directly opposite the Clifton railroad station and is within two blocks of the center | of the city. It can be reached quickly by car, train, or bus.

A sales office in New York will maintain constant touch with the plant (3) through messenger service and direct telephone lines. Deliveries will be made by our own trucks, which will make daily trips to | the city. Our rapid delivery service will not be disturbed because of our new location. On the contrary, you will | receive even quicker service because of additional employees on our staff.

Several new presses will be installed | in Clifton when they are delivered. When this new machinery is ready to be put into operation, the necessary (4) men will be transferred to Clifton from New York. Then, the rest of our equipment will be moved in such a way that there will be | no interruption in our service. This gradual moving of our plant may take as long as two years.

We are certain that you will | be benefited by this action on our part.

We take this opportunity to thank you for the interest and confidence | that you have shown in us in the past and to express the hope that we shall continue to merit your business. Yours very truly, (5) (1.46)

97.

[shorthand outlines]

Key: (1) I wonder, familiar, American, sum, finest, supplied, presentation, entitle. (2) Accident, bring, wealth, current, enjoyable, bureau, relating. (3) World, points, bounds, to become, movement, promote, furthering. (4) Broaden, activities, dues, card, accept, privileges, to do so, friends. (5) Literature, persons, leather, research, we are sure, advantages.

Dear Friend: I wonder whether you are familiar with the many advantages that will be yours when you join the American | Travel Club. For the small sum of $4 a year, you will receive the following benefits:

1. You will be given | reduced rates in the finest hotels and shops all over the United States. If you travel abroad, you will be supplied with | a list of hotels in which the presentation of your membership card will entitle you to special rates.

2. You will receive (1) an accident insurance policy in the sum of $2,000. Each year for ten years the value of this policy | will be increased until it reaches the sum of $4,000.

3. Each month you will receive the Travel Magazine. This | magazine will bring you a wealth of current information that will make your travel more enjoyable.

4. You will have the | use of our information bureau, which supplies to members all types of general information relating to travel in (2) any part of the world. This bureau also will provide maps to the points to which you wish to travel.

The American Travel | Club is growing by leaps and bounds.

At the present time it has a membership of over seventy-five thousand. Wouldn't you | like to become a part of this national movement to promote travel?

No doubt you are familiar with the work of the | American Travel Club in furthering such matters as good roads, preserving forests, and other activities.

In order to (3) broaden our activities, we are inviting you and some others whose names have been suggested as being interested | in travel to become members. The dues are only $4 a year.

You need not send the $4 now. Just mail the enclosed | card to tell us that you accept this invitation. If you should care to do so, however, enclose your check and thus take | immediate advantage of all the privileges of membership.

If you have any friends who might be interested in (4) membership, we should be happy to have their names so that we may send them literature about our club. If you will send us the | names and addresses of five persons, we will show our appreciation by presenting you with a special leather edition | of the atlas prepared by our research staff. This atlas is on the market for $10. We are sure you will wish to own | a copy of this book; so act now. Get your friends interested in our club and let them know of all its advantages. Yours truly, (5) (1.46)

98

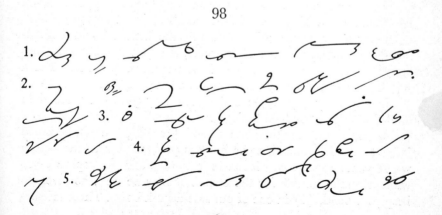

Key: (1) **Various, referred, needless to say, recommend, denominations, slightly.** (2) **Involved, United States, Government, program, effect, adopted, deducting, organization.** (3) **Highly, maturity, possible, absolutely, redeem, post office, you should understand, ordinary.** (4) **Specific, anyone else, another, payable, appears, undue, trouble.** (5) **Safe-deposit, next time, courteous, attendants, facilities, hestitate.**

Dear Mr. Brown: Your letter asking for information regarding the various types of savings bonds has been referred to | me. Needless to say, your decision to invest in these bonds is a wise one.

There are three types of savings bonds—Series E, Series | F, and Series G. In view of your income, I would recommend that you invest regularly in Series E.

These bonds come | in five denominations, ranging from $25 to $1,000. The bonds bear interest at slightly less than (1) 3 per cent.

In the purchase and sale of savings bonds, no commission is involved. We shall be happy to arrange for your | purchases of bonds, as we are authorized agents of the United States Government. You might inquire, however, whether a savings | program is in effect in your own organization. Many organizations have adopted the plan of deducting | so much each month from the employees' salaries for the purchase of bonds. If your organization has such a plan, by all (2) means take advantage of it.

While it is highly desirable for you to hold all the bonds until maturity in order | to get the best possible return, it is not absolutely necessary. You can redeem the bonds at any time that | you feel you need the money. You can do that in this bank, at any post office, or at any other agency authorized | by the United States Government. You should understand, however, that you cannot sell savings bonds in the ordinary (3) sense of the word. Bonds are issued to a specific person and are not redeemable by anyone else.

In any given | year, no one person may purchase more than $5,000 worth of bonds in Series E.

Should you at any time lose a bond, | another one will be issued in its place. The fact that the bond is payable only to the person whose name appears on | it makes it possible to make replacements without undue trouble for the owner. It may be wise, however, to keep your bonds (4) in one of our safe-deposit boxes. These safe-de-

posit boxes cost very little and may save you a good deal of grief. |
The next time you are in the bank, visit the Safe Deposit Depart-
ment. Courteous attendants will be glad to show you sample | boxes
and also the facilities for safeguarding them. You can get a box for
as low as $5 a year.

If there | is any other information you would like to have re-
garding savings bonds, do not hesitate to write me. Cordially yours,
(5) (1.47)

99

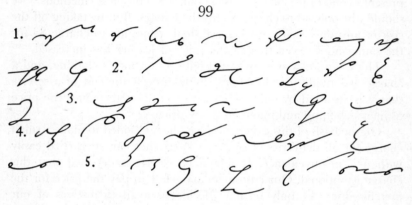

Key: (1) Customers, extend, policy, greater, starting, remove, unnecessary, merchandise, privilege. (2) Delivery, example, prefer, suddenly, experiences, inconvenience. (3) Let us, women's, quality, obliged,
leather. (4) Alterations, to make, packages, carried, clearly understood,
optional, elect. (5) Themselves, approval, original, propose, to do,
economic.

Dear Madam: In the best interests of our customers and in spite
of rising prices, we are going to extend our lowered-price | policy so
that it will bring even greater savings to our customers.

Starting today, we will remove from the | prices we charge for
our goods the cost of all those unnecessary services that often our
customers do not want. In other | words, the prices you pay will be
for merchandise only. It will be your privilege to decide for yourself
whether you wish (1) to make use of such service as delivery, for
example. You may choose whether you desire the service or prefer
to | take the savings in the price of the merchandise.

This step was not taken suddenly on our part. It followed the actual | experiences we have had with our customers, who have shown that they are far more interested in savings than in services | that can be omitted without inconvenience. By doing this, we can offer merchandise at prices that are lower than (2) they would be under our old methods of doing business.

Let us take our $3 women's shoes, for example. We have maintained | the quality and price of these shoes for over ten years. Under present conditions, if we used our old business methods, we should | be obliged to charge $4 for these shoes. But, by taking off the cost of all unnecessary services, we shall | continue to charge $3 for the same shoes—even though the price of leather has increased.

This new policy was also tried out (3) on men's clothing, and a charge was made for alterations. By taking off the cost of a service that was required by only | a few, we were able to reduce the price of men's clothing and maintain a low price.

On the basis of this experience, we | have decided to make a small charge for all deliveries of small packages that can be carried easily without | inconvenience. It should be clearly understood that this charge is optional. Our customers may elect to pay the price for the merchandise (4) only or may decide to avail themselves of our delivery service. If this plan does not meet with the approval | of our customers, however, we will go back to our original policy. We are determined to devote our efforts | to the best interests of our customers.

We propose to do all in our power to prevent waste in business. We are | going to do our part to prevent inflation so that once again our economic life will run smoothly. Very truly yours, (5) (1.47)

100

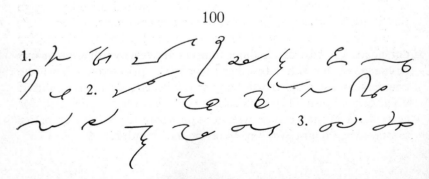

Key: (1) Future, transportation, sometimes, we have been, worried, possibility, expect, glad to say, however, rest. (2) Studied, replies, questionnaire, to our, definitely, ground, they want, impossible, complete, analysis. (3) According, families, generally, themselves. (4) One of the, radio, equipped, results, favorable, enjoyment. (5) Individual, speakers, really, many other, described, appreciation, given.

Dear Mr. Brown: During recent years the public has done a good deal of dreaming about what future air transportation would | be like. Much of this romance has made good reading. It has sometimes been a little embarrassing, however, to those of us who | actually have to deliver the job. We have been a bit worried about the possibility that our customers | might be influenced to expect too much and to expect it too soon.

We are glad to say, however, that our fears were set at rest after (1) we had studied the 19,000 replies we received to the questionnaire we recently sent to our customers. These replies | definitely indicate that, no matter how much our customers fly, their feet are still on the ground. They want better and faster | air transportation, and they want more of it. They are not, however, looking for the impossible.

What they do want and | expect is told in the pages of the booklet that is enclosed. The booklet gives a complete and detailed analysis of the (2) answers we received to the 125 questions we asked in our questionnaire.

One thing is sure, according to the | answers we received. Air travel in the future is going to be enjoyed by the whole family, more than ever before. It | is clear that families going on their vacations will quite generally travel by air and thus insure themselves of more | time at their vacation spots. The same thing is true of pleasure trips and business trips of all kinds. The answers to the questions show clearly (3) the travel trend of the future.

One of the many interesting facts brought out by the answers is that nine out of ten | of our customers are in favor of a radio in the planes. Before the war, several of our planes were equipped with radios | as an experiment. The results of that experiment were favorable, and you may be sure that any new | planes we build will have radios for your enjoyment. About 80 per cent of the answers indicated, however, that our (4) customers were in favor of individual speakers at each seat. Answers to other questions indicated that our | customers are really interested in the future of the air-line business.

Many other interesting facts were brought | out; but we shall not go into them in this letter, as they are described fully in the enclosed 16-page booklet.

Once more, | we wish to express our appreciation of the help you have given us by answering our questionnaire. Very sincerely yours, (5) (1.47)

PART VI

100 WORDS A MINUTE

101

Key: (1) Town, announced, intention, country, mind, guarantee, pointed, might not, a thousand. (2) Invested, advised, to forget, strong, anyone, successfully, men and women, justified. (3) Usually, of course, especially, summers, except, perfect. (4) Survive, result, healthy, anywhere, I want, photographs, descriptions, around. (5) Exactly, elsewhere, you want, attach, proper, amount, reserve, finest.

Dear Friend: Twenty years ago, people in my town laughed at me. I had just announced my intention to plant evergreen trees and sell them by mail | all over the country.

They asked why I was planting evergreens when the country all around was covered with them. They thought I had lost my mind | when I decided to guarantee that my trees would live. They pointed out that my customers might not plant them correctly or might let the roots | get dry or do any one of a thousand different things that would kill the trees. They were sure that I would lose every penny that I (1) invested in the business. My best friends advised me to forget the whole matter and go into some other line of business.

I knew that my trees | would be strong and that almost anyone could plant them successfully with a few simple instructions. But most of all, I had faith in the people | who plant trees. I was sure that men and women who love trees would take good care of them. I was sure that if I were honest with them, they would be | honest with me.

I am glad to say that my faith was justified. I have sent thousands of trees to my customers. Very few write me for (2) replacements because trees have died. When they do, they usually tell me that one tree has died out of a shipment of perhaps fifty or one hundred. | Some people have planted as many as one thousand or more and have written me that every one of them lived.

Of course, I cannot take | too much credit for that. Nature is especially kind to trees here in Maine and makes them healthy and strong. The trees have to stand some hot summers | and very cold winters. I do not give the trees any special care after the first year, except transplant them at the right time. Only perfect (3) trees survive under those conditions. The result is that every tree that is shipped is a healthy specimen that will grow almost | anywhere under any weather conditions.

As I write you today, it is still winter. But it will be spring planting time soon, and I want you to have | first call on the finest of my trees. My new spring catalogue is enclosed. Read it now, while the matter of trees is in your mind. Examine the | photographs of the beautiful trees you will find there and read the descriptions of them. Can't you picture a row of these trees around your home and (4) the beauty they will add to it? Notice, too, how little they cost. My evergreen specials are as low as fifty for $2, or exactly | 4 cents each! The other trees are also priced far below what you would have to pay for them elsewhere.

Choose the trees you want. Enter their numbers | on the enclosed order blank, attach your check for the proper amount, and mail it to me today. I will see that your evergreen trees reach you | right in time for spring planting.

By ordering now, you give me an opportunity to reserve for you the finest of my trees. Yours truly, (5) (1.31)

102

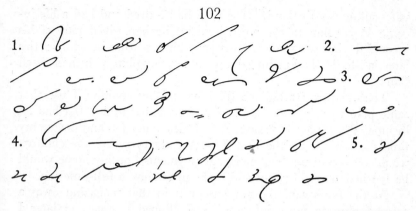

Key: (1) Devote, retired, I had, to do, to be, writer. (2) Moments, today, earning, earned, idea, years ago, afford, family. (3) Article, I wanted, turned, picture, wife, England, according, couldn't, really. (4) By the time, mortgage, coupon, in a few days, seemed, adopted. (5) Went, as soon as, first, dreamed, short stories, general, subscribe, Sincerely yours.

Dear Friend: I have always said that a man could make a hobby pay real money if he could devote to it as much time as he devotes to his | regular job. That is what I am now doing—making my hobby pay real money. However, it was not until I was fifty-five and | retired with a life income of $150 a month that I had a chance to do what I have always wanted to do. Ever | since I can remember, I have always wanted to be a writer. As a matter of fact, I did a little writing while I was working (1) for the Brown Manufacturing Company; but I had to do it in my spare moments, which were very few. Today I am spending all my | time at it, and I am earning more than I ever earned in the office at my regular job.

I got the idea about fifteen years ago | when I was forty. At that time I had a good job that paid me fairly well. I could not afford to leave the job and give full time to my | hobby. I had my family to consider.

Then one night in the spring of 1931 I was running through a magazine, planning (2) an article I wanted to write in my spare time. As I turned the pages, I noticed a picture of a man and his wife sailing for England. | The man had retired and had a life income. According to the advertisement, he had saved part of his income during the years he was | working, so that he could retire later in life. He had arranged a special saving plan with the Russell Bank.

That picture started me thinking. | Why couldn't I use that same plan to help me do what I really wanted to do? If I had an income of $150 a (3) month, I could leave my job and devote my time to writing. By the time I was ready to retire, the children would be grown up. The mortgage payments | on my home would be finished. I could retire and make my hobby a full-time job.

At the bottom of the advertisement in that magazine | was a coupon offering more information. I clipped it out, and later I mailed it. In a few days I received a booklet telling | me all about the Russell plan. It seemed to be just the thing for me. Fifteen years from the day that I adopted the plan, I would be getting (4) an income of $150 a month for as long as I lived.

That very week I applied for the Russell plan. The fifteen years | went fast. As soon as my first check arrived, I retired to do what I dreamed of doing. I have made out pretty well, selling short stories and | articles of general interest. With my income of $150 added to my earnings, I am making more money than | I have ever made before.

You, too, can have the life income you desire if you subscribe to the Russell plan. Do it today. Sincerely yours, (5) (1.32) .

103

5.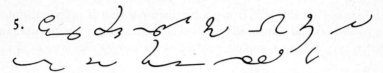

Key: (1) Running, more and more, dividends, attract, customers, certain, amount, otherwise, doubt. (2) Worth while, assistance, employee, managers, results, to be done. (3) Required, campaign, carried, normal, approved, control. (4) Clerks, example, observe, ideas, in the future, nothing, advance, one of our. (5) Approximate, various, crowds, assured, endeavor, effective, don't, longer, sooner, volume, guarantee, part.

Dear Mr. Smith: As a merchant, you realize, I am sure, the importance of running a real sale now and then. More and more stores are doing | this every year, and they find that it pays big dividends. The larger stores often run two or three big sales each year.

These sales attract customers, | and you lose to the store conducting the sale a certain amount of business that would otherwise come your way. People like to shop in stores that | have sales because they have the feeling that they are saving money by shopping in that way. Consequently, there seems to be little doubt that sales (1) are a necessary and desirable part of the business of retailing.

Now the question for you to decide is whether it is worth | while for you to employ outside assistance or whether you can conduct the sale satisfactorily with the help that you have. We believe | it will pay you to employ an experienced organization like ours to run the sale for you.

Our staff of sales managers is especially | trained. Each man has managed and planned hundreds of sales. He knows just what should be done to get the best results. He knows the type of advertising (2) required to put the sale across. He knows how the entire campaign should be planned and carried out. He takes the entire load of work off your hands, | leaving you free for your normal routine work.

Before we take each step, we outline it for you completely. We tell you what is to be done, how | much it will cost, and the people who should do the job. Every advertisement that is prepared must be passed on and approved by you before it | goes to the printer. In that way you have complete control of the program as well as of its cost. ✕

In addition to the income you will receive (3) from the sale, you will get certain other benefits. Your clerks, for example, will have an opportunity to observe our trained employees | for two or three weeks. They will get many new ideas on ways to arrange and display merchandise that they can use in the future.

You pay | us nothing in advance. Our fee is payable after the sale has demonstrated its success and the money is coming in.

Isn't it | worth a trial? We shall be glad to give you all the facts and figures based on your own store. It will take less than an hour for one of our men to make (4) a survey of your store, outline a plan, and give you the approximate cost. He will gladly discuss the various means that can be employed | to make the crowds flock to your store. You can rest assured that he will have your best interests at heart and endeavor to plan a sales campaign that will | prove to be the most effective you have ever had.

Don't put the matter off any longer. The sooner you start, the sooner your sales volume | will increase. We guarantee that you will be so pleased with our service that you will make it a regular part of your business. Sincerely yours, (5) (1.33)

104

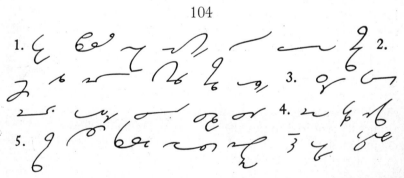

Key: (1) Property, apparently, carbon, notified, tenant, on the market, I have not been able. (2) In fact, to see, one of them, definite, agency, requested. (3) I understand, permission, something, lowest, amount, accept, another. (4) Sooner, possession, you would be able. (5) I shall be able, to make, balance, collection, you may be sure, interests, report, self-addressed.

Dear Mrs. Smith: Your letter of January 24 was on my desk when I returned to the office after a long trip.

On December | 10 I wrote you about your property. The letter was addressed to you in Flint, Michigan; but apparently it did not reach you. I | am enclosing a carbon copy of the letter.

I have notified the tenant that the house is to be placed on the market, but he is | not interested in buying the property. I have taken several people through the house, but up to the present time I have not been (1) able to get an offer of more than $7,000 for it. We are, however, still working on the sale. In fact, I am taking | two people to see the house this afternoon. One of them is very much interested, and I may have some definite news for you soon.

As | I wrote you on December 12, the rent for this house has been fixed at $35 a month. I wrote the renting agency that this figure | does not cover the payment of the loan you have on the property, and I requested that they permit you to raise the rent to at least (2) $50 a month. I understand that this permission is usually granted. At any rate, I shall follow up this matter of | a rent increase until we get something done about it.

November and December were very slow on all real estate sales. January | sales are picking up a little, however; but the entire situation is still not too bright. It would be a big help to us if you would | let me know the lowest amount that you would be willing to accept for your house. Another thing that makes the house difficult to sell is the (3) fact that, after the house has been sold, the present tenant must be given six months' notice. I have talked to the present tenant, and he tells me | that he will not move until he has to. The only way you could get the tenant out sooner would be to take possession yourself. In that case, | the tenant would have to be given thirty days' notice. You would, however, have to live in the property at least six months before you would | be able to sell it to another tenant.

I have been making payments on your loan each month, and

the enclosed statement shows the amount spent (4) and the amount on hand. I shall be able to make the February payment with the balance we have on hand plus the February rent | collection. If you would care to have me do so, I shall be glad to send you a statement each month.

You may be sure that I am looking after | your best interests and that I shall get in touch with you as soon as I have something to report.

I am enclosing a stamped and self-addressed | envelope for your convenience in writing me. Please be sure to let me know the lowest amount you will accept for your house. Cordially yours, (5) (1.35)

105

Key: (1) Judged, vocabulary, ability, language, formed, as soon as, heard, sentences, poorly, favorable. (2) Improved, master, acquires, as a result, faithfully, I am confident. (3) Priceless, find, yourself, words, selected, awkward. (4) Distinction, meanings, literature, grammar, one of those, edition. (5) Urge, approval, useful, card, in a few days, merely, remit, look.

Dear Mr. Jones: All of us are judged by what we say and how we say it. Whether we are talking or writing, we are rated by our | vocabulary, by our use of words, and by our ability to handle the English language. Haven't you often formed your opinion of a | person just as soon as you heard him say a few sentences? If he spoke well, your opinion of him was good. If he spoke poorly, your impression | of him was not favorable. You will notice that the man who is a good leader is a good speaker and one who has command of the (1) language. Only through good speaking can he win the good opinion of groups of people.

Now a person's vocabulary can be improved and | increased. No one is born a master of the English language. He acquires that mastery as a result of training. You can master the English | language if you are willing to put in the necessary time and study.

All you have to do is spend ten or fifteen minutes a day | reading and mastering just one page of Doctor Smith's new book called "English for Everybody." If you do this faithfully, I am confident (2) that in less than a year you will have a grasp of the English language that will be priceless to you.

"English for Everybody" is a guide to | the correct use of the English language. It is so interesting that you will soon find yourself spending much more than ten or fifteen minutes | a day on it. The book shows how words work for you and how they are a part of living speech.

The book contains 498 pages of | material carefully selected for its importance in everyday speaking and writing. Doctor Smith shows you how to avoid awkward (3) expressions and how to distinguish between fine meanings of words. He gives you many interesting facts about words and presents information | about literature that everyone should know. The essential rules of grammar are fully and thoroughly covered. If you are one of | those who never could master grammar, you will be delighted at the new method of presentation that Doctor Smith has devised.

This is one | book that you will use over and over again. It is a book that can mean much to you. The cost of the new edition is only (4) $2.75.

We urge you to send for a copy on approval. You can keep the book for ten days and see for yourself what it is | and how useful it can be to you. Just fill in and mail the enclosed card, and a copy of the book will reach you in a few days. You need send | no money right away. You merely agree to return the book in ten days if you feel you cannot use it. There is always time to remit | for the book should you decide to keep it.

Take advantage of this opportunity to look through the book. **It** can help you a great deal. Yours truly, (5) (1.36)

106

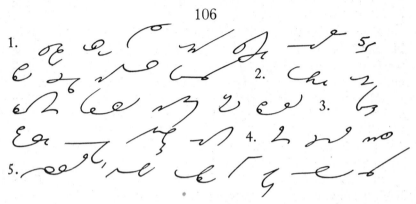

Key: (1) Accept, writer, demand, resulted, advance, modern, five hundred thousand, appeared, simply, you would like, permitted. (2) Pleasures, reason, certificate, brilliant, you do not have, offered, excellent. (3) Bonus, explains, membership, descriptions, notify. (4) Effect, secondly, worth while. (5) Guarantee, at least, last year, down, to purchase, mail, needed.

Dear Friend: Will you accept without charge a copy of James Brown's new novel, "Red Valley"? The world has waited more than four years for a new book by | this fine writer. The demand has been so great that it has resulted in the largest advance sale in the history of modern publishing. | More than five hundred thousand copies were sold before the book appeared in print. Yet you may receive a copy of this great book, which sells for | $3.50, without charge simply by telling us that you would like to join the Book Club at this time.

The publisher has permitted (1) us to present a limited edition of "Red Valley" to those who indicate that they would appreciate the gift and would enjoy | the additional pleasures of joining the Club. It is for this reason that we send you the enclosed gift certificate. Your copy of this | new and brilliant novel will be sent entirely without charge through the regular channels. You do not have to buy a book each month. You need | buy only four out of the twelve that are offered during the year.

In addition to the excellent reading that will be available to (2) you, you will make a cash saving when you accept our books. After you have purchased four books, you will receive without charge one book as a bonus. | This explains why so many people make their book purchases through this Club.

Another advantage of membership in the Book Club is that you | will receive each month a copy of Book News, which serves two purposes: First, it tells you in advance about the books that will be offered in coming | months. From the descriptions of the books you can decide whether you would like to own them. If you do not think those books would be of interest (3) to you, you simply notify us to that effect. Secondly, in addition to containing news about the books that will be sent to Book | Club members, it contains reviews of twenty or thirty other books that make good reading.

Your membership in the Book Club will bring you the best | in books. It will enable you to devote your limited reading time to books that are worth while. You will no longer have the experience | of reading halfway through a book only to lose interest in it.

We should like to urge you to accept our invitation at once. If you (4) join now, we can still guarantee that there will be no increase in the cost of your books for at least one year. The cost of paper and binding has | gone up more than 50 per cent during the last year, and we do not know whether we can hold down the cost of the books much longer. You will pay | only $3 for the selections you decide to purchase plus a few cents to cover the cost of shipping.

Accept this invitation | now. Sign the certificate and mail it today. No stamp is needed. Your free copy of "Red Valley" will be shipped to you at once. Yours truly, (5) (1.36)

107

1.

2.

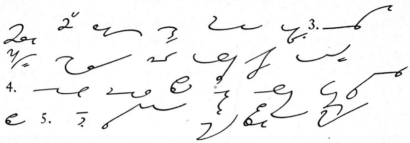

Key: (1) In the past, learned, operates, out of date, millions, subscriptions, everything, to know, various, gradual. (2) Some weeks ago, department, conference, two o'clock, years ago, consisted, floor, reporting. (3) Many times, Washington, completed, one of the, largest, debate, London. (4) More or less, summary, appeared, newspapers, marvel, perfection, admit, easier. (5) Interesting, editorial, informed, expires, up to date.

Dear Reader: In the past three months I have learned that my idea of the way the News Magazine staff operates is out of date by four or five | years. I have been with the News Magazine for eleven years now as its publisher. I have sent out millions of letters trying to sell | subscriptions. I thought I knew everything there was to know about our magazine. But I found that I still have much to learn.

The editors of the News | Magazine could not tell you how the various changes have taken place, because the changes have been too gradual. Let me tell you a few (1) of the changes that have taken place.

Some weeks ago Jack Smith was off on his vacation; and, to help out, I decided to edit his | department. On the first day I called a conference for two o'clock in my office. Ten years ago this department consisted of two men; | so it did not occur to me that seating would be a problem. But, when I arrived at my office, I found all the chairs filled and, in | addition, six or eight men sitting on the floor. All these men have had many years of experience and training in reporting business conditions. (2) In the short space of four or five years, this department has grown many times. The same thing is true of all the other departments of the News | Magazine.

Some years ago we had only one man in our Washington office.

That man worked for us for a few hours each day after he completed | his work for one of the Washington papers. Today we have the largest news staff in that city.

I remember that at one time we had a | long debate about whether we should have a part-time man to cover the news in London. Now we have eight men who cover the news for us there. (3)

What does all this add up to? Even though the News Magazine was good ten years ago, it was more or less a well-written summary of | the news that appeared in the newspapers. Today more than half the information given in the News Magazine cannot be found in the | newspapers. We use the newspapers for help in deciding what stories are important, but our men begin where the newspapers leave off.

Now I | am not going to try to tell you that the News Magazine is a marvel of perfection. I will admit that it was much easier when (4) we simply rewrote news reports in an interesting style. But, as each week goes by, we are solving more and more of our editorial | problems. No other news magazine has ever had such a collection of writing talent to prepare the material for its readers. |

We are confident that, when this period is over, we shall be proud of the part we have played in keeping the public informed of latest developments. |

Your subscription to the News Magazine expires today. Send in your renewal now, and make sure of keeping up to date. Yours truly, (5) (1.37)

108

Key: (1) I am sure, to us, retired, worrying, future, circle, dissatis-fied, being able, words, hopeless. (2) Millions, I had, lifetime, concern, postman, amount, to know. (3) Protect, provide, permanent, disabled, ordinary, require, today. (4) I want, comfort, typical, to find, obliga-tion, without, explains, starting. (5) Possible, large, of course, district, personally, request, catalogue, to serve you.

Dear Mr. Brown: As a businessman, you will be interested, I am sure, in reading the following letter that was sent to us by a | man who recently retired:

"Fifteen years ago I made a discovery that changed my whole life. When I was forty, I was worrying | about my future. I wasn't getting ahead. I seemed to be living in a circle, and I was dissatis-fied. I used to dream of being | able to relax and forget my money troubles. In other words, I longed for security.

"But it seemed hopeless. I was not rich and (1) probably never would be. Like millions of others, I had spent a lifetime trying to make both ends meet.

"But that was fifteen years ago. Now, | I have retired on a life income. I have no business worries and no concern over my future. I can work or play as I like. Each | month the postman hands me a check for $150, and I know that I shall receive a check for the same amount every month | as long as I live.

"My friends want to know how I ever managed to retire on a life income. The answer is simple. When I was forty, (2) I discov-ered the Mutual Savings Plan.

"The minute I read about this plan I realized it was just what I needed. Through it, I | could get a life income of $150 a month in fifteen years, and protect my family. In addition, the plan provided | for a permanent income in case I had been permanently disabled before I reached fifty-five.

"Best of all, I could do all this | through easy payments and for far less money than most ordinary investments require.

"Today, at the age of fifty-five, I have the (3) things I want, with no worries. I can be sure of comfort in the years ahead with a permanent income of $150 a | month."

This letter is typical. Wouldn't you like to make sure of your own future? Wouldn't you like to find out for yourself how the Mutual | Savings Plan works? You can get the facts without obligation by sending for our free booklet. A post card will bring it to you without charge. In | a simple way, this booklet explains how to get a life income of $10 to $200 a month or more starting at the age (4) of fifty-five, sixty, sixty-five, or seventy. It is possible to fit the Mutual Savings Plan to your own needs, whether they are | large or small. Don't delay much longer. Send for your copy now.

Of course, if you prefer, our agent in your district will be happy to tell you | personally about the Mutual Savings Plan or any other plan that will better fit your needs. Along with your request for our | catalogue, just say that you would like to see our agent; and he will be at your door at your convenience ready to serve you. Very truly yours, (5) (1.37)

109

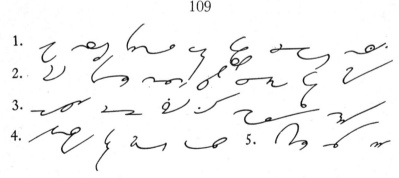

Key: (1) To present, carefully, booklet, on the subject, preparation, simplify, creating. (2) Found, biggest, connected, ideas, I am sure, probably, up to date. (3) No doubt, someone, hasn't, handed, completed, consulted. (4) Described, possible, solution, likely. (5) Difficulties, any time, worth.

Dear Mr. Jones: The facts we are about to present are so close to the heart of every man who uses direct-mail advertising that we | know you will read them carefully. What is more, we are confident you will agree with every sentence in the letter. After you have read the | letter, we are confident that you will send for a copy of the free booklet on the subject, which is now in preparation. A copy | is yours without charge for the asking.

We believe we can simplify by about 50 per cent the job of creating and printing your (1) direct-mail advertising pieces. We believe we can do this because we have found an answer to the three biggest problems connected with | direct mail. These problems are: (*a*) obtaining a good mailing list; (*b*) finding good ideas that can be made into a mailing piece that will create | interest; and (c) getting co-operation between the man who prepares the final copy for your advertising and the printer.

I | am sure we don't have to say anything about these problems. You have probably long wished that you could obtain a list that is up to date so (2) that you would not have to waste your advertising on people who have no interest in your line. You have, no doubt, wished you had someone on your | staff who could produce a new idea, one that will interest the reader when he sees your advertising piece. Hasn't your printer often told | you, when you handed him your completed copy, that the advertising piece would not be easy to print and that he should have been consulted | before the final copy was prepared?

We believe we have worked out a plan that will save time and money in preparing mail pieces from the (3) very first step to the final printed piece. This plan is described in detail in the booklet that is now in preparation. The title of | the booklet is "Selling by Direct Mail." A copy will be sent to you by mail free of charge. All you have to do is ask for it.

It is | possible that after reading this booklet you will find that it does not supply a solution to your particular problem. In that case you | will have lost only the fifteen minutes that it takes to read it. But it is much more likely that in the booklet you will find the answer to (4) at least some of the difficulties that face direct-mail advertisers today. In that case, you will have gained something valuable.

We are | going to print a large supply of this booklet, and you

can obtain a copy at any time. But we suggest that, if the booklet is,
worth | looking into, it is worth looking into now.

A stamped envelope is enclosed for your convenience in sending
for a copy. We shall be | happy to send the booklet to any of your
friends who may be interested. Simply list their names, and we will
do the rest. Yours very truly, (5) (1.38)

110

Key: (1) Short time ago, to know, wife, thoroughly, if anything,
hardly, mortgage. (2) $100, of course, mother's, capital, amount,
premium, policy. (3) Earnings, honest, families, solution, described.
(4) Mind, fulfilled, obligation, certain, moreover, comfortably. (5)
Emergency, perhaps, booklet, representatives, convenience, I am sure,
briefly, simply.

Dear Mr. Woods: A short time ago a man sat at my desk and
told me a remarkable story. He is the type of man you like to
know. | He pays his bills, has a wife and two small children, and .
is thoroughly happy.

He said, however, that one evening he and his wife were |
discussing what would occur if anything should happen to him. He
has some life insurance and some savings. But all this would hardly
cover the | mortgage on their house and pay his last bills. What
would happen to her and the children after that?

They decided that they would need at least (1) $100 a month,
that they could not get along satisfactorily with less than that

amount. Of course, his wife might get a job again; but | this would deprive his children of their mother's time, the very thing he did not wish. What could he do about it?

Well, to provide $100 | a month means a capital investment of $40,000 because this amount, safely invested at 3 per cent, will yield about | $100 a month. The premium on a $40,000 life insurance policy is $887. (2) This man feels that out of his earnings of $3,000 a year he should not pay more than $400 for insurance.

What | is the answer? Until fairly recently there has been no honest answer to this problem. Men like this man did what they could. They saved a little | and bought as much life insurance as they could. If they died early in life, their families just had to carry on as best they could.

Today | this problem can be solved quickly. Perhaps the solution will interest you. It is described fully in the booklet that is enclosed.

Once you (3) have taken advantage of this new opportunity in life insurance, you can put your mind at ease and really enjoy life. You will have | fulfilled a very important obligation to your family. You will have made certain that, come what may, the ones you love will always have | money for the necessary things in life. Moreover, you will have provided them with an income at the time that they will need it most, while | the children are young. You will have done all this easily and comfortably with this new policy for a fraction of the usual (4) insurance cost.

Finally, if any emergency arises, you will find a clause in the policy that will enable you to carry | the policy during the period of emergency.

Perhaps you will have some questions about the policy after you have read the | enclosed booklet. You may want to know exactly how the plan operates. I shall be more than happy to send one of our representatives | to see you at your convenience and tell you more about the plan. I am sure he can answer all your questions briefly and simply. Yours truly, (5) (1.40)

111

1.

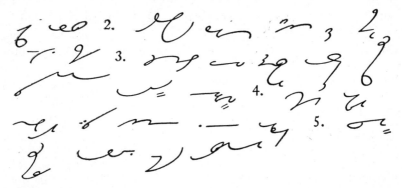

Key: (1) Do you know, 67 cents, smaller, contributors, popular, word, to pay, rewrite. (2) Intelligent, years ago, undertook, yourself, evenings, entertaining, afford. (3) Significant, almost, subscribers, languages, we have been able, editorial, London, Moscow. (4) Confidential, reports, correspondents, ahead, to come, a million, research. (5) America's, favorite, learning, informed, entitles. .

Dear Friend: Do you know what it costs to get the News Magazine to you each week? It costs 67 cents a word.

Some of the smaller magazines | pay contributors 1 cent a word, perhaps 2 cents. A few of the larger ones pay 5 cents a word, and one popular weekly pays as | much as 15 cents a word. But, in times like these, the News Magazine has to spend well over 67 cents on every word it prints.

It does | not spend this amount to pay famous authors, but to get the news at the source and to write and rewrite it until it is suitable (1) for publication in the News Magazine. Our purpose is to get all the important news in these times of stress into the head of the intelligent | person—and to make it stick. That is why it costs so much for each word that you find in our magazine.

About twenty years ago, the News | Magazine first undertook to help busy people like yourself keep up with the week's news in an evening's entertaining reading. At that time, | the only service we could afford to promise our friends was to read for them hundreds of newspapers and magazines and to boil down all the (2) significant news that we found.

The News Magazine still covers almost every important newspaper and magazine for its subscribers. | It covers so many that it would take you more than 460 hours of steady reading to go through them all, even if you could | read all the languages. But each year, as more people have purchased our magazine, we have been able to increase our service. For example, | we now have our own editorial offices in London, Moscow, and eighteen other capitals so that we can get vital news (3) to you more fully and quickly. We are now able to get confidential reports from special correspondents all over the world. These reports | give our editors information that no newspaper has published, information that will help us help our readers think ahead and plan | ahead and be prepared for things to come.

With more than a million names on our mailing list, the News Magazine can and does spend as much each week | for research and writing as we could spend in a whole year at the start.

So, try the News Magazine for yourself. See why the editors of (4) America's leading newspapers now call the News Magazine the most important and useful magazine in their work. See why seven out of | eight of our subscribers vote it their favorite magazine.

While you, too, are learning to get full value from your reading of the News Magazine, | we will do our weekly job of keeping you well informed for the next eight months for less than our editorial costs for four words in a | single issue—eight months for $2.67.

The enclosed card entitles you to this special offer. Very sincerely yours, (5) (1.41)

112

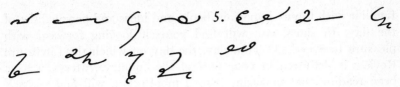

Key: (1) Heard, woman, literature, informed, found, theater, something, suddenly. (2) Front, looked, actually, all right, ourselves, you will find, many of the. (3) Articles, specialists, complete, accurate, clever, becoming, familiar, personalities, forward. (4) Country, you have been, one of the, on the market, prove, card. (5) Excellent, two million, persons, enjoyment, we are sure, one of the best, investments, thoroughly.

Dear Friend: We heard about a woman who used to carry a copy of the Literature Review wherever she went. She never read it, | you understand. She just carried it with her under her arm. She thought it made her look intelligent and well informed. She thought that it would help | her make a better impression on the better class of people.

One day that woman found herself at the end of a long line of people waiting | for tickets to the theater. She realized that she would have a long wait and so looked for something to help her pass the time. She suddenly (1) remembered that copy of the Literature Review under her arm and began reading it. Before she knew, she had read it from cover | to cover. By the time she reached the front of the line she not only looked intelligent and well informed, but she actually was.

All right, | this is not a true story. We made it up ourselves. The fact remains, however, that once you start reading the Literature Review some nice | things begin to happen to you. You will find, for example, that many of the important issues of the day start to make sense. That happens (2) because you have an opportunity in the Literature Review to read articles by people who are in close touch with those issues. | Those people are specialists in their line; and, when they write an article, you can rely on their information to be complete and accurate. |

You will find yourself suddenly saying some clever things in your discussions with your friends. You will find yourself becoming familiar with | more important books and ideas and personalities of the day. In short, you will find yourself looking forward with pleasure to every (3) Thursday, the day on which the Literature Review is delivered in your part of the country. After you have been reading that magazine | for a month, you will find yourself telling other people exactly what we are telling you now, that the Literature Review is one of | the finest magazines of its kind on the market today.

What is more, we will prove this statement. If you will return the card that is enclosed, | we will send you a sample copy of the Literature Review. You will then have an opportunity to go through the magazine and (4) enjoy the many excellent features it contains. You will have an opportunity to learn for yourself why more than two million persons | in all parts of the world read it with interest and enjoyment.

If you find that the magazine is all that we say it is, and we are sure | you will, send us a check for $5; and we will see that a copy of the Literature Review is sent to you once a week for the | fifty-two weeks of the year. It will be one of the best investments you have ever made. You will enjoy each issue thoroughly. Yours truly, (5) (1.41)

113

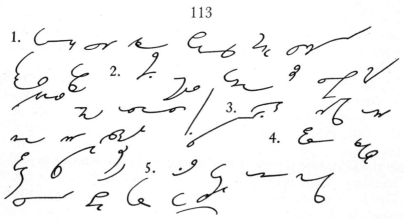

Key: (1) Promotion, another, to sell, approximate, furnishings, accustomed, businesslike, prepare. (2) Everything, inventory, personal, excess, imagine, up to date, destroy, insured, recollect, judging. (3) Themselves, you would not be able, result, one of our, worth, thousands, he did not think. (4) Experiment, surprise, expensive, items, several hundred dollars. (5) Handy, provides, room, you will be able, amount, assistance, bring, program.

Dear Mr. Barnes: Suppose for a minute that you had just received a promotion in your organization, but that the promotion would make | it necessary for you to move to another city and to sell all your household furnishings. What would be the first thing you would do? Would | you place an approximate value on these furnishings and then sell? Or would you make a complete list of what you own and decide on the | actual value of each item? As you are a businessman who is accustomed to doing things in a business-like way, you would prepare an (1) inventory of everything you own. After you had completed that inventory, you would probably find that the actual value | of your goods and personal property was far in excess of any estimate you would have made.

Because this is true, can you imagine | the situation you would be in without an up-to-date list of your furnishings if they were suddenly destroyed by fire? Even though | your things were safely insured, would you be able to list them all and recollect their approximate value? Judging by the experience (2) of many of our clients who have found themselves in that position, we are of the opinion that you would not be able to list all of | them, with the result that you would have to sustain a loss.

About a month ago I suggested to one of our good clients that he make an | inventory of his furnishings. His house was beautifully furnished, and the furnishings were worth thousands of dollars. He did not think it | was necessary to make an inventory, as he was sure he could remember everything in the house and how much it cost. Just as (3) an experiment, however, I got him to list all the things that he thought he owned and their approximate value. We then took a copy | of our booklet and made an actual inventory. To this man's surprise, he found that he had omitted many expensive items that | would have meant a loss of several hundred dollars in case of fire.

Therefore, decide to take steps at once to prevent taking a loss if fire | should suddenly strike your home. What steps should you take? That is easy. Simply prepare a list of your furnishings and personal property. We (4) have a handy inventory booklet that will help make such a job a simple matter. This booklet provides space for a listing of every | item in your home, room by room. With this booklet completely filled out, you will be able to make a claim for the full amount covered by | your insurance policy.

We shall be glad to send you our inventory booklet. If you would like the assistance of one of our | representatives in bringing your insurance program up to date, we shall be glad to have him call on you at your convenience. Sincerely yours, (5) (1.45)

114

Key: (1) Immediately, down, educated, elementary, difficulties, speech, paragraphs, serious, any one of these, ability. (2) Principal, vocabulary, inability, himself, sufficient, words, something, you want. (3) Pronunciation, effort, doubt, grammar, common, recognize, commit, many of them, they are, improves. (4) Fortunately, few minutes, coupon. (5) Lessons, to purchase, otherwise, nothing, why not, studying, criticism, toward.

Dear Mr. Banks: What impression do you make on people when you speak? When people hear you speak, do they immediately put you down as an | educated man? Or do they wonder whether you have completed elementary school?

If you have any one of the difficulties | of speech that are discussed in the paragraphs that follow, you do yourself a serious injustice every time you speak. Any one of | these difficulties can give people the wrong impression of your ability and your education. These difficulties of speech can hold (1) you back every day of your life.

One of the principal difficulties is a small and weak vocabulary. The inability | of a person to express himself clearly is often due to the fact that he does not have command of a sufficient number of words. He | may have a good idea but loses out in the end because he cannot put it into words. If you can call upon a large body of words | whenever you have something to say, you can win any position you want to reach. People will be eager to listen to you.

Then there is (2) the matter of pronunciation. Do you pronounce correctly each word that you use? Do you make a constant effort to improve along these | lines? When you are in doubt about a word, do you look it up?

How about grammar? Do you know that there are four hundred common errors in grammar? | Would you recognize them if you saw them? Are you sure you do not commit many of them without even knowing that they are errors? It | improves your personality to know that every word and phrase you use is correctly used. *Stop*

Whatever your goal in life is, your speech will (3) be a factor in helping you reach it. You have probably recognized this fact before. Perhaps you have not tried to do anything about | your speech because you thought it would be too difficult. Under ordinary methods, it is difficult. Fortunately, there is a new method | by which you can acquire better speech by spending only a few minutes on it each day. That method is built into the series of | lessons called "Improve Your Speech," which has just come off the press.

If you will return the enclosed coupon, we will send you the first lesson, which will show (4) you how easy it is to learn how to speak correctly. The entire series of lessons sells for only $15. Before you decide | to purchase them, you must satisfy yourself by the first lesson that the lessons will do all that we say they will. Otherwise you pay nothing. |

Why not have some of your friends join you in studying these lessons? You will be able to help one another and receive much valuable | criticism. You will also enjoy working with others.

Take the first step toward improving your speech by returning the coupon. Yours truly, (5) (1.45)

115

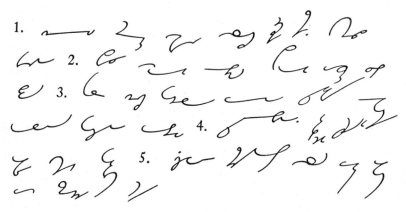

Key: (1) One of the most, functions, competent, carefully, sufficient, everything, definitely, picture. (2) Aptitude, qualities, measured, abilities, occasions, initial, he was not. (3) Bring, unusually, personnel, on the market, adopted, improved, learned, procedure, let us know. (4) Administering, specialists, findings, report, confidential, prospective. (5) Whether or not, if you would like to have, card, on the subject, representative, of course, as a result, forward.

Dear Mr. Bennett: One of the most important functions of the sales manager is to hire competent salesmen who will increase the business | of the organization and be a credit to it. No doubt you choose each new salesman carefully and check up on his references | and his personal history. But are these interviews and checkups sufficient to tell you everything that you should know about your men? Research | has shown quite definitely that they do not. To get a complete picture, the sales manager should ask each new sales-man to take the Brown (1) Aptitude Test. This test reveals the salesman's hidden qualities and character traits. It enables you to compare his measured abilities | against your impressions of him.

No doubt you remember some occasions when you hired a man because of the good initial impression | that he made. Then you spent a good deal of money training him, only to find eventually that he was not suited for the job. The Brown | Aptitude Test will tell you what you need to know about a man before you spend any money on him in the way of training.

Very often (2) the Brown Aptitude Test will bring out the fact that, while the man does not have the qualities of a salesman, he is unusually well | suited for an advertising or a personnel job.

The Brown Aptitude Test was first placed on the market about ten years ago. Since that | time it has been adopted by hundreds of organizations. The test has been improved from year to year, as we learned from the experiences | of those organizations.

The procedure in giving the test is simple. When you decide to hire a new salesman, let us know and (3) we will send you a copy of the test. Complete directions for administering the test will be enclosed. After the salesman has completed | the test, you mail it to us. Our staff of specialists, each of whom has had more than twenty years of experience in handling men in business, | then analyze the test. They then meet to discuss their findings, after which a report is written. A copy of this report is submitted | to you and a confi-dential copy is kept in our files.

After you have read the report, you will learn many things about your prospective (4) employee that will be valuable in help-ing you reach a decision as to whether or not you should employ him.

If you would like | to have further information about the Brown Aptitude Test, return the enclosed postage-free card, and we will send you our booklet on the | subject. If you would care to have us do so, we shall be glad to have our representative call and discuss your personnel problems with you. | There will, of course, be no obligation on your part as a result of his visit. We shall look forward to hearing from you. Sincerely yours, (5) (1.46)

116

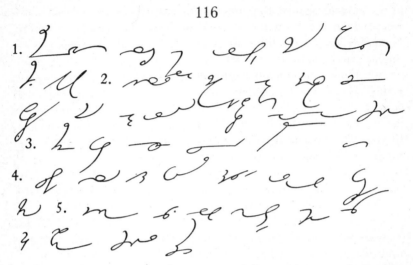

Key: (1) Several months ago, carefully, engineers, relationship, assumed, obligation, everything, dependable. (2) To carry, established, inspection, subscriber, women, appreciated, found, instances, rendered, especially, normal, factor. (3) Everyone, privilege, mind, amount, determine, of course. (4) Attached, card, to us, promptly, substituted, regardless, provide, assured. (5) School, anything, nearest, classified, in the future, any time, social, we hope you will, factory, Very sincerely yours.

Dear Mrs. King: When you purchased your Monroe Cleaner several months ago, you received a machine that had been carefully designed and | manufactured to give you the best possible service. That machine is the answer of our large staff of engineers to your cleaning problem.

When | we sold that machine to you, our relationship did not end with the sale. We assumed the obligation of doing everything in our | power to make sure that you received from it many years of dependable service. We assumed, further, the obligation of keeping the (1) cost of maintaining that machine as low as possible. To carry out these obligations, we established a half-yearly inspection plan, | to which you are a subscriber at the present time.

Thousands of women in all parts of the country have appreciated the advantages | of this inspection plan. We have found, however, in some instances that Monroe owners prefer service to be rendered once a year rather | than twice. This is especially true in homes where cleaners may receive less than normal use because of one factor or another.

So that (2) everyone will receive the kind of service best suited to his particular needs, the Monroe organization feels that each user should | be given the privilege of selecting the plan he prefers. In deciding whether you prefer a half-yearly or a yearly plan, please | keep in mind that the amount of use and the care given your cleaner should determine how frequently it should be inspected. For all owners | who feel that the use that their cleaners receive justifies inspection twice a year, we will, of course, continue on the old basis.

Please indicate (3) your desire on the attached card and mail it to us at once. Unless this card is received promptly, the half-yearly inspection will be | discontinued and the yearly inspection substituted.

Regardless of the plan you select, please remember that the Monroe organization | maintains service stations all over the country that provide prompt and efficient service at a reasonable cost. Only in these stations | can you be assured of receiving Monroe parts whenever replacements have to be made. The men who do the repair work in these stations (4) have been especially trained for that type of work in our school in New York. If anything should happen to your cleaner, look up the name and address | of the nearest station in the classified section of your telephone book.

We wish to assure you that we appreciate your business | and hope that we may have the pleasure of serving you in the future. If at any time your business or social relations should bring you to | New York City, we hope you will give us an opportunity to take you through our school and our main factory. Very sincerely yours, (5) (1.48)

117

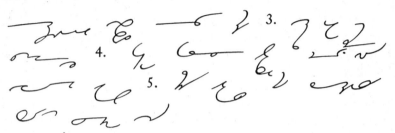

Key: (1) **To us,** summer, delivery, school, occupying, attention, officials, probably, 75 per cent. (2) Expected, last year, operate, efficiency, economy, worker, manufacturers, capacity, many of them, forced. (3) Considerably, represent, investment, economically. (4) Purchaser, premium, taxpayers, something, won't, columns, to place. (5) If you would, to supply, further, illustrate, article, I am sure, count.

Dear Mr. Hale: Your letter of June 17 comes to us at a time when we are at the beginning of our summer rush. At this time the | production and delivery of school busses before the fall term begins in September is occupying all our attention.

    I do | not know whether school officials generally buy other equipment as they do school busses. I do know from many years of experience, | however, that probably 75 per cent of all new busses are ordered after the middle of July and that delivery (1) is confidently expected about the first week in September. Last year we received several orders as late as the middle of | August with the request that the busses be delivered on the first of September.

    No business can operate with anything like maximum | efficiency and economy on such a schedule. It is bad for the worker, and it is bad for the employer. Most manufacturers | are now working to full capacity, and many of them are working overtime. All of them have been forced to take on a great many (2) men who have had no experience in this type of work to help them take care of orders.

    We are now working night and day to meet the orders | on which our customers expect delivery in July and August. After a few weeks our staff will be considerably cut, as | we shall have to wait for the new models to come out.

    School busses represent a large investment in the way of carrying charges. In order | for us to manufacture the busses economically, we should have the orders about six months before delivery is expected. (3) Every saving that we are able to make in the cost of manufacturing the busses is passed on to the purchaser. I do | not think that school boards realize that they are paying a premium for every late order that they place. I do not think that the taxpayers | realize this either, or they might have something to say about the matter.

Won't you do something through your magazine columns to urge those who | do the purchasing of school equipment to place their orders early enough so that they can take advantage of all these savings and to help us (4) and other manufacturers serve them more efficiently? If you would consider the publication of an article along these | lines, I should be happy to supply you with any further information you might need, as well as photographs to illustrate it. A good | time to run such an article would be in February or March, at which time orders for school busses should be placed.

I am sure we can count | on you to help us with our problem. We shall look forward to hearing from you soon regarding this important matter. Very sincerely yours, (5) (1.49)

118

Key: (1) Attention, in the past, Chicago, referred, original, letters, person, in the future. (2) Especial, assistance, opened, correspondence, distributed, department, record. (3) Affect, first, contents, overlook, recommend, form. (4) Communications, New York, concern. (5) I understand, devotes, up to date, consequently, disposed, possibilities, practice, anxious, efficient, system.

Dear Mr. Smith: It has come to my attention that our mail has not been handled very satisfactorily in the past. Just recently, | the manager of our Chicago office wrote me that several important letters were referred to the wrong persons. Because the original | letters are no longer available, it is difficult to place the blame on the proper person and to make necessary changes. | In the future, when mail is referred to the wrong person, the letter should be sent to the general manager for his attention.

It (1) might be wise at this point to review, briefly, our methods of handling the mail. This review should be of especial assistance to the new people | who have joined our staff within the last six months.

All mail that is addressed to the Davis Publishing Company is opened by the office | girl. Each piece of correspondence is then stamped with the date and distributed to the proper departments. All mail addressed to the magazine | department is delivered to Frank Brown, who stamps it with a receiving stamp. A record is made of all cash that is enclosed. If cash is mentioned (2) in the letter but is not enclosed, Mr. Brown makes a note of that fact for later attention.

Some letters affect two or more departments | or offices. These letters are the ones that cause most of our difficulty. The first step should be to refer each part of the letter to | the proper department. This should be done before any action is taken on the contents of the letter. Because it is easy to | overlook necessary information in making this reference, we recommend that the enclosed form be used. We have used this form in the (3) New York office for several years and have found it quite satisfactory.

Then there are the communications that are addressed to the New | York office but do not concern the New York office at all. In such cases, the entire communication will be referred to the proper | department. If that communication should concern two or more departments, a copy of the entire letter will be sent to each of the | departments. This seems the most satisfactory method of handling such communications.

Some of the communications that are received (4) by the New York office call for additions or changes in our mailing list. I understand that Miss Jones devotes one day a week to keeping | our mailing list up to date. Consequently, care should be taken not to refer a letter to Miss Jones until all other matters have been | disposed of. You can easily see the possibilities for delay unless this practice is followed.

If any questions should arise in | your office about the handling of correspondence, feel free to write me.

We are anxious to set up an efficient system. Cordially yours, (5) (1.50)

119

Key: (1) Desirous, concern, attract, humorous, cartoons, forced, circulation, efforts. (2) Otherwise, appearance, reasonable, established, qualified, special, subscribers, fields. (3) Entirely, different, exclusive, situations. (4) Of course, however, to choose, discard, we are sure, nominal, illustrations, many of the, countries. (5) Professional, in a position, extend, idea, complete, enthusiastic.

Dear Mr. Brown: As the editor of your company publication, you are always desirous to obtain greater reader interest. | That is always the main concern of a publisher of a magazine. One way to attract more interest is to have well-drawn, humorous | cartoons. We believe that the service we have to offer will be of especial interest to you.

Many editors have been forced either | to reprint cartoons from other magazines of general circulation or to depend upon the efforts of an employee whose work (1) detracts from the otherwise fine work and appearance of their publications. To satisfy the need and demand for a cartoon service at | a reasonable cost, the Smith Agency was established for the exclusive use of editors like you.

The men on our staff are well | qualified to supply you with any type of cartoon you may desire. They can provide special cartoons for any type of work that you may be | in. Our list of subscribers is a long one; and, as you will see by a check of their names on the enclosed blank, they cover a wide range of fields. (2)

As a regular subscriber, you will receive from us ten new and entirely different cartoons each month for your own special use. These cartoons | will not be issued to any other publication. You will have exclusive rights to them. Each cartoon will be drawn to appeal to your | company employees, from department heads to shipping clerks, and will feature situations that arise only in your company life.

Each | month's set of cartoons will be packed in special folders to insure their reaching you in first-class condition. Ten cartoons are released each month. We (3) realize, of course, that you will not have the space, nor will you desire, to use all of them in your publication. It is our plan, however, | to give you a selection from which to choose. Reprint the cartoons that appeal to you and discard the others.

The charge for this service is only | $5 a month, which we are sure you will agree is a very nominal sum for cartoons drawn especially for you.

In addition | to this service, we make up illustrations for your reading matter. We have been supplying many of the country's largest book publishers (4) and professional magazines for years, and we are now in a position to extend this service to other editors.

We are | enclosing a folder that will give you an idea of our work. As you will see, the cartoons illustrated have been used by a number of well-known | magazines. The editors of these magazines have expressed their complete satisfaction with our service and are very enthusiastic | about it.

The order blank enclosed will make it convenient for you to subscribe to our service. Mail it in today. Cordially yours, (5) (1.50)

120

Key: (1) Because, some of these, involved, I hope this, mind, men and women, reports. (2) To give you, writers, specific, reputation. (3) Accompany, combat, unusual, to gather, sometimes, you may be sure, was not, co-operation. (4) Exists, armed, forces, facilities, standard, started, various, to do. (5) Firmly, hesitate, regarding, come.

Dear Friend: During the past year or two, many letters that have come to this office have contained the same few questions. Because some of these questions | involved matters of policy, I feel that the answers should be made available to everybody. I hope this letter will clear up some | of the questions that may have been in the back of your mind but that you have not expressed on paper.

Many readers have asked how our men and women | got the photographs and reports that we printed about the war. Some of you have wondered whether the pictures we published did not give (1) information to the enemy. I wish it were possible for me to give you the complete picture of our photographers and writers at | work, for I believe you would find it very interesting. I will, however, confine this report to the specific points that have been raised. |

Because of their long experience in getting into difficult places and getting unusual pictures, our photographers quickly | adjusted themselves to wartime conditions. And because our men have made a fine reputation among Army and Navy authorities, (2) these authorities made it possible for our men to accompany combat units. Working with these units, our men had unusual | opportunities to gather information.

Sometimes our men were asked by the authorities to use old photographs of battlefield | scenes until such publications could not be of help to the enemy. No matter how revealing our pictures and reports may have seemed to you, | you may be sure that they contained no information that was not known to the enemy.

Another evidence of the co-operation (3) that exists between our organization and the armed forces is our School of Photography. This school was organized at the request | of our armed forces to make the facilities of our organization available to the Army and the Navy and to raise the | general standard of war photography. Since the school was started, scores of men who were trained there have entered the various branches of the | services and are now making photography history all over the world.

The final question has to do with our editorial (4) page. Many of you have praised us for our method of reporting the news. Some have wondered, though, if our policy of giving all the facts might | not be damaging to the morale of our readers. We firmly believe that it is the responsibility of the press to tell the truth, | no matter how bitter it may be.

I am very glad that these questions have been raised, for I have enjoyed writing this letter to you. I hope | that you will not hesitate to write me freely again should other questions regarding our magazine come to your mind. Yours truly, (5) (1.54)

PART VII

110 WORDS A MINUTE

121

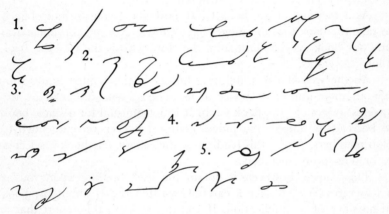

Key: (1) Originally, judges, announcement, last minute, distribution, club, represents. (2) Considerable, combined, prominent, opinion, obliged, chosen. (3) United States, to us, it is not, unusual, single, recommended, selected, to our, advance. (4) You want, nothing, merely, report, if you want, one of these, instead, system, to choose. (5) Carefully, don't, definite, you will find, whether, sometimes, dividends, Sincerely yours.

Dear Reader: This month, members of the Book Club will receive two books for the price of one. Originally, the judges decided that the novel, "The | Traveler," would be the book for our members this month. The announcement had already been printed when, at the last minute, a book that came up for consideration | demanded immediate distribution. This book was Frank Smith's "Victory Through the Air." It was therefore decided to send it to the members of | the club along with the other book.

The two books may be obtained from the Book Club—by its members only—for $3. Needless to say, this price represents (1) a considerable saving over the combined retail price of the two books.

A prominent official in the Government said, after he had read | "Victory Through the Air," that it was, in his opinion, a book that every person should read.

This is the comment of many thoughtful readers about this | book. It is clear now that aviation is the great key to the future —"Victory Through the Air" will tell you why.

As a member of the Book Club, however, | you are not obliged to take the book that the judges have chosen. Nor are you obliged to buy one book every month from the club. This is the way the Book Club (2) works.

All the well-known publishing houses in the United States submit all their important books to us. These books are read by the various judges of | the Book Club. It is not unusual for a single book to be read by nine or ten judges before it is even recommended to club members. After | this reading by the judges, one book is selected to be sent to our members.

This choice, however, is not in the least binding upon you as a | member. You receive a carefully written report about the book in advance of its publication. If you decide from this report that it is a book (3) you want, you do nothing—and the book comes to you in due course. If you decide you do not want the book, you merely sign and mail a slip to us telling us not | to send it.

With the advance report about each month's book, you receive a little magazine giving brief reports about all the other books that have been | reviewed by our judges.

If you want to buy one of these books from the Club, you can get it merely by asking for it. Or you can use these reports to guide you | in buying books from your own book dealer. In other words, instead of limiting your reading, this system widens it. It enables you to choose your reading (4) carefully.

One of the advantages of joining the Book Club is that you don't miss the books you want to read. In addition, there is a definite | moneysaving factor when you buy your books from the Book Club. The choices of our judges are usually at the top of every list of best sellers. Time | and again you will find yourself buying these books anyway, whether you are a member of the Book Club or not.

By buying these books from the Book Club, you | sometimes pay less than the retail price. In addition, for every two books you buy, you receive free of charge one of the Book Club dividends. Sincerely yours, (5) (1.38)

122   3/30

Key: (1) You will be glad, program, $50,000, to make, results, do you want, to promote. (2) Begun, popular, selection, town, cards, streetcars. (3) Publicity, third, to supplement, if you wish, management, if you do not. (4) A hundred dollars, co-operate, answer, of course, include, mentioned. (5) We hope that, problem, likely, to me.

Dear Sir: You will be glad to learn that the National Company is going to start a big advertising program to bring more customers into your | store. It is a program that will cost us over $50,000. It is a program that we hope will increase your profits. In order to make sure that | we get the results you want, we are asking you to help us.

The first thing that we want you to tell us is this: Which of our products do you want us to stress | in our advertisements? In the past two years we have not done much to promote the merchandise that you sell easily. We have felt that this merchandise does not (1) need to be advertised. We have promoted other National products so that the public would ask you for them, too. In recent months, however, we have | begun to wonder whether we should not do more to build up your sales of our popular merchandise. What do you think?

The second thing on which we need your help | is the selection of the best kind of medium for reaching the customers in your town. In some sections of the country, newspaper advertisements | get the best results. In other sections, display cards in busses and streetcars are most profitable. In a few large cities, advertisements in local (2) magazines seem to do more to interest customers than does any other kind of publicity. What is best in your town? What will bring the most | customers into your store?

The third thing we need to know is whether you would care to supplement our advertising program with one of your own. If you wish to | advertise that you sell National products at the same time that we advertise the value of those products, we shall be willing to spend much more money in | your town. If you do not care to share in the advertising program, we may spend as much as a hundred dollars for publicity. For each dollar that you (3) spend to advertise National products during the week of June 10 to 14, however, we will spend three dollars. If you spend a hundred dollars, | we will spend three hundred. Do you wish to co-operate with us?

The fourth thing that we hope you will tell us is this: Do you want us to mention the name of your | company in the advertisements we place in your town? Your answer to this question will depend on how you answered the other questions, of course. We | like to include the names of our dealers. Some dealers, however, do not want their names mentioned because they have made promises to other manufacturers. (4) We feel that using your name is a boost to our product, but we also feel that using your name will bring the customers into your store. We hope that you | will tell us that you do want us to use your name.

The fifth matter on which we would like your advice concerns the problem of timing the advertisements so that | they reach customers at a time when they are most likely to be interested. We are planning at the present time to conduct the advertising | program during the second week in June because that is the time when National products are most timely.

We are enclosing a form for your answers. Cordially, (5) (1.39)

123

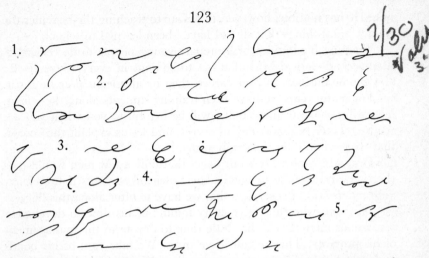

Key: (1) Statement, school, rapidly, who have been, become, men and women, have been able, demand. (2) Items, employees, drop, introduce, special, beginner, fundamental, learned, stenographic, clerical, to be done. (3) Career, prepare, helpful, courses, trouble, investments, developing, various. (4) Management, property, to us, records, connection, prevented, control, assures, without, owners. (5) To understand, to do, more and more, persons, it is not, as soon as.

Dear Sir: There is one statement with which all people will agree, and that is that better jobs go to people who are trained.

Our school has been serving this city | for a great many years, and during that time we have seen thousands of boys and girls take positions in business and rise rapidly to important places. | Others who have been trained, although they have not all become leading men and women of business, have been able to earn a better living than they could have earned | had they been given no training at all.

Business houses demand trained workers; and, if they fail to get them, they will have to set up training centers. However, with (1) this expense added to the cost of doing business, the prices of the items you buy will increase, or the wages paid employees must of necessity | drop. So the businessman of today expects his employees to be trained well when they leave school. He realizes that he will have to introduce them to the | special duties that apply to his own business. He has no time, however, to devote to teaching the beginner the fundamental things that should have | been learned in school.

Training for business will prepare young people to do the stenographic and clerical work that has to be done in every office. If (2) you choose business as your career, then by all means prepare for it.

For many years we have been training students along these lines. You will receive training that | will be helpful to you when you are ready to enter business. Pay us a visit, and let us explain the courses that we have to offer. Sincerely yours, |

Dear Mr. Smith: It is our belief that only a few men would take the time and trouble to handle their own investments if they knew and understood | the services that we have to offer along this line.

The man who must give every minute of his time to developing his various interests (3) has little time to devote to the management of his property. This he can leave to us. We take care of his bonds and help him maintain proper records. | We also handle all details that come up in connection with his investments.

Many persons have had no experience in these matters, and the help of | our bank is not only desirable but necessary if losses are to be prevented.

The trained personnel of the National Bank offers an | effective service. Our organization assures care of investments without in any way limiting the owner's control. There is nothing difficult (4) to understand about arranging an account with the National Bank. All you do is call at our head office, or at one of our branches, and decide | the things you want us to do for you. You decide on the services you want us to render in connection with your investments. You write a letter stating | these things and sign it. That is all there is to the matter.

As the years go by, more and more persons have given us the job of handling their investments.

While | it is not possible to state the cost to you, we can give this information as soon as you tell us what you want the service to cover. Cordially yours, (5) (1.41)

124

1.

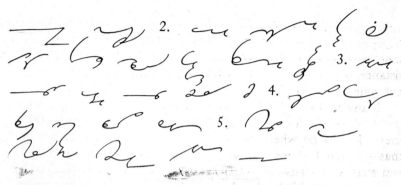

Key: (1) Advice, I am sure, community, capital, invest, experience, required, management, you will find. (2) Owners, customers, businesses, hard, to understand, biggest, concerned, prospects, bargains, specialize. (3) Toasters, many other, resistance, many of the, worried, usually. (4) Incidentally, please understand, cheerful, you can be sure, certainly, years ago. (5) Definitely, quality, different, development, district, more and more.

Dear Mr. Bland: You have asked me to advise you about starting a new business. You realize, I am sure, that I do not know your business community. | I do not know whether your community needs a store for men's clothing. I do not know how much capital you plan to invest. I do not know | how much experience you have had in operating a store, in keeping the books, or in the other details required for successful management | of a business.

What I do know is this: In most cities, opportunities for starting new retail stores are not good. You will find nearly as many store (1) owners looking for customers to buy their businesses as for customers to buy their goods.

It is hard to understand how this can be true in view | of the fact that the past Christmas season saw the biggest buying rush in our retail history. But the truth is that most big store owners are concerned about | the prospects for the next few months.

For one thing, customers are complaining about prices and are buying only when they can find bargains. The fur market | has been very bad. Stores that specialize in clothing for men have to hold special sales to get merchandise moving. Furniture stores are overstocked. Stores that sell (2) electric merchandise, such as irons and toasters and radios, have found that the market is flooded. I could go on and name many other kinds of stores | that are meeting more and more customer resistance. When you meet customer resistance, you have to cut prices; and, when you cut prices, you also cut your | profit.

Many of the manufacturers are worried about the problems of the store owners, for the store owners are not laying in stock the way they | usually do when they expect good markets. I do not doubt that you can find many manufacturers who will be eager to help you start a new business. (3) They will give you credit, good advice, and many kinds of help. That, incidentally, is one point in favor of going into business right now.

Please | understand, Mr. Bland, that the picture is not entirely dark. Many businessmen are very confident and cheerful about the future. The way things stand | today, you can be sure that a new store will be a success if you know a great deal about store management; but you will certainly have to work hard. You will | have to look for customers. A few years ago customers would have looked for you.

Before you decide definitely about starting your store, perhaps you should study (4) your business community and the buying habits of the men you would expect to come to your store. Have they used up the money they saved in bonds or in | the bank? Do they look for quality merchandise or for bargains? Do they talk about their fine salaries or about the difficulty of paying all | their bills?

The customer in your community may be entirely different from the average customer in the rest of the country. There may be a | big real estate development in your district. On the other hand, if business is getting more and more quiet, you might be wise to wait a few more months. Yours truly, (5) (1.41)

125

1. *[shorthand outline]*

2. *[shorthand outline]*

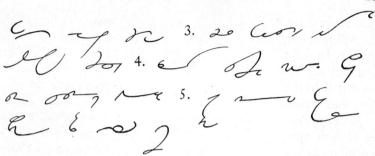

Key: (1) Application, Chicago, territory, approved, welcome, document, definitely. (2) Perfectly, clear, let us know, receipts, premium, program, knowledge, security. (3) Worry, protected, at all times, intelligent, financial. (4) Seldom, advance, warning, approach, young, accumulation, at a loss. (5) To be sure, one of the most, problem, I hope you will, experience, card, convenient.

Dear Friend: Your recent application for an accident and sickness policy has been received. We sent it to our Chicago office, which handles the | territory in which you live. You will be glad to know that the application has gone through the necessary channels and that it has been approved. We take | pleasure in welcoming you to our large family of friends. Your policy is enclosed. It is a valuable document, and you should keep it in a safe | place. Before you put it away, however, it would be wise for you to read it so that you will know definitely what situations it covers. If, (1) after you have read your policy, there are any clauses that are not perfectly clear to you, please be sure to let us know. We will do our best to explain | them to you.

Also, we suggest that you keep your receipts with your policy. They, too, are important. Each year you will receive a notice from us when your | premium payment is due. You will be given ample time to arrange for payment.

The program of protection that you have made possible with this policy | for yourself and your loved ones is a fine start on the road to better living. The knowledge that you are protected will give you a feeling of security (2) and freedom from worry. Your small premium investment may some day pay you or the members of your family a big dividend. The wisdom of | being fully protected at all times is apparent to every intelligent man and woman. I believe that you will never regret the day that you | decided to take out this insurance. In our files we have many letters from men telling us how glad they are that they made an investment in our | insurance because it helped them meet emergencies. One man made the statement that without this insurance he would have faced financial ruin.

Accidents and (3) sicknesses very seldom give any advance warning of their approach. The time to take steps to protect those who depend on us is when we are still young and | have the power to earn money.

Therefore, I urge you sincerely to keep this insurance in force. Perhaps there will be times when heavy expenses may tempt you | to give up your insurance. You may have such a large accumulation of bills that you may be at a loss to know how to pay them. That is the very | time you should put forth every effort to pay your premiums. The cost of your policy is not large. It amounts to about three cents a day. That is a (4) small investment, to be sure; but it is one of the most important investments you can possibly make.

You will be interested to know that we | handle not only accident and sickness insurance but all other types of insurance as well. Whenever you need help with any insurance problem that | may arise, I hope you will remember to call us. We shall be glad to send a representative to see you at any time. Our representatives | are trained men, who will be only too happy to give you the benefit of their training and experience. Keep the enclosed card for convenient reference. Sincerely yours, (5) (1.42)

126

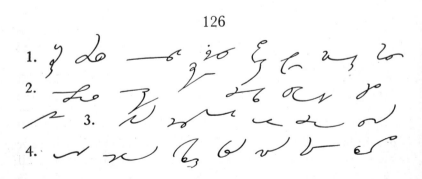

Key: (1) Officials, variety, many of those, hesitate, expensive, typical, solutions, frequent. (2) Machinery, moved, we have done, simply, accomplished, satisfactorily, do not. (3) It is not, schedules, wrong, single, week end. (4) Worked, installed, dangerous, point, won't, furthermore, certainly, another. (5) One of our, experts, investigates, recommends, careful, inspected, several times, kept, preventing, accidents, Very sincerely yours.

Dear Mr. Martin: Ask company officials why they continue to use floors that are rough and hard to clean. You will receive a variety of | answers. Many of those answers will be based upon incorrect ideas of how to maintain floors. Officials hesitate to take action because they think the problem | is a difficult and expensive one. The purpose of this letter is to discuss a few typical questions and to suggest solutions. Here are | a few typical objections of the man who needs a new floor right away but who hesitates to take definite action:

Perhaps the most frequent objection (1) we hear is that heavy machinery cannot be moved in order to put in a new floor. Of course, the moving of heavy machinery is a | difficult task, and one that may often lead to a good deal of expense. It is possible, however, in many cases to solve this problem by not moving | the machinery. We have done this in many cases by simply laying a new floor around the machinery. This can be accomplished quickly and | at a very small cost and in most cases very satisfactorily.

Another objection is that the company officials do not feel they (2) can close their plant while a new floor is being laid. It is not necessary to close down the business while a new floor is being laid. You do not have to | stop your work schedules. Floors can be replaced in sections. One part can be laid while workers keep right on producing in the other sections.

Still another objection | is that the laying of new floors will take too long. This is based on a wrong impression—that the laying of a new floor is a long process. With our | methods, we can lay as much as 3,000 square feet in less than a single day. If necessary, our men can work over a week end to save time. This plan has (3) worked very well in many plants in which we have installed new floors.

A very dangerous objection made by some officials is that, even though their | present floors are not in good condition, there is no point to putting in new floors—the new ones won't last very long. Of course, there is no point to laying a new floor | if in a short time it will be in as bad shape as the old one. Furthermore, if the old floor did not give satisfactory service, you certainly | would not want to install another floor of the same type. Material that is satisfactory in one situation may not do at all in another. (4) Before we install flooring material, one of our experts investigates the conditions under which the floors will be used. On the basis of | his investigation he recommends the flooring that will be most satisfactory.

The careful official makes sure that the floors in his plant are in good | condition. Furthermore, he takes steps to see that the floors remain in that condition. He has them carefully inspected several times a year by one | of our experts, who sees to it that the floors are kept in the best possible shape. This is an important step in preventing accidents. Very sincerely yours, (5) (1.42)

127

Key: (1) Thank you for your, compiling, families, guarantee, to our, have been, telephone, directory, approximately. (2) However, determining, to make, two hundred, 5 cents. (3) Listings, called, women, proportion, prefer, in a position, our understanding, further. (4) Prepared, results, submitted, United States, postage, applicants, subscribing, tested. (5) Heard, liberty, to join, previous, consists, worth while, throughout the, period, topics.

Dear Mrs. Day: Thank you for your reply to our advertisement.

We are compiling a list of families that have children under twelve years of age. We | guarantee to our customers that the names on these lists have been verified over the telephone.

The work consists of telephoning each family whose | name we send you in order to get the information. The name of each family is typed on a card, together with the address and telephone | number, which have been checked with the telephone directory. We find approximately one family out of every four families has children under twelve. (1)

The work is not difficult, but it does require a great deal of telephoning. You can do this work in your own home over your own telephone, however. | The money you earn is clear.

As there is no way of determining the amount of time given to the work, we base the rate of pay on the number of | names verified. To make it worth your while and ours, you would need to make at least two hundred calls a day. We pay 5 cents for each completed card showing that | there are children under twelve in that family. If you obtain four hundred names a week, you receive $20; if you obtain three hundred names, (2) $15. As only one family in four has children of the right age, two hundred listings a day must be called in order to earn $15. Some | women make three hundred to four hundred calls a day, and their earnings are in proportion. Your time is your own, and you may work as hard as you care to. We | prefer that you do not accept the work unless you are in a position to spend six hours a day, to earn from $20 to $25 | a week.

The first question you ask is: "Are we correct in our understanding that you have children under twelve years of age?" If the answer is "No," no further (3) comment is needed. These calls take very little time; and, if you will keep to the prepared talk, you will save time. Few people will ask further questions.

The | results of your work would be submitted to us each week by United States mail; and your check, plus postage paid, would be sent at once. We are ready to start in your | city; and, to save time, we have written several other applicants. If you are interested, please fill out the enclosed application and return it | to us at once. Yours very truly,

Dear Mr. Carson: You will recall that we wrote you recently about subscribing to "Tested Sales-Building Ideas." As (4) we have not heard from you, we are taking the liberty of writing again, for we know you will want to join the company of the many successful | businessmen who are subscribing to our service.

As we pointed out in our previous letter, our service consists of ideas that proved most worth while in sales | operations throughout the country. Over a period of a year, our staff chooses a minimum of twenty-five such ideas, covering such | vital topics as selection of salesmen, sales contests, and sales plans.

To join our family of subscribers, just mail the enclosed form. Very cordially yours, (5) (1.43)

128

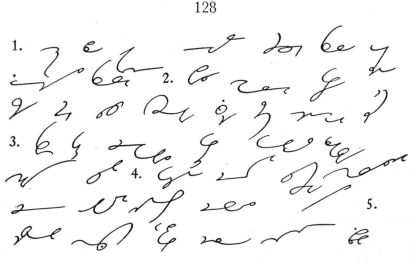

Key: (1) Considerable, easier, to become, modern, financial, barrier, register, home-study, balance. (2) Aptitude, compliments, prepaid, afford, furnish, without, developed, highest, effective, instructors, supervision. (3) Basic, positions, simplicity, previous, pleasantly, surprised, costume, ideas. (4) Procedure, sometimes, advanced, graduates, women, independence, you would like to have, smartly, to do. (5) Stylist, creative, self-expression, skill, contentment, happiness.

Dear Miss Jones: This letter contains an announcement of considerable importance. It represents a new plan that makes it much easier to become | a student at the Modern School for Dress Designing. With this new plan, we are breaking down every financial barrier and making it so easy for | you to take up our training that you will not want to lose any more time in getting started.

You can now register for our complete home-study course by | paying only $2.50 with your enrollment, and you can pay the balance of the fee in small monthly installments of $4 each. If you (1) have talent and aptitude for fashions, we believe you will want to act promptly.

After you enroll, you will receive with our compliments a student's | dress-designing kit, which will come to you with all charges prepaid. When you open it, we are confident that you will wonder how we can afford to furnish all | these items and supplies without cost.

The Modern School for Dress Designing has developed home-study teaching methods to the highest point of efficiency. | By our effective teaching methods you learn costume designing by simple steps, all under a capable instructor's patient supervision. This opens (2) the way to more rapid progress and explains why so many students finish this basic training in only six to eight months. At the end of that time | they are ready for their first positions in the field of dress designing.

In speaking of the simplicity of our training, we should like to stress that our sketching | lessons are very clear. Students with no previous training in drawing are pleasantly surprised because they are soon able to make rough sketches. It | is well to remember, too, that there are famous costume designers who do not draw or sketch at all. They merely work out their ideas by draping. If you do (3) not like to sketch or draw, you may follow the same procedure.

A student may sometimes find it possible to earn money while studying by doing work | for neighbors and friends. It is even possible for an advanced student to obtain a position before she graduates, just as many of our students | have done.

Like so many modern women today, you no doubt desire greater independence. You would like to have money for travel and to buy the things· | you want. You would like to be able to dress more smartly on much less money. In addition, of course, you want to do the type of work that will in itself keep (4) you happy. As a dress designer and stylist, you have a never-ending opportunity for creative work and self-expression.

The designer | of smart fashions enjoys creating new dresses. Here may be the opportunity for you to develop a skill that will give you a new interest. This | skill can lead to greater contentment and happiness and can open the door to the possibility of increasing your earning power.

The enrollment | blank is easy to fill out. Do it now and mail it. As soon as we receive it, we will send you the first lesson and the designing kit. Your truly, (5) (1.45)

129

Key: (1) Directors, announce, suspended, summer, reopen, notified, contracts, serious, ourselves, former, pupils, desirability, town. (2) Operate, next year, moved, facilities, children, accommodate, successfully.

(3) Several months, residents, complained, conclusion, board, recognize, community, expect, source. (4) Another, appointed, as a result, increasingly, quality. (5) Circumstances, meantime, corporation, inactive, grateful, supported, answered.

Dear Friend: The directors of the Jones School regret to announce that at the end of the present term the activities of the school will be suspended. There | will be no summer session, and the school will not reopen in the fall. The teachers have been notified that we cannot renew their contracts.

We have taken | this action only after serious study of the situation in which we find ourselves. Those of us who serve as directors are all parents of | present or former pupils in the school. We are, therefore, fully aware of the desirability of a well-run school such as this in our town. Furthermore, (1) we are aware that the services of a school of this type are now more necessary than ever before. But our experience convinces us | that we could not operate the school next year on the same basis as we operated it this year.

At the beginning of the present school year, we increased | the size of our staff and moved the school to its present desirable location on North Avenue. Here we had ample facilities to take care of | all the children who were enrolled. We were able to accommodate sixty children.

Unfortunately, after the school had been running successfully for (2) several months, some of the residents complained to the authorities that we were operating the school in violation of village laws. We had | a number of discussions with the authorities, but we could reach no satisfactory conclusion.

Believing that the school was providing a necessary | service, we asked the village board to amend its regulations. We hoped that that board would recognize the value of the school to the community | and that it would help us find some way to carry on. After several sessions, however, it became clear that we could expect no help from that source. In (3) the end, the most the board felt it could do was to permit us to continue until the end of this present term.

We have been looking for another site, | but we can find nothing in the village itself. A committee of four directors and one teacher was appointed to see whether we could use one of the | public school buildings, but that plan also fell through.

As a result of all these factors, it has become increasingly more difficult for the school to maintain | the high quality of the work it has been doing with young children for the past ten years. Therefore, until such time as arrangements can be made to run the (4) school under more favorable circumstances, the operations of the school will be suspended. In the meantime, the corporation will continue | on an inactive basis. The directors will meet from time to time to consider what action can be taken to reopen the school.

We are grateful to | all parents and friends of the school who supported us during the years in which the school has carried on its work. If any of you have questions that are not | answered by this letter, or if you have any suggestions to offer about the future, please write or telephone any of the directors. Your truly, (5) (1.47)

130

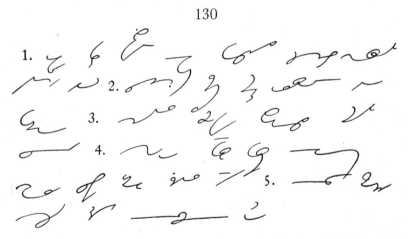

Key: (1) Report, pieces, has been done, improve, proudly, significant, clients, directed, toward. (2) Educating, effectively, furnishes, retirement, to our, personal. (3) Country, $2,000,000,000, approximately, funds, amount. (4) Greater, enterprise, private, mortgage, complete, attached, officers, history, entered. (5) Many of them, as a result, gained, substantial, men and women, superior.

Dear Mr. Jones: The annual report of a large organization such as ours should supply two vital pieces of information. It should tell | exactly how well the organization did during the year. It should also tell what has been done and what is being done to improve its service to the | public.

In our report to you for this year, we can proudly say that the year has been a very successful one. We feel, though, that our most significant gain | has been in the improvement of our service to new clients as well as to our old and valued ones.

For many years our efforts have been directed toward (1) educating our people in the field to help clients fit life insurance into their general finance planning. Our men have been doing this so | effectively that we have many letters in our files expressing appreciation of this service.

As you know, our company furnishes health insurance and | retirement plans in addition to life insurance. The fact that we make these forms of insurance available is very helpful to our men when they | try to meet the personal needs of their clients.

Life insurance companies in general have experienced a high level of activity during (2) the year. We feel that you will be interested in some of the figures. In 1948 our insurance company became one of the | few insurance companies in the country to have more than $2,000,000,000 of life insurance in force. This represents a gain of approximately | 25 per cent over 1947, which was also a good year.

No doubt you will also want to know about the investment of the | funds that stand back of your insurance. During the war years our company invested a large amount of those funds in war bonds. This is also true of all (3) other insurance companies. Now that the war is over, we are investing the greater part of our funds in private enterprises.

With the increase of | private building of homes, a large part of our funds is being invested in mortgage loans. A complete listing of the many investments we have made is | given on the attached table. A careful study of them will quickly convince you of the thought and planning that have gone into the investments the officers | of the company have made.

Our staff is now larger than at any previous time in our history. Most of our people who entered the armed forces (4) have been released, and most of them have come back to their regular positions. Many of them have been promoted as a result of the experience | they gained while serving in the armed forces. In addition, we are adding a substantial number of young men and women to the staff. We are also actively | working to develop superior methods for training and promotion throughout the staff. That program will help us to carry out the aim of the | entire organization to improve our service to you.

If you have any questions after reading this report, please feel free to write me. Sincerely yours, (5) (1.48)

The Following Congressional Record Shortcuts Are Used in the Takes That Follow

Key: Mr. Speaker, Mr. President, Mr. Chairman, committee, appropriate, appropriation, legislation, legislator, legislature, legislative, administer, administrator, administration, agriculture, agricultural, democrat, democracy, Gentleman from Nebraska, Senator from Ohio.

131

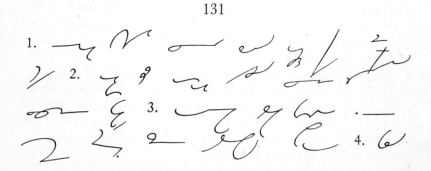

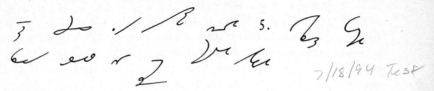

7/18/94 Test

7/16

Kathy

11/6/3

Key: (1) Mr. President, dividends, amount, earned, refuses, judged, Senator from New Jersey, forward. (2) Respect, exist, workers, decent, American, standard, enactment, proposed. (3) Lumber, terrible, picture, a million, government, functioning, assume, intelligent, ability. (4) Point, interests, family, a dollar, to do so, one of those. (5) Dangerous, profits, period, thoroughly, other, investment, ventures, deposits.

Mr. President, I agree entirely with the Senator that no employer has a right to pay dividends in terms of the amount of money | that the employees have earned and which he refuses to pay. I say that the employer has no right to pay dividends based upon such conditions, and that | the profits and the success of the business are falsely judged if they are based on such a foundation.

I return to the thought of the Senator from New | Jersey. He is afraid of what this Congress may do now; but he does not look forward to the Congress of the future, which will be able to take care of the (1) situation that will then exist. The conditions with respect to labor to which I refer do not exist in the case of workers who are receiving | 80 cents an hour, but they do exist among those who are receiving 40 cents an hour. The Senator from New Jersey states that there is a minimum | wage in his factory of $32 a week. In some states there is a minimum of $16 a week, which will not pay for a decent | American standard of living. The purpose of the bill is to take care of such situations.

It is said that the enactment of the proposed bill would (2) increase the price of lumber by 5 per cent. That would be a terrible situation to picture, would it not? We might save a million lives, but we would | have to pay 5 per cent more for lumber.

When all is said and done, the fear of what is going to happen in the future does not impress me so long as the | American Government is functioning and so long as Congress will continue to meet. I assume that future Congresses will be just as | intelligent as is the present Congress, and will have just as much ability to look forward and, if necessary, say, "This wage is too high. Things have reached the (3) point where living costs are lower, and it is no longer necessary to maintain such a high minimum standard." Why should we say that the next few years | will produce a Senate and a House that will not look after the interests of American labor? What right have we to say it as to the present | Senate and House ? No Member of the Senate will say that a family of four can be supported on the minimum wage.

Mr. President, many | businesses are paying a wage of a dollar an hour in cases in which they are able to do so. I am not one of those who wish to say that it is (4) dangerous to mention profits. I say that without profits there cannot be proper living conditions in America during the coming period. | We must have profits for the businessman, and I agree just as thoroughly to that as does any other Senator. I believe there must be profits. |

The Senator from Minnesota wondered whether there would be enough money available for investment in business ventures. I am hoping that there | will be enough money. If the present amount is not enough, there will be an increase in bank deposits, unless the money is invested in business. (5) (1.40)

132

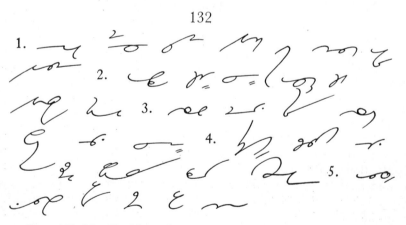

Key: (1) Mr. President, Senator from Maine, I do not, discussion, to have been, connection, report, document. (2) Last year, South America, reactions, situation, described, false. (3) Carries, something, voted, careful, approval, anything, American. (4) Justified, executive, nothing, existence, isolated, certain, development. (5) Required, handicap, obtain, effect, opportunity, concur.

Mr. President, following the remarks of the Senator from Maine, I do not wish to go into all the matters discussed by him. The discussion | seems to have been brought about by a discussion in connection with a request that a report by the Senate Committee on Commerce be made a public | document. I regret that I was called from the Chamber for a conference with one of the departments, because I would have objected to the request. | I have always felt that a document of this type should not go out in such a way as to give the impression that it is the official action of the (1) Senate.

That question arose here last year when the Senator from Nebraska, after making a tour of South America, returned to the Senate and | made a speech about what he saw and his reactions to what he saw. He requested that his speech be made a Senate document. I objected to that request. | It was finally agreed that the views on the other side should be printed along with his comments, so that there would be a fair expression, thus | presenting both sides of the situation that he described.

The general public does receive a false impression with respect to Senate documents and public (2) documents. A public document carries with it the impression that it is an official document of the Government of the United | States. It may create the impression that it is an act of Congress or something that Congress has voted upon. Therefore, I feel that we should be careful in | giving to such documents the impression of our approval. However, it is too late to do anything about it.

I am as much interested | in American aviation as is the Senator from Maine or any other Senator, but I do not believe that because of that interest (3) we are justified in taking the position that the Executive Department cannot enter into executive agreements. The matter | of executive agreements is nothing new. It is brought up now as if it were a new device, but actually it has been in existence in our | Government for a long time.

It may be that in some isolated case a contention could properly be made that a certain executive agreement | should have been a treaty requiring a two-thirds vote of the Senate. But, in the development of our commerce, the Executive Department must have (4) the authority, in my judgment, to enter into these agreements, which are not required to be treaties in the sense that they must be approved by a | two-thirds vote of the Senate.

It seems to me that it would handicap our Government in entering into arrangements on such matters if all such agreements | and arrangements had to come before the Senate as treaties and had to obtain a two-thirds vote of the Senate before they could go into effect. |

When the Senator from Maine has had an opportunity to read our report, I think he will find that we concur in the Senator's view on the bill. (5) (1.52)

133

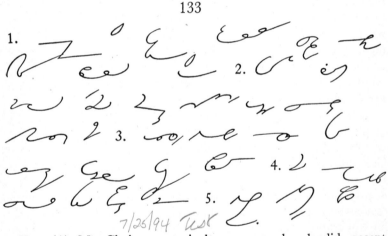

Key: (1) Mr. Chairman, agriculture, proposal, splendid, accept, measure, devoted, excellent, agricultural. (2) Pertains, heretofore, so-called, transferred, functions, conducted, result, administration, duplication, effort. (3) Required, at least, mind, burden, removed, personnel, provided, appointment. (4) Further, employee, annually, board, expenses, sum. (5) Traveling, discovered, I hope that.

Mr. Chairman, the pending bill comes from the Committee on Agriculture, and I assume that that great committee has given much study to this | proposal. Knowing the members of that committee and knowing the splendid job that committee has done throughout the years, I am willing to accept to a large | extent their judgment upon this measure. My state is well represented upon that committee by a gentleman who has devoted much time and | study to agricultural problems, and I am confident he has given careful study to this very problem. His judgment is excellent upon (1) matters of this character; and his position will carry much influence with the Members upon this question, which pertains to agriculture.

Heretofore, | Mr. Chairman, we have had a number of so-called lending agencies, all of which are mentioned in the pending measure. I am in complete accord that all | these lending agencies should be transferred and their functions conducted by one person. That will result, I am confident, in a far better administration | of this agency. I am also convinced it will result in doing away with the duplication of effort and that it should result in (2) reducing the personnel required to administer the functions of this agency. At least, that is one of the items that all have in mind, because the | cost of these many agencies of our Government is imposing a very heavy tax burden upon all of our people. It is the hope of all that | this policy may be changed and this very heavy burden removed in large part from the taxpayers of our Nation.

Mr. Chairman, while there is the hope | that this measure will reduce the personnel required to run these several lending agencies; yet this measure provided for the appointment of a (3) seven-man board, one member of which shall be the Secretary of Agriculture. Further provision is made for the appointment of a special | Assistant Secretary of Agriculture, who will serve as a full-time employee. Each member of this seven-man board will receive the sum of $10,-000 | annually. Therefore, this board will cost the taxpayers the sum of $70,000 a year in salaries. Provision is also made | for the necessary expenses for travel on the part of each of the members. While there may be a saving; yet, at the very outset, the sum of (4) $70,000 plus the necessary traveling expenses of the seven members of the board, is authorized, and that will result in | reducing any saving.

During my service as a Member of Congress, I have discovered that, if a proposal is made to save the taxpayers some | money on the one hand, at the same time some other proposal is made for spending all that saving, and in the end the taxpayers have not been given any | relief at all.

I hope that some effort will be made to reduce the Federal spending of a taxpayers' money by cutting down on personnel. (5) (1.54)

134

Key: (1) Proposed, permanent, nothing, promptly, receive, measure. (2) $1,000,000,000, annually, amount, Government, Senator from California, criticized. (3) Manner, civil, committee, conducted, adequate, substitute, requested, report, procedure, classifications. (4) Judicial, legislative, discussing, compelled, submitted, to do so, favored, another. (5) Personally, refuse, substantial, disposal, permitted, agreed, disposed.

7/27/94 Test

Mr. President, the increase proposed by the bill is a permanent increase. There is nothing temporary about it. Once the bill is passed, it will | remain on the books for many years to come; and it will continue in force after the cost of living goes down. While it is true that Federal employees | do not receive increases promptly when the cost of living goes up, it is also true that they will continue to receive increases, such as the one | proposed by the pending measure, long after the cost of living goes down.

The pending bill would mean an increased cost upon the Federal Treasury of (1) $1,000,000,000 annually. I think that is a vital question. The amount involved is as much as the total cost of the Government was in | 1916. The amount involved in this bill is one-fourth the total cost of the Government when I came into the Senate in 1932. | At that time the total cost of the Government was $4,000,-000,000 a year.

Mr. President, I did not in any way intend to suggest | that the Senator from California had criticized me, because, so far as I know, he has not done so. The only criticism I have made (2) of the Senator from California is in regard to the manner in which he, as chairman of the Civil Service Committee, has conducted | the hearings. I criticized his haste in reporting this vitally important bill without holding adequate hearings and then his offering a substitute | for a bill that five out of ten members of the committee had requested him to report. It should be said that I voted against it. I say, Mr. | President, that that is an unusual procedure in the Senate.

There are sixteen classifications of the civil service, embracing all kinds (3) of employees. Then there are the judicial branch and the legislative branch. I believe that a vital question of that kind that confronts us at the present | time should be settled in committee instead of being settled by discussing it on the floor of the Senate. The Senator from Iowa, the | Senator from Connecticut, and I were compelled to offer in the Senate a schedule of rates that had not been submitted to the committee because | we had no opportunity to do so. Instead of a flat increase of 20 per cent, we favored another plan. The Senator from California (4) knew that.

Mr. President, I have no criticism to make personally of the Senator from California; but I have never known | a chairman of a committee to refuse a substantial membership of the committee an opportunity to examine witnesses.

I | do not wish to delay the disposal of the pending bill. The Senator from California has from time to time permitted other legislation | to be considered by the Senate.

I stated yesterday that I was willing that an hour be agreed upon at which time the bill could be disposed of. (5) (1.56)

135

3. [shorthand symbols]

[shorthand symbols] 4. [shorthand symbols]

[shorthand symbols]

5. [shorthand symbols] 7/29/94 [shorthand symbols]

Key: (1) Mr. President, associate, myself, Senator from Ohio, experiment. (2) Exception, history, substance, column, country, article, floor, Union. (3) Some of these, unusual, exists, speech, Rhode Island, length, point, respect, postponement, gathering. (4) Commission, for the purpose, studying, can be done, military, president, nomination, empowered, weapon. (5) Something, America, to make, complete, situation, reason, I hope that this.

Mr. President, I am happy to associate myself with the able Senator from Ohio in attempting to carry out the purposes | of the resolution that has been submitted by the Senator from Ohio and is now before the United States Senate. I presume the | resolution will go to the Committee on Foreign Relations or some other appropriate committee of the Senate.

Mr. President, it was | on January 31 that the Senator from Illinois rose in his place in the Senate Chamber and discussed the question of the experiment. I (1) took exception at that time to what I believed to be an unnecessary experiment at this particular hour in the history of the | world.

My friend Tom Smith, who is an able newspaper man, was good enough to take the substance of what I said and report it in his column, which was carried | throughout the country.

In response to that article and in response to the statement I made on the floor of the Senate, letters came from a great number | of States in the Union. Among all the letters I received, only one took issue with the position I stated on the floor of the Senate at that time. (2)

Mr. President, some of these letters, which came from people throughout the country, are unusual. They are among the most intelligently written | letters I have ever received. In my opinion, they are fairly typical of the feeling that now exists throughout the country.

I may also say that | in a speech that I delivered in Rhode Island last Saturday I spoke at length upon this very question. Every point that was made with respect to | the postponement of the experiments was applauded by the people who attended that gathering.

Mr. President, I wish to repeat a little (3) of what I said on Saturday night with respect to this question.

A commission has been set up for the purpose of studying the situation, for | one reason and one reason only; that is, to see what can be done to keep the world from using this power for military purposes. The President | of the United States has sent to the Senate the nomination of one of the outstanding men of this Nation, to be a member of that | commission.

This commission has been empowered by the United Nations to study atomic power and to eliminate it as a weapon for (4) military purposes. At least our representative on the commission ought to have something to say about whether or not he considers this | experiment one that is in keeping with the best interest of America. He should be given an opportunity to make a complete study of | the matter. He should be given time to look into all phases of the situation. There is no reason why we should take action at this time. This matter | can safely rest for another three or four weeks.

Mr. President, I hope that this resolution will be given the most serious consideration. (5) (1.57)

136

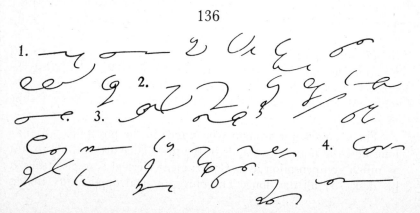

Key: (1) Mr. President, amendment, offered, gentleman from Texas, proposals, adequate, alarmed, private. (2) Unable, government, provisions, I repeat, postmaster, administering. (3) Entitled, equalize, to do, adopt, applicable, woman, post office, compensation, clerical. (4) Practical, afforded, postal, adjustments, atomic, investigations, recommend, separate. (5) Support, 900,000, to provide, opinion, indirectly, legislators.

Mr. President, the bill before us is a very difficult one. I have a high regard for the members of the committee. It seems to me that | the amendment to increase salaries by $400, offered by the gentleman from Texas, is probably the best of any of the pending | proposals. It has been said that all salaries should be increased. I favor adequate salaries for all Federal employees. I am not alarmed | that some Members of Congress are retiring to private life for the larger salaries. I would not want to be a Member of the House of Representatives (1) if the time should come when no Member of the House should be worth more than $10,000 or unable to earn more than $10,000 in private | enterprise. I am not alarmed when some people leave the Government service because they can get more than $10,000 in private employment. I | want to remind you now that there are provisions whereby experts can receive much more in times of peace than $10,000 a year.

I repeat that the | proposal of $400 is probably the best we have had yet. In my judgment, a postmaster administering a $50,-000,000 (2) business is entitled to just as much compensation as the administrator in any department of the Government. So, until we equalize | and adjust the salaries of the postal employees and the salaries of the Federal employees generally, it occurs to me that the wise | thing to do is to adopt this $400 increase, making it applicable to all.

For my part, the woman who stands in the post office all | day long and the man who stands in the post office are entitled to just as much compensation as a Government clerical worker sitting at his desk (3) all day long. The only practical opportunity that is afforded to the House now to equalize these salaries is to vote for this | $400 increase. The bill probably will go to conference. The bill we passed for the postal employees has gone to the other body, and it will | probably go to conference. There will be an opportunity to work out and make adjustments that will be fair to all the employees in the Government. | If we need experts for atomic investigations and other work, I recommend separate provisions for making the talent available (4) to the Government. I believe it does not support the main contention for increases for 900,000 employees when we say it is | necessary to provide additional compensation for about 200 employees. In my opinion, the salaries of Members of Congress should be | increased directly rather than indirectly.

Mr. President, there was a time when legislators took into consideration the taxpayers; | but today the taxpayers are the forgotten people in this country. Unfortunately, we are at present faced with a very serious condition. (5) (1.58)

137

Key: (1) **Mr. Chairman**, committee, agricultural, appropriations, result, authorship, report, considerable, sum. (2) To our, Treasury, effort, amendments, recommended, evidence, developed, observe, something. (3) In a position, justified, disagreeing, familiarized, yourselves, spirit. (4) Majority, minority, co-operated, accomplished, of course, assistance, one of the best, represents. (5) Endeavored, mind, can be done, forgotten, financial, burden.

Mr. Chairman, your committee on agricultural appropriations brings to you the agricultural appropriation bill for the coming year. | This bill is the result of long hearings that began on January 14 and continued for several weeks and of careful study on the part | of the membership of the subcommittee.

We have no pride of authorship in any of the provisions of the bill. As you will note from the committee | report, it carries a very considerable sum of money. We have sought to write a bill that would be fair to the interests of agriculture in (1) the United States and at the same time fair to our National Government in view of the condition of our Treasury at the present time. We shall | welcome any effort by any member to improve the bill through the offering of amendments.

We do ask, however, that, before any member of | the committee shall undertake to bring about changes in the actions that have been recommended by the subcommittee, he shall give | consideration to the evidence that was developed in the hearings. You will observe from an examination of the hearings that they comprise something over (2) two thousand pages. I am not in a position to say that, after you have studied the evidence, you may not be justified in disagreeing | with the actions that have been recommended by the subcommittee. But I do feel that, in view of the efforts that we have devoted to the production | of this bill, you ought not to disagree with us without having first familiarized yourselves with the evidence.

The committee has approached the | consideration of the many problems that are taken up in this bill in a spirit of public service. There has been no evidence of politics on the (3) part of any member of the committee on either the majority or the minority side. All its members have co-operated in the | work that we have accomplished; and, of course, we have had the able assistance of one of the best of the executive secretaries who serve the | Committee on Appropriations.

The bill carries in direct appropriations about $600,000,000, which represents a reduction below | Budget estimates for next year of $15,000,000. Of course, direct appropriations are not the only subject matters that are considered in (4) this bill.

In making the reductions that have been made in the bill, the committee has endeavored to keep in mind the needs of agriculture and to | serve those needs as best it can be done through the various agencies of the Department of Agriculture. At the same time, we have not forgotten the difficult | financial condition of our National Government and of the heavy burden of taxation that must rest upon our people. We have tried, | therefore, to effect economies in appropriations without endangering the ability of the Department to serve the needs of the farmer. (5) (1.60)

138

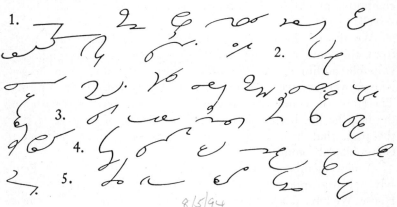

Key: (1) Mr. Chairman, afternoon, appropriations, gratitude, skillful, expert, rendered, devotion, attempting, includes. (2) Gentleman from Nebraska, amount, confronting, fortunate, energies, as a result, accurate, reports, observation. (3) Addition, lawyer, connection, civic, has been able, accept, appointed. (4) Benefit, attendance, was not, municipal, in the past, likewise, functioning. (5) Generally, thankless, certainly, personally, property.

Mr. Chairman, the House has before it this afternoon the annual supply bill for the District of Columbia for the coming year.

The committee | this year had for the first time the services of Mr. Bob Jones, who has been a clerk of the House Committee on Appropriations for many years. The | committee desires to express gratitude to Mr. Jones for the skillful and expert help he rendered to the members of the committee and for his | devotion to his work. He worked night and day in attempting to obtain the facts for the committee.

The membership of the committee this year includes the (1) gentleman from Nebraska, to whom the country, as well as the people of the District of Columbia, owes a debt of gratitude. He has devoted | a tremendous amount of time to the work of solving the problems confronting the people of the District of Columbia. We in Congress are | very fortunate in having the valuable services of the gentleman from Nebraska, because he has given of his energies on many | occasions. He has, as a result, been able to bring to the sub-committee and the full committee accurate reports of what he observed.

We also (2) have on the committee a new Member of Congress from the state of Virginia. The gentleman from Virginia is a valuable addition | to the subcommittee because, as a lawyer, he was very active in connection with civic affairs in Virginia. Therefore, the committee | is pleased, because of his experience and the help he has been able to render by reason of those services in the past, that he saw fit to accept | service on the District of Columbia subcommittee.

A new member of the committee, the gentleman from Pennsylvania, was appointed (3) just before the bill was reported to the House. We have not had the benefit yet of his attendance at the hearings of the committee.

The gentleman | from Massachusetts was not able most of the time to be present at the hearings. We missed him very much because of his great experience as a | municipal official in the past.

The gentleman from Washington, likewise a member, gave valuable service to the committee because of | his knowledge of municipal functioning in his own area.

Mr. Chairman, service on the Subcommittee on the District of Columbia is (4) generally regarded by our colleagues of the House as a thankless job. Certainly no one can claim that there is much advantage to be derived by | reason of service on the committee. Personally, I regard it as a valuable opportunity for public service because the District | of Columbia and the city of Washington are the property of the entire Nation, and not just the property of the people who reside | here.

I have found in my service that the opportunity to learn more about the functioning of city government has been valuable to me. (5) (1.61)

139

Key: (1) Chairman, committee, interstate, foreign, I want, attention, disagreement, conference, program, contemplates, period, worthy, report. (2) Record, favoring, ignore, established, pattern, Congress, appropriation, postwar, accordance, assistance, recall, attempt, certainly. (3) Administered, government, existing, appropriate, political, construction, similar, comparable, to provide. (4) Measure, expected, required, proposed, indeed, practice, approve, opposite. (5) Let us, concentration, colleague, we want, confusion, governmental, legislation.

Mr. Speaker, the statement made by the chairman of the Committee on Interstate and Foreign Commerce covers this bill. I want to address my remarks | to one special phase of it and to call your attention to the fact that I have no disagreement with the chairman of the committee or with those who signed | the conference report.

After all, this is a program that contemplates the expenditure of $500,000,000 over a six-year period; | and it is one worthy of our most serious consideration.

Mr. Speaker, this conference report should be defeated. I do not believe that (1) the Members of this House desire to go on record as favoring a program that would ignore the long-established pattern that built the highways of | this Nation.

A few years ago, as you know, the Congress authorized a $1,500,000,000 appropriation for postwar highways. In | accordance with the established Federal-state pattern, that whole program is to be carried out with the assistance of state agencies.

As you will | recall this House passed a bill to set up a program of Federal aid for school lunches. Did that bill attempt to ignore the states? It certainly did not. The school-lunch (2) bill recognized that such a program could best be administered by working through the states. It recognized that, in our American system of government, | the states should and must play an important role. Finally, it recognized that existing state agencies are the appropriate bodies to deal with | their own political subdivisions. Federal aid for the construction of airports should be handled in a similar manner.

Even more comparable | to the pending airport-aid bill is a bill recently passed by the Senate which seeks to provide Federal aid for the construction of hospitals. This (3) measure is now being considered by the House Interstate and Foreign Commerce Committee, through a subcommittee headed by the gentleman from | Tennessee. I believe a favorable report is expected in the near future. No one has suggested that the head be required to deal with the thousands | of subdivisions in the proposed program of Federal grants for hospital construction. Indeed, the United States Public Health Service has no desire | to change the practice of working through duly established state agencies. Why, then, should we approve the pending conference report, which is opposite to (4) the system of co-operation that has been developed over a long period of years?

Let us face this issue squarely. Do the Members of this | House want further concentration of power in Washington? As our colleague, the gentleman from Texas, said, do we want to add to this great confusion | of governmental powers here in Washington? Make no mistake, that is exactly what the pending conference report proposes to do.

I believe | that a federally aided program of airport construction is most desirable. I believe that legislation for this purpose should be enacted. (5) (1.61)

140

Key: (1) Mr. Speaker, committee, occasions, appropriation, legislation, agriculture, reported, already. (2) Expedite, beneficial, gratification, agricultural, administration. (3) Government, budget, population, centers, oppose. (4) Together, country, interdependent, indirectly, certainly. (5) I hope, notwithstanding, counties, I had, detain, insert, that can be understood.

Mr. Speaker, the Committee on Rules has said on several occasions that it would not bring in a special rule on appropriation bills that | include legislation. Nevertheless, we have granted such a rule for the Department of Agriculture appropriation bill. Most of the important | provisions that would be subject to a point of order have received favorable consideration from the Committee on Agriculture. That committee | has reported two bills that would make in order the main provisions in this bill, and the House has already acted favorably on the school-lunch bill. (1)

Consequently, the Committee on rules felt the rule on this bill should be granted, in spite of points of order, to expedite beneficial appropriations | for agriculture and the farmers of the Nation.

It is with real gratification that I again offer a rule for agricultural | appropriations.

Mr. Speaker, the bill before us carries appropriations of more than $1,000,000,000 for the operation of the Department | of Agriculture alone and for the administration of the many laws entrusted to that vast Department. These expenditures are almost wholly (2) for the direct benefit of American farms and American farmers. The appropriations in this bill are greater than the entire cost | of running the United States Government for a whole year before the First World War. It was not until 1910 that the annual budget for | the Federal Government exceeded $1,000,000,000. Little of this appropriation will directly benefit those of us who live in the | large population centers; nevertheless, it would not even occur to me to oppose a rule making it possible for us to vote on these appropriations. (3)

It has always been clear to me that we must all live together. There is no reason why the people of the cities should be at odds with the | people in the country. We are interdependent. We who live in the big cities are benefited indirectly by appropriations made directly | to help the farmers.

Certainly I shall not make any objection to this rule or to the appropriation bill; yet, whenever we come in here | with legislation in the interest of the big population centers, all kinds of objections are raised. Last week we heard frequently of states' rights. I hope (4) we shall hear none of that in regard to this bill, notwithstanding that we are making appropriations here to be spent in the states and counties and through | the many divisions of the Department of Agriculture.

I had intended to read some of the individual items in this bill; but I shall | not detain the House. You have no doubt read the bill. However, in order that the whole country may know what we are doing here for the benefit of | agriculture and for the farmers of the Nation, I ask permission to insert in my remarks certain figures that can be understood by the farmers. (5) (1.62)

PART VIII

120 WORDS A MINUTE

141

Key: (1) Mr. President, for a long time, worry, lifetime, immediately, children, remove, mind, citizen, United States. (2) Lifeless, describes, suffering, years ago, effects, let us, significance, recommended. (3) Serious, 10-pound, consumer, power, moderate, controls, further, doubled. (4) Confined, one of our, typical, to build, million, common sense, excuse. (5) Dangers, ahead, to do, something, knowledge, remind, already, to understand, I hope, situation.

Mr. President, we have been talking about inflation for a long time as if it were a threat about which we do not have to worry during our lifetime. Actually, | we are facing this threat now; and we must deal with it at once.

Unless we deal with it immediately, the consequences may haunt us and our children for many | years. Now, on the other hand, if we look at the problem with clear vision, we can remove the threat. If we keep the interests of our country as a whole in mind, we | can prevent inflation from overtaking us.

That task calls for clear thought on the part of every citizen of the United States as well as every department (1) of the Government.

The word "inflation" is cold and lifeless, but it describes a process that can cause a great deal of suffering. I wonder how many of you | remember what happened the last time we had price inflation some twenty-five years ago. The effects of that inflation lasted for many years and caused considerable | suffering throughout the nation.

Let us look at the record to see just what happened at that period. In 1916, the cost of living began to rise, but there | were few who saw its significance. It was only when prices had risen 70 per cent that the President recommended any steps to prevent inflation.

The (2) consequences were so serious that many people today will still remember them. By 1920, a 10-pound bag of sugar cost $2.60 and | a 10-pound bag of flour cost 88 cents. The consumer found that items for which he paid $1 in April, 1916, cost as much as $2 in | 1920. The family with no increase in income found its purchasing power cut in half.

We have now, just as we had in 1916, moderate rises in | the cost of living. If we fail to use the controls at our disposal to prevent a further rise, we may once more find the cost of living doubled.

The rise in prices (3) is by no means confined to food and clothing. I have before me, for example, the actual figures on the cost of building a six-room house in one of our typical | cities. This home that could have been built a year ago for $6,000 now costs over $7,000 to build. Here we have an increase in price of nearly | 20 per cent.

Not only is the cost of building homes rising, but higher rents are also being charged to the millions who do not own their homes.

We must decide | now whether we shall have the common sense to avoid what we previously experienced. There is no excuse for us to be too late in meeting this threat of inflation (4) that faces us. We know what is going on. This time our eyes are open to the dangers that lie ahead of us. We know now that the time to do something about | inflation is before it occurs. We should profit by the knowledge and take prompt action now.

There is no need for me to remind you of the reasons that prices have already | risen. But we need to understand the issues, and we need to see clearly the consequences of delay. I should like to point out what has already been done. Then, I | should like to call your attention to what still must be done in order to keep prices from rising further. I hope Congress will take steps soon to meet this situation. (5) (1.37)

142

Key: (1) Mr. Chairman, I hope that the, committee, argument, discharge, quarrel, if you want, perfectly, disagreement, amendments. (2) Clearly, determining, certain, gentleman from Ohio, triple, benefits, expecting, first attention. (3) Railroad, men and women, engaged, included, related, industry, ourselves. (4) Propose, bankers, word, solvent, one of the, sponsors, enacted, formula, report. (5) Competent, person, actuary, testimony, appeared, exactly, support, require, above that, fund.

Mr. Chairman, this is a serious matter, and I hope that the Committee will not get off on the wrong track in the argument as to what happened in the committee | or what did not happen. That is water over the dam. It does not make any difference to me whether you signed a discharge petition or whether you did not. | That is your right as a Member of Congress, and I have no quarrel with those who did. If you want to do those things, it is perfectly all right. But there is a vast difference | in the area of disagreement between the original bill and the committee amendments to the original act. Members should get those differences (1) clearly in mind in determining what action and what position they are going to take on this legislation.

There is one thing that is certain. If you adopt | the Jones bill as introduced by the gentleman from Ohio, you might just as well get ready to increase these taxes on the employer and the employee. You will | have to triple them if you are even to begin to pay the benefits provided by the Jones bill. It just simply cannot be done by passing the Jones bill and | expecting the men to get those benefits.

There are five major differences between the Jones bill and the committee amendments. The first one I want to call your attention (2) to is that of coverage. Under the original law, the railroad men who are employed generally in railroad service are covered; and that is all. The taxes | are levied in order to take care of those men and women who are engaged in railroad work. But what does the Jones bill do? What is the coverage of that bill? It provides | for an increase in the coverage to include many things not related to the railroad industry at all. We may just as well be honest with ourselves. You and | I know that, if you extend the coverage, there is only one way it can be done; and that is to increase the tax rate against both the employer and employee.

Now, (3) what does this bill do? We propose in the committee bill that there shall be no change whatever in this coverage as provided in the present law. I might add here that | the gentleman from New York said that some bankers had testified before our committee and that he was taking their word for it that his fund would be solvent. Mr. Lee | is one of the original sponsors of the legislation who testified before the committee when the original act was enacted, and he helped set up | the formula for the tax basis. He was wrong then, and I say to you that he is wrong now. You Members of Congress paid for the report that was made to your committee (4) by a competent person. The actuary did not take just Mr. Lee's word and the word of the other actuaries to whom he referred. He took the testimony | of every witness who appeared before the committee. He considered the bill and worked out from the bill and the testimony just exactly what it would cost, | so that we could present this matter to the Congress and to the people of the railroad industry so that they would know what they would have to pay to support the Jones bill. | It would require an increase of about 3 per cent above that which the bill provides to give all the benefits covered by the Jones bill and still keep this fund solvent. (5) (1.40)

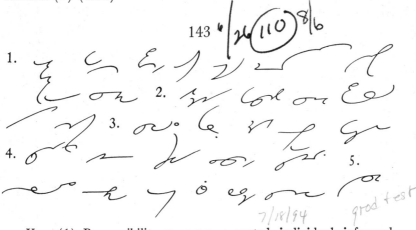

Key: (1) Responsibility, program, expected, individual, informed, some time ago, timetable, I am sure. (2) It is understood, practice, announce, explained, to do, could have been. (3) Accordingly, bringing, substantial, majority, procedure. (4) Identical, to him, vetoed, enacted, I do not think. (5) Guilty, measure, legislation, highly, earliest, ignore, demands.

Mr. Speaker, since I have been charged with the responsibility for planning the program of the House and for advising the Members as to what might be expected | in our schedule, I have tried to give Members of the House information on which they could depend. I have tried to arrange the program so that Members might depend upon | it in making their individual plans. I believe that I have been successful in keeping the Members informed.

Some time ago, Mr. Speaker, I referred to the | program for this week in a statement on the floor. That statement told about the timetable for action on the bill that we have been trying to expedite.

I am sure it (1) is understood by all of us that conference reports are in order at any time. It has never been my practice to announce this fact every time I take the floor, | for this fact is explained in every one of the notices that are sent to every Member of the House, both on the Democratic and the Republican sides.

√ What we | are trying to do here today, Mr. Speaker, is to consider the tax-reduction bill as a conference report. True, it is not a conference report; but it | is just like one. This bill could have gone to conference, the usual agreements could have been made, and the bill could have come out as a conference report and have been (2) voted on today. We are trying to get a vote on it today. All Members certainly knew that the tax bill was being completed in the Senate and might be brought | into the House at any moment.

Accordingly, Mr. Speaker, in my opinion, it cannot be fairly stated that any of us have engaged in bad faith in | bringing this tax-reduction bill to the floor at this time for final revision. The House has already passed the bill with a substantial majority. We have been waiting | for the Senate to complete its revision. Now we are ready to consider those changes that the Senate has thought to be important. Our procedure, therefore, is (3) identical with our procedure for action on a conference report.

Now, apart from the matter of the program and procedure, the gentleman from Texas | indicates that there should be a delay in acting on a tax reduction. I point out to him and to the membership of the House that in our first session we worked on | tax relief for our people. We passed two tax bills that were vetoed. The veto was overridden in this body; it was not overridden in the other body. So, | a tax bill was not enacted. The bill before us today represents the tax bill passed by the other body on Monday of this week.

I do not think that we are (4) guilty of any undue haste in proceeding to act on this measure today when we have spent about a year and a half in trying to get such legislation enacted. | I also call attention to the fact that the bill dates back to January of this year. For that reason, if for no other, all Members certainly knew that the | tax bill was being completed in the other body and might come to us for action at any moment. It seems to me highly important that action be taken | on this measure at the earliest possible moment, which is today. For this House to delay one day longer would be to ignore the demands of those who sent us here. (5) (1.41)

144

Key: (1) Mr. Chairman, support, called, lowest, gentleman from Michigan, respects, was not, accepted, sincerely, reconsider. (2) To do, expecting, recognize, legislation, I want, anyone else, furthermore. (3) Himself, borne, to testify, at all times, not only, country, also, to spend, I hope the. (4) Certainly, minimum, beyond which, requiring, contribute, emphasis, above. (5) Result, conclude, conflicting, everyone, argue, Christmas, except, favored.

Mr. Chairman, I propose to support this bill, and I speak as the author of a different tax bill from the one in question. My tax bill called for a tax reduction | all the way from 35 per cent in the lowest incomes to 7 per cent at the top.

But I cannot go along with the gentleman from Michigan in two respects. | The first error I believe he is committing is in deciding to vote against any tax reduction just because his particular bill was not accepted | by the Committee on Ways and Means. I sincerely hope he will reconsider that decision.

In the second place, I cannot go along with him in the statement that (1) the majority leader has been trying to tell him what to do. I did not submit my bill never expecting it to go through. I introduced it, and I fought for | it with the members of the Ways and Means Committee with all the force I could muster. But I recognize the fact that legislation is a matter of give and take.

I | want to assure the membership on both sides of the aisle that neither the majority leader nor anyone else has tried to tell me what to do. I do not propose | to have anybody tell me what to do. Furthermore, I am confident that he has not told anybody what to do. I resent the fact that the gentleman from (2) Michigan has allowed himself to create any such picture of the majority leadership in this body, which has the respect of the members of the House on | both sides of the aisle.

I believe the fight I put up has borne fruit, and I am happy to testify that the leadership has at all times been ready and willing to hear | us.

I feel it to be my duty to support this legislation and am confident that it will bring not only new hope to the people of this country but also will | give them more money to spend on the good things of life.

As I stated when the bill was introduced, I hope the time is not too far distant when the present exemptions of (3) $500 for a single person and $1,000 for a married person can be raised somewhat to a greater figure. There certainly is some minimum, | it seems to me, beyond which we should not go in requiring a man to contribute out of his income to the expenses of running the Government. This minimum | might well be set somewhat higher than the present figures.

Although special emphasis should be placed on relief in the lower incomes, it would not be fair, it seems to | me, to deprive of the benefits of tax reduction single men with incomes over $700 or

married men with incomes above $1,200. (4) This would be the
result if we adopt the suggestion of the gentleman from Rhode
Island.

Therefore, I conclude, a bill has been brought before us that
takes into | consideration the conflicting opinions and positions of
many members. There are those who sincerely contend that a
straight reduction should be given to everyone. | Others claim that
reductions should take the form of a raise in the present exemptions.
We could argue here until next Christmas if we all opposed any tax-
reduction | bill except the particular one that we favored. The
country looks to this Congress for accomplishment. We must get
on with the great work that lies ahead of us. (5) (1.41)

145

Key: (1) Mr. President, construction, respect, in the world, unfor-
tunately, improved, 2,000,000, pavement. (2) Probably, definitely, engaged, hard-surfaced, concerned, become, occurred. (3) Economy, program, already, one of the best, a billion dollars, expenditure, number.
(4) Explanation, discuss, portion, reason, immediately. (5) Director,
appointed, drafting, flexible, effort.

Mr. President, last November I introduced a bill providing for
the construction of good farm roads. I wish to make a brief state-
ment at this time with respect to | the bill.

Throughout the country, we have many fine roads, perhaps the
finest in the world. We have many excellent roads, but unfortu-
nately about 42 per cent | of our farm roads have never been im-

proved. I believe the improvement of these roads is one of the most important problems that is before this Congress at this time.

In the | forty-eight states, there are over 2,000,000 miles of roads. However, only 45,000 miles have good pavement and about 99,000 have fair pavement. (1) The rest of the roads probably do not need pavement, but definitely do need improvement of some kind.

Many county and state highway departments have for years been engaged | in improving local roads, and there are now sections of the country that are well supplied with hard-surfaced roads. But this amounts to only a small part of the total | roads.

I have been long concerned with getting the farmer in my state out of the mud. I believe it has now become a responsibility of the National Government. | It is high time that we should give a hand to the farmer.

In considering this problem, it occurred to me that, if we are to spend Federal money to aid in (2) enforcing peacetime economy, we can find no better enterprise than a program for improving local roads. As senators already know, the building of roads is | one of the best job providers. It goes without saying that any reduction in the farmer's cost of getting his produce to market will bring about economies | for the city man as well as the country man.

With these considerations in mind, I introduced in the Senate last November a bill calling for a billion | dollars' expenditure at least for building all types of farm roads. The expenditure of this money should provide jobs for almost a million men for a number of (3) years.

At the time I introduced the bill, I gave no explanation of it on the floor. Since that time, several members of this body have expressed to me their interest | in the measure and have asked me to discuss some of its provisions.

Under my bill, both the Federal and state governments will supply the funds. However, the | Federal Government will supply the greater portion of the funds. The reason for this is that, because of the great need, this work must get under way quickly. Few county governments | would be ready to make such a heavy expenditure for roads immediately. Even those counties that have the money available would not be able (4) to release it quickly enough.

In my bill a director appointed by the President would work with the local and state highway departments. One of the chief problems | in drafting a bill of this type is to make it flexible enough so that it will apply to all states. I have made every effort to do just this. Let me point out | that in five of our states, the state highway departments construct and maintain the local roads as well as the state roads. In other states, the towns maintain agencies for road | building. All these cases have been considered and provided for. One provision would allow two or more counties to act together in setting up a highway agency. (5) (1.42)

146

Key: (1) Stranger, inquired, one of our, word, soundest, in the world, fundamentally. (2) Anything, period, development, expect, assured, establishing, reputation, affected. (3) Justice, securities, railroads, in addition to that, shippers, thousands, families, legislation, years ago. (4) Let us, whereby, empire, amount, contract, of course, soldiers, transport. (5) Forts, surely, destroying, statute, limitations, there is not, beyond, approach, fair understanding.

Mr. Chairman: I recall the visit, when I was about six or eight years old, of a stranger to our home. He inquired of my father as to the character of | one of our neighbors. My father replied that his word was as good as a Government bond. From that day until now, I have looked upon a Government bond as one of the | soundest and best investments in the world.

Why is a Government bond so sound? Not nearly so much because of the value of the country as because of the character | of the 130 million people who make up the country. Our people are fundamentally sound; they are fundamentally fair. So, for all these years, we have (1) been taught to look upon anything issued by the Government as one of the best and soundest investments in the world.

More than that, Mr. Chairman, during this period | of the development of our country, our people have come to look upon their government as being fair and just in every sense of the word. Why? Because the | people are just and fair and believe in fair play. They expect their government to treat its people fairly. Each and every one of us to that extent is assured of | a fair deal, having had a part in establishing this reputation for the Government.

A great number of our people are affected by this bill today, and these (2) people expect justice and fairness on the part of the Government. Who are these people? They are the holders of the securities in the railroads; they are the common | people in all parts of the country who have put their savings into the railroads. In addition to that, we have the shippers who use the railroads, and these include thousands | of farmers. We also have the employees of the railroads and the future of their families to consider in this legislation.

When this agreement was entered into | about seventy years ago, neither the Government nor the railroads could foresee the situation that we have today. If they could have foreseen it, they never (3) would have entered into such an agreement. Let us look at what happened at that time. The only way that the West could be developed was through the aid of the railroads. Therefore, | an arrangement was made whereby the railroads were to help in the building of an empire. They undertook the task and did it well. In return for their services, the | Government gave them a certain amount of land.

That was the principal contract. As the railroads were built, settlers made their homes in the West and they needed protection. Forts | were built to protect these people. Of course, these forts had to be supplied with soldiers and food and guns. So the railroads agreed to transport the soldiers and their supplies free to (4) these forts. From that agreement, the present contract was developed, and it is now slowly but surely destroying the railroads.

Simple justice, Mr. Chairman, demands that | this bill be passed
because, as I said, our people believe in justice and demand that it
be passed. The statute of limitations has long since run against this
agreement. | It is now seventy-five years since it was entered into.
There is not a state in the Union that has a statute of limitations of
any kind that extends beyond | a period of thirty years.

Every member of the House should approach the matter con-
tained in this bill with a fair understanding of what is involved. (5)
(1.42)

147

Key: (1) Mr. Speaker, commerce, suspension, ordinary, to us, perfectly, candid, opposition, upon the subject, entered. (2) Freight, transportation, commercial, profit, built, as you know, excellent, financial.
(3) Outstanding, some of them, heretofore, develop, they wanted, to
build, millions. (4) Contract, they are not, unsold, according. (5)
Worth, resolution, notwithstanding, myself, conscience, quite understand,
urged, servant, moment.

Mr. Speaker: The bill that we are about to discuss comes from
the Committee on Interstate and Foreign Commerce, and its author
is the distinguished gentleman from | New York. We are able to dis-
cuss it at this time because of the suspension of the ordinary rules that
apply to debate. Two hours have been allotted to us. |

To be perfectly candid with the members of the House, there is some opposition to the bill. Nevertheless, the Committee on Rules feels that the House should have an | opportunity to pass upon the subject.

At the time these grants were made by the Government, an agreement was entered into by which the railroads would transport Government (1) freight without charge. The Government office would furnish all the transportation equipment. Later, the Government asked the railroads to furnish transportation equipment, | which the railroads did. The railroads then agreed that they would carry the freight of the Government for 50 per cent of the regular commercial rate. The purpose of | this bill is to eliminate that rate.

A great deal of the land that was given to the railroads has been sold by them, in many instances at great profit. In addition | to making money on these lands, they have built up those sections, which meant more traffic on their roads. Today, as you know, many of those railroads are in excellent financial (2) condition. I think they are in a better position today than they have ever been in the history of our country. Most of them are making money. They are | taking care of their outstanding debts, and some of them are even paying back the interest on the bonds on which they could not heretofore make payments.

I fully | appreciate that the railroads have helped to develop the West. I think, though, that it is only fair to say that the men who built the railroads were not mainly interested in | building up the country. They wanted Government help to build the roads. The Government did help by giving these men millions of acres of land. The railroads later sold these (3) lands at high prices.

At the present time, the railroads still own about 150 million acres of that land. They desire now to cancel the contract by which they | agreed to carry Government traffic at 50 per cent of the commercial rate, but they are not willing to return the land. I would favor the bill if the railroads | would return the unsold land to the Government.

This bill aims to cancel the contract calling for transportation of Government freight at 50 per cent of the commercial | rate. If the bill is passed, it will cost the Government about half a billion dollars in the next two years, according to the War Department. I feel that the unsold (4) land these railroads still have is worth many times that amount.

Although I have called up this resolution to give members an opportunity to vote on it, I do not | believe the bill should pass.

Notwithstanding the fact that I have requests by some bankers to vote for the bill, I cannot bring myself to favor it; my conscience will not permit | me to vote for it.

I cannot quite understand why this bill should be urged at this time when the railroads are doing so well. However, I am a servant of the House | of Representatives. The Committee on Rules felt that the bill should be considered at an early moment, and I felt that today was a good time to consider it. (5) (1.42)

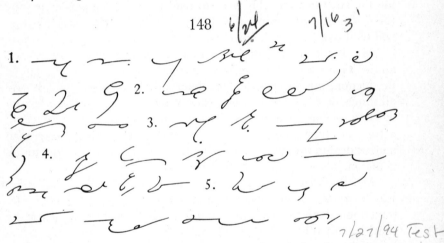

148

Key: (1) Mr. President, coming, legislation, industries, Senators, something, heard, in the past, converts, approve. (2) Recognize, especially, alarmed, occasion, telegrams, immediate. (3) Contributing, disposing, management, statistics, objectives. (4) To speed, program, to understand, record, manual, unions, cards, opposed, furthermore. (5) Fault, ourselves, they want, some of them, misled, similar, enacted.

Mr. President, since coming to the Senate last August, I have insisted on legislation that would tend to stop strikes in our industries. Consequently, I want | to express my thanks and appreciation to the ' Senators who have shown themselves as being in favor of doing something about this matter.

On the floor today | we heard from Senators who are well known to have been in favor of legislation of this character in the past. We have possibly heard from a few converts to this | cause. It is an especial pleasure to see those who opposed legislation of this type raise their voices here today and approve of what we have done. I think that is a (1) good sign. To me it indicates that they recognize the weakness of their cause. I think it is an indication that the voice of the people is being heard, and I think | that in this great country of ours it is well that the voice of the people be heard.

The people of this great nation and especially those of the state of Texas are alarmed | at the way production is getting behind, and they are expressing their views very definitely. I took occasion during the last week and this week to read many | telegrams expressing the desire of those people that Congress take immediate action that will tend to speed up the production of needed materials. (2)

Mr. President, I realize that there is more than one side to this affair. There are many different causes contributing to the lag in production, but the people | are interested in disposing of any and all things that are causing the delay. Whether labor is responsible or whether management is responsible, | the people are interested in getting full-time production. I do not think the people are interested a great deal in the statistics showing that there are only | a few strikes going on. Those statistics will not help the cause in any way.

Mr. President, when I came to the Senate, one of my objectives was to try to (3) do away with strikes in our factories and to get something done to speed up our production program. When I say that, I want you to understand that I am not fighting | labor. I believe I have as good a labor record as any member of the Senate. I worked at hard manual labor from the time I was small until I was | over twenty-five years old. I might also say that I belonged to labor unions. I belonged to unions at the time when they did not even have cards printed. I am | not opposed to the organization of labor unions.

Furthermore, I wish to say, Mr. President, that I do not believe the honest laboring people of (4) this country are at fault in this situation in which we find ourselves at the present time. I think the laboring people want to work and they want to speed up production, | but some of them have been misled. Very often the laboring people cannot voice their own feelings and must do what they are told to do by their leaders or else run | the risk of losing their jobs.

Let me tell you a little about the history of the bill that I introduced in the Senate. It is similar to the bill that we | have in Texas. On March 31 last year, as Governor of the state of Texas, I recommended that legislation be enacted to correct this situation. (5) (1.42)

149

Key: (1) Mr. Chairman, calendar, already, on the subject, to make, reply, first, entrance, retract. (2) Private, misunderstood, effect, permitted, absent, whether. (3) Himself, I should like to know, refused, accept, duties, to find, report, records, some of the. (4) Another, pleasant, uniform, delegates, myself, willingly, intend, account. (5) Ordinarily, my understanding, contracted, facilities, established, consequently, logical, transaction, how much, paid.

Mr. Chairman, when I prepared the following remarks, I did not have a calendar before me. I did not know, therefore, how many special matters were already | waiting to be considered. I shall try to make my remarks brief.

Mr. Chairman, after I finished speaking in the House on the subject of the food conference, the | gentleman from Texas tried to make a reply to all the points I brought up. It seems to me, however, that in several instances he missed the point.

In the first place, he | mentioned the fact that I sought entrance to the conference without having been invited. The purpose of my remarks yesterday was to retract the statement that Judge Brown (1) had invited every Member of Congress to attend the session. Judge Brown's invitation was a private one to me. I misunderstood his invitation to include | any Member of the House, and I passed this information on to the membership. It was for the purpose of clearing up this question and retracting the invitation | that I took the floor yesterday.

Now, the gentleman from Texas made several remarks to the effect that Members of Congress should stay here in Washington. He | even went so far as to say that we should not be permitted to draw our pay when we are absent from Washington. I want to ask the gentleman right now whether he (2) has always done the same thing himself. I should like to know whether he has always refused to accept his pay for those days on which he has been absent from Washington.

I | tried to make it clear yesterday that I really felt that I was discharging my duties to the country by trying to find out what is being done to feed the peoples | of the world. I was told that we could later call members of the conference before our committee and get a full report at the proper time. Let me point out to you | that Judge Brown made the statement that no minutes would be taken and no records made of some of the discussions. In other words, they were to be private meetings.

May I ask (3) by whose authority these meetings are to be private?

There is another matter to which I made reference yesterday and which I should like to discuss today. I | refer to the hotel rate of $5 a day that I paid in Hot Springs for a pleasant room and excellent meals. I did not make it clear that this is a uniform | rate applying to all the delegates and their staff. The gentleman from Ohio and myself are both willingly paying our own expenses. We do not intend to | submit any expense account to anyone or to any department. I doubt that this is true of anyone else presently living at that hotel.

I pointed (4) out that ordinarily the hotel charges $14 a day for that room and meals. I assume that the owner of the hotel felt that this was necessary | in order to make a fair profit. It was my understanding that the Government had contracted with the hotel for the use of its facilities during the | conference. The rate I refer to is, I assume, the one established by the Government. Consequently, it is logical to assume that the Government is going | to accept some loss in this transaction. Just how much it will be for each person I do not know. The fact remains, however, that I paid my own bill out of my own pocket. (5) (1.42)

Key: (1) Mr. President, reorganization, functioning, improve, control, selected, one of them, all right, I cannot understand. (2) Enact, to make, departments, complained, justification, occasion, in the past, criticism, patronage. (3) Political, appoints, extend, deprive, participate, to become. (4) Education, respect, country, residents, preferred, terms, Wisconsin, Iowa, moved, sometimes, ability, dedicate. (5) One of the, compensations, it is not, affords, someone, struggling, I hope that, be able.

Mr. President, I am not saying that the Congress does not need some overhauling and some reorganization; but, when we reorganize it, we should do so | with a view to eliminating that which now is not satisfactory and which now is not functioning properly. We should try to enact legislation that will make | changes that will improve the situation.

But we have before us a bill that places all Senate employees under the control or direction of a man to | be selected by the leaders of the Senate and the leaders of the House of Representatives. If one of them makes the selection, that will be all right. But I cannot (1) understand why it is proposed that we enact this legislation in an effort to undertake to make a change in all the departments here that are doing the | work efficiently now. I dare say there has been no complaint; and, consequently, there can be no justification for the proposed change.

Suppose we pass the bill. My own | opinion is that there will be just as much occasion for complaint after the bill is enacted as there has been in the past. We hear a great deal of criticism | of the patronage system. I have never cared anything about patronage. I do not think it is of very much benefit or value to Members of Congress. (2) I do not wish to retain the right to select pages because of any political advantage that that right might give. Actually, I do not know whether it | would give any advantage at all. If a Senator appoints a page, perhaps that page's father and mother might vote for the Senator; but I do not know that it | would extend much farther than that.

I do not see why I should deprive myself of the right to participate in the appointment of pages. If some boy from my state wishes to | become a page in the Senate, I wish to have the right to help him if I can. I wish to help that boy by giving him an opportunity to obtain a good (3) education; and I wish to see that the boys of my state have a right in that respect equal to that of boys who live in the other parts of the country. I see | no reason for placing some residents in a preferred status. A boy living here can serve as a page; but, under the terms of the pending bill, a boy living in Wisconsin | or Iowa or any other state could not serve as a page unless his parents moved here.

Mr. President, sometimes we wonder why men with great ability | dedicate their lives to the service of their country and of their state here in the Senate or in the House of Representatives for the small salaries that they are (4) paid. Mr. President, what is one of the finest compensations of serving in the Senate of the United States or in the House of Representatives? It is | not the check that a Member of the Congress receives each month. That is not what keeps him here. It is the opportunity to serve those who need help. One of the finest | compensations of service in the Congress, one that I value most, is the opportunity that service in the Congress affords the Member of Congress to help someone | who is struggling to get an education or to meet some of the other problems of life. I hope that I shall always be able to be of service to my fellow man. (5) (1.42)

151

Key: (1) Mr. Chairman, I do not believe, anything, single, unwise, founders, established, fundamental. (2) Legislation, they are not, courts, repealed, danger, require, two-thirds, distinguished, respect, I cannot understand. (3) Accordance, population, various, precedence, majority, country, regardless. (4) Agriculture, heard, bureaus, capable, houses, advocate, regulations. (5) Sympathy, personally, short time.

Mr. Chairman, I do not believe that anything I might say now will change a single vote. I simply want to record my opposition to this resolution because, | in my opinion, I think that it is unwise.

I realize that the world has changed and that the distances between nations is no longer an important factor. | I do not think this is a good reason, however, to change the system of government that the founders of our country established when they wrote the Federal Constitution. |

Certain things are fundamental; they do not change with the

times. I refer particularly to such matters as treaties between nations. Treaties are not like other (1) legislation that is enacted by the Congress. They are not subject to review by the courts, and they cannot be repealed by the Congress without great danger that | the United States might be drawn into war. Because of this fact, the men who wrote the Constitution found it desirable to require that all treaties be approved by | a two-thirds vote of the Senate of the United States.

I regret very much that I find myself unable to agree with the distinguished chairman of the committee | on this matter. I have a great deal of respect for him, but I cannot understand how he can advocate a resolution of this kind that would make the (2) consideration of treaties so easy.

Of course, I do not want to be sectional about this thing; but the House of Representatives is made up in accordance with the | population of the various states. Again, it must be remembered that treaties take precedence over all state laws. As a protection for the interests of the | small states, they were given equal representation in the United States Senate. That is not the case in the House. The time might come when a majority of this House | might come from eight or ten large states in the country. If we change the Constitution, the representatives of those states could write a treaty regardless of its effect on (3) agriculture or other industries in other parts of the country.

I have heard the argument made in the past few years that our methods of passing legislation | need revision. I have heard it said that government by bureaus is more capable of legislating than are the elected representatives of the people. They | say that these government agents who visit the farms and business houses are in closer touch with the people and with what the people need than are their own representatives. | Thus they advocate that those agents can write orders and regulations that will much better serve the people's needs than will the laws enacted by the Congress.

I know (4) that my good friend from Texas is not in sympathy with such a policy. He does know, however, that that school of thought will be found in many places. There are a great | many people who think that this generation must accept the challenge and that we must build an entirely new world for them to return to. Personally, I am willing | to respect their judgment on treaty making. They will have seen a lot of this world, and they are going to be in the legislative halls of the states and in this Congress | within a short time.

It is interesting to note that the United Nations in San Francisco decided to apply a two-thirds voting rule on all major issues. (5) (1.45)

Key: (1) Possible, further, attending, requirements, heard, distinguished, gentleman from Virginia. (2) Possession, administration, afternoon, room, across, advise, concerning, negligence, I wonder. (3) Justified, accept, of course, connected. (4) Included, something, supervisors, adopt, everything else, touch, personnel. (5) You want, to do, destroy, reasonable, certainly, recommendations, investigated, thoroughly, discovered, has been able, practices.

Mr. Chairman, I am sorry that it will not be possible for me to yield any further. My time is limited and there are several matters that I must | discuss in the time that I have remaining.

I do not blame the chairman of the committee for not being present and attending the hearings. However, since he was not | present at the hearings, I do not feel that we should rely on his judgment as to what the requirements of this organization may be.

I think that we should place | our confidence in the judgment of those gentlemen who did attend all the hearings and who heard all the evidence.

The distinguished gentleman from Virginia says that (1) he has in his possession a number of newspaper clippings that show that the Farm Administration has not done its duty. The gentleman is a member of this | committee. He must have been advised during the last two or three months that we have been holding meetings every afternoon, and during a large portion of the time we | were considering the affairs of the Farm Administration. A great deal of the time he has been working in the room just across from us. Yet he did not come before | our committee to advise us of evidence that he claims to have concerning the negligence of the Farm Administration.

I wonder whether the House is now (2) justified in revising the judgment of the committee on the basis of these newspaper clippings. If we accept the gentleman's judgment, we shall deal a blow to the | farmers of the United States. That is one sure way to defeat our end.

A great deal of incorrect information has been given on the floor of the House. I wish it were | possible to take the time to correct it all. I realize, of course, that that is not possible. Men have been talking here about $40,000,000 and | $50,000,000 for expenses just as if they knew what they were talking about.

I hold here a copy of the budget for 1948. The expense connected (3) with this particular item in connection with the Farm Administration is less than $6,000,000. There is also included in this item of | $50,000,000 an item of $10,000,000 for grants. Is that something that we ought to cut out?

The gentleman from Illinois said that that item will not be cut | out. He said that he will cut out some of the farm supervisors who are traveling around the country. How do we know that this $10,-000,000 in grants will not be | cut out if we adopt that aim? It has been my experience that Government departments always reduce everything else before they touch personnel. This grant of (4) $10,-000,000 is very small.

May I ask just what you want to do with this organization?

If you want to destroy it, then adopt an amendment to strike the | appropriation for it out of the bill. But, if you want to carry it on in a reasonable way, then certainly you must take the recommendations of the | committee.

We have investigated the Farm Administration. We have gone over its work thoroughly. We have discovered a great deal more than the gentleman from | Virginia has been able to call to our attention. We have taken steps to correct some practices that called for correction.

Gentlemen, this is a poor man's bill. (5) (1.46)

153

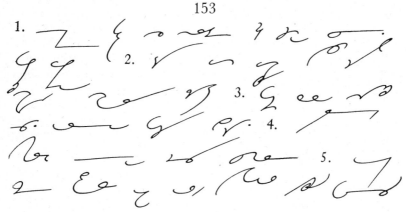

Key: (1) Mr. Chairman, possible, committee, criticism, Social, Security, amending, previously, original. (2) System, of course, occupied, to make, studies, competent, completed, extensive. (3) Perfect, earlier, continuously, anything, remainder, proceeded, that understanding. (4) Determination, difference, minority, submitted, agreement. (5) Legislation, assume, explain, represent, regarded, temporary, **designed, permanent.**

Mr. Chairman, I appreciate very much the action of the House in making possible the consideration of this bill reported by the Ways and Means | Committee. I say that with no criticism whatever of those who took a different view. The matter of changing the Social Security law and amending it | is an important subject. As I stated previously, I have lived with this subject ever since 1935.

I had the privilege of being chairman | of the Committee on Ways and Means when that committee reported the original bill; I have always been very proud of that. At that time we set up the Social (1) Security System; and, while the law has been amended from time to time since, it still retains its original form. The present bill is the best we can get under present | conditions.

Mr. Chairman, we held long hearings on this matter from February to June. It is said that we had months and months. Of course, there were months and months occupied | in the consideration of this matter; but most of that time was used by our staff, which had to make many long and difficult studies. I think that we had the most | competent staff I have ever known.

After the staff had completed its work and made its report, we began an extensive consideration of the subject. The reason (2) we got at it rather late was not that we were slow in getting out a report. While our committee is not perfect, it does work. Our committee would have been able | to report a bill earlier had it not been for the fact that we had to consider another report.

We began work on the bill as early as we could and worked | as continuously as it was possible to work. We realized that it would be impossible to get anything enacted during the remainder of this | session of the Congress that was of an important nature. We proceeded all the way with that understanding; that is, that we would have to leave some matters for future (3) study and future determination. We proceeded that way until we had completed our work and got ready to bring out our bill. When we did that, we found there was | a difference of opinion as to what we could get through and as to what should go in the bill. When we reported the bill, we had a minority that would not yield | in any way. They believed that certain provisions that the majority wanted should not go into the bill. But we reported the bill with these provisions. We thought | perhaps we could take care of those differences. The minority submitted a very strong report; so we could not reach an agreement on the bill as reported. (4) Finally, to make possible enactment of legislation, we made changes in two titles of the bill. If we had not done this, it would have been impossible to | get through any legislation and we could not assume responsibility for it.

I should like to explain briefly the provisions of this bill. I want to make it | plain that this bill does not represent the final consideration of Social Security legislation by the Committee. It should be regarded largely as | a temporary measure designed to freeze the old-age insurance tax rate while permanent changes in both the insurance and assistance programs are being perfected. (5) (1.47)

154

Key: (1) Amendment, control, something, construction, last year, recall, included, conceded, one of the most, treacherous, greatest. (2) A hundred, destruction, property, engineers, evolved, strongly, emphasize, distinguished. (3) Handicaps, elected, representatives, bound, project. (4) Recommendation, warrant, conclusion, contrary, notwithstanding, accepted, mandatory, duty, to pursue, common sense. (5) Dictate, maintained, regardless, power, presidents, badly, constrained, I want, funds.

Mr. Chairman, my amendment proposes to increase the present sum for flood control to $135,000,000. The object of that increase is to | give us something with which to begin actual construction on the Red River flood-control plan, which has been approved by the Congress. The Members will recall that very | important item, which was included in the flood-control bill and approved by the President about a year ago.

The Red River is about 1,200 miles | long, and it drains a great part of four states. It is conceded to be one of 'the most treacherous rivers in the entire Nation. In 1945 we had the greatest (1) flood we had had in a hundred years. We had considerable destruction of crops, homes, cattle, and other property.

I am seeking by this amendment to get | a small sum with which to begin this work. The engineers tell me that with this sum they can start the plan that was evolved by the engineers and that has been approved by | Congress, after many years' study.

I cannot too strongly emphasize the importance of this. I know that the distinguished gentleman heading the subcommittee | will probably say there is no sum in the budget for this construction work. I am not here to criticize the gentleman from Michigan and the other splendid (2) gentlemen on that subcommittee. They have worked hard and they gave us a very courteous hearing, and I am not here condemning them. I fully recognize the fact that | they were working under budget handicaps. But, Mr. Chairman, I take a position today when my party is in the minority as I did when my party | was in the majority; namely, that it is the business of the elected representatives of the people in this Congress to pass on these matters, and that we | should not be bound by what a few men in the Budget Bureau include in a budget estimate. I contend that, when Congress sees that a vital project is left out without (3) any budget recommendation, it is the business of the Congress to do what the facts of the case warrant; and, if Congress, after due consideration, reaches | the conclusion that a certain project ought to be included, then we ought to include it, the budget to the contrary notwithstanding. In other words, I accept | the recommendations of the Budget Bureau as a guide but not as mandatory and infallible. I am not contending that their recommendations should | be passed over lightly; but I am insisting that Congress has not only the right but also the duty, upon proper showing, to pursue the course that reason, common (4) sense, and good business judgment dictate, even though it be contrary to budget recommendations. I have maintained that position, as I said, regardless of which | party was in power.

Now, here today, I admit that the President's budget did not contain a cent for construction on the flood-control plan on Red River as passed | previously. But, Mr. Chairman, I feel the need of starting this work so badly that I am constrained to present this amendment anyway and do my best to get | a sum large enough to start construction work.

I want to say here also that we need some funds to start work on the Red River Canal, also approved by the Congress. (5) (1.47)

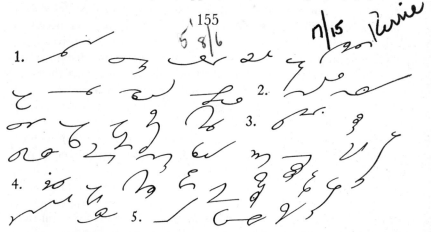

Key: (1) Detained, anxious, length, words, on the subject, domestic, represent, many of the, concerned, machinery. (2) Country, created, another, will be able, to perfect, effectively, definite. (3) I do not think, exists, outline, formation, conclusions, period, successful, emphasize, foundation, obvious. (4) Hesitate, repetition, difficulties, expect, to form, association, special, privileges, standards, entire. (5) Indeed, promised, afford.

Mr. President, the statements of the gentleman from Oregon are very true. I did not have those amendments in the bill originally. I thought, at that time, | that it would be very difficult to pass any radical measure. Nevertheless, for a long period of time I have had it in mind to bring up the bill.

I | did not bring it up solely because of the coal strike. As a matter of fact, the bill has been pending for a year and a half when there was no coal strike going on. However, | as I said before, when certain persons testified that they would not regard the agreement as binding, I thought that this was a good time to bring up the bill. The

Record (1) will show that, even before that time, I indicated a desire to bring up the bill and had several discussions with the Senator from Kentucky about | it. He indicated to me that the bill would be considered later on.

I do not want to be unreasonable about the measure. I am agreeable to | accepting any amendment that would improve the bill. I do want to say, however, that the Congress of the United States should have a part in all Government | activity. It should pass the necessary laws and not leave everything to the power of the Executive. I am not hostile to the Executive, as all (2) Members of the Senate know. But, Mr. President, the people of the United States expect the Congress to play a greater part in the actual running of affairs. |

Mr. President, the bill is a general bill. It applies to every situation. It may be needed six months from now in connection with some situations | arising perhaps in an airplane factory or other factory. It is intended to cover the whole field. Certainly it is better to pass this | legislation now.

Senators say they do not want to legislate in haste and passion. It is better to legislate now before difficulties arise, so that we may (3) not be met with a charge that we are trying to correct only one situation. Mr. President, I am not seeking to correct only one situation. I | am seeking to correct every situation falling within the terms of the bill. I am seeking to anticipate such things and to try to prevent them if possible. | I hope that all other members of the Senate will consider this measure during the evening and will consider it carefully.

I do not want the bill to be | sent back to the committee. I regret that the Senator from Kentucky suggested that the bill should go back to that committee. He said, on one occasion, that the (4) committee has been at fault. I deny that the committee has been at fault. The committee gave this matter careful consideration over a period of a | year and a half. It tried to get consideration of the measure on the floor of the Senate. It has never been able to obtain consideration by the Senate. | That bill was not subject to some of the objections that are now being brought up against the pending bill.

I hold in my hand a copy of the hearings held before | the committee. At the hearings, the Secretary of War urged the passage of the original bill and said that it was needed and would meet the situation. (5) (1.50)

156

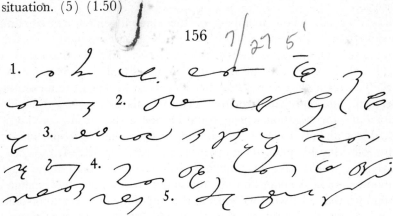

Key: (1) Committee, everyone, listening, argument, enterprise, considerable, recommendations. (2) Agreement, last time, approval, I hope that, report. (3) Thoroughly, record, to us, witnesses, representative, collected, costs, so much. (4) Conflict, accept, obligation, interpret, outstanding, contradictions, clarify. (5) Very important, materials, standard.

Mr. Chairman, I think it is a very interesting thing that our committee has been called together to discuss a topic that is so much in the public press | today. Everyone is talking about housing. Everyone is reading about housing. Everyone is listening to both sides of the argument about whether | housing should be left entirely in the hands of private enterprise or whether the Government should step into the picture and try to provide new homes for the public. | It seems to me, Mr. Chairman, that there will be considerable interest in the recommendations of this committee; and I sincerely hope that we shall be (1) able to come to an agreement without a long delay.

The last time I was on a committee that was considering a matter of great interest to the | public, some members of the committee were so afraid that they would not produce a recommendation that would meet public approval that they debated the subject | until public interest had moved on to other matters. I hope that we shall not avoid the issue in that manner. I hope that we shall be able to investigate | the problem and make a report to the House within two weeks.

After all, fellow members of the committee, an investigating committee of the Senate has (2) already gone thoroughly into this same subject. The record of their meetings is available to us. I do not think that we need to call the same witnesses that the | Senate committee called, because the statements of those witnesses are all on the record. The representative from Pennsylvania has suggested a plan for our | investigation which would be fine if the Senate committee had not already collected all the information that we could obtain by following his plan. The | plan of the representative from Pennsylvania would take us four months to complete. In those four months the facts about housing and about costs would have changed so much that (3) what we learn at the end of the investigation would be in conflict with information we would get at the start of the investigation.

I think that we should | accept the record of the Senate committee and make it a part of the record of this committee. We are under no obligation to accept the recommendations | of the Senate committee. We can study the facts given in the record of the Senate committee and interpret them as we may believe is proper. If there | are outstanding contradictions in that record, we can call witnesses to clarify those points.

I have noted that there are some contradictions of that kind. There is one (4) contradiction that I think is very important; I refer to the different estimates given by different witnesses about the cost of some of the | materials that would be used in any housing constructed by the Government. I cannot see how standard grades of steel can have so many different prices. I | would want to investigate that one point. But I do not believe, Mr. Chairman, that we should pretend that no one has ever investigated the problem, however, | just because I want to know more about the price that the Government should have to pay for steel. I believe that we should study the report of the Senate committee first. (5) (1.51)

157

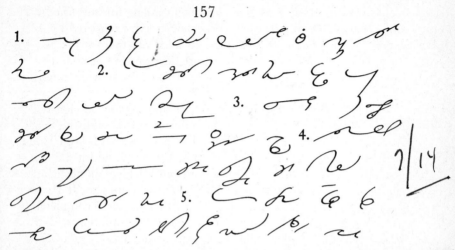

Key: (1) Mr. President, effective, possibility, farther, alertness, highly, cautious, doubts, fully. (2) Executive, Constitution, foreign, properly, legislative, negative, rendered, development. (3) Administration, initiate, execute, shared, senior, Senator from Michigan, I understood, compared. (4) Declaration, continuously, informed, more and more, citizens, advance, situation, different, adventure, gathered, source. (5) Progress, power, enterprise, past, measure, prominent, testified, exception, warned, decided, course.

Mr. President, I plan to vote for the loans in question. They can be and should be effective in pushing the possibility of war farther and farther away. | Those who deny the possibiliy of war are living in a dream world. We must not dream again. We must keep awake. We must be wide awake. We must be actively | awake. The proposal we are considering requires alertness and gives an opportunity for highly useful activity.

While the loans will have my vote—and | I believe a vote of the majority of my fellow members of the Senate—the support that we give them should be cautious. Our doubts and our suggestions should be fully (1) expressed. Not to express them would be unfair to the Chief Executive, who, by our Constitution, is charged with the conduct of our foreign relations. Should he fail | properly to estimate the state of opinion of the legislative branches of the Government, he might find himself at some point asking for authority that | would be denied him. That is the negative service rendered by a free expression of opinion on this floor. In addition, there is the positive service that can | be given to the future development of policy by the expression here of different opinions derived from wide ranges of experience.

The (2) administration does initiate and execute foreign policy. Much of that foreign-policy responsibility is shared with the Senate. At other policy | levels the responsibility is shared with both Houses of the Congress. While recognizing this, I, for one, find it difficult to go all the way with the senior | Senator from Michigan in his fine presentation of this undertaking to the Senate two days ago. If I understood him correctly, he was suggesting | that we yield completely to the administration. He compared this particular situation with a request from the President that the Congress vote a (3) declaration of war.

I submit that the two situations are not the same. A declaration of war comes after a long series of events of which the public has | been continuously kept informed. More and more the whole mass of citizens of the Nation have seen the coming of war in advance of the declaration.

This situation | is different. We are starting on a long, new adventure. We have set out to achieve peace actively rather than enjoy it passively. We must place on this | adventure every ray of light that can be gathered from every source. Those rays of light must be directed on the difficult path that lies ahead.

What is the situation (4) we face? Putting it briefly, we are trying to stop the progress of a new power bent on expanding its rule as far as possible. This great power is telling | its own people, and has been telling them for years, that free enterprise is a thing of the past.

Recently we held hearings on this important measure. At this hearing | several prominent men, who have made a study of the whole matter, testified. Without exception, they warned us that we should not take any hasty action and that the | matter should be discussed freely. They felt that once we decided on a course of action, it might be hard to change that course, even though it was not a satisfactory one. (5) (1.53)

158

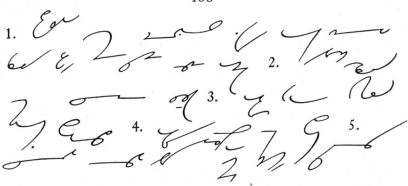

Key: (1) Expenditure, government, something like, a billion dollars, legislation, one of the most, period, opposed, I do not, anyone, reasonable. (2) Discuss, concerned, involving, amendment, equitable. (3) Respect, postal, different, approximately. (4) Reported, majority, unjustified, approve. (5) Amounts, many of those, testimony, to furnish, admitted.

Mr. Chairman, this bill involves an expenditure by the United States Government of something like a billion dollars annually. It is legislation | affecting more than a million people. It is one of the most important measures that have come to the House for consideration for a long period of time.

It has | been inferred in the newspapers that there are Members in this House who are opposed to any raise in the pay of Government employees. That inference is not correct. | I do not know of anyone in the Civil Service Committee or outside that committee who is not in favor of granting fair and reasonable pay to (1) the employees in the Government, and I shall discuss that a little later on. Let me say, on behalf of those who work in Federal service, I am in favor | of their receiving a fair and reasonable pay. Let me say that, so far as pay raises are concerned, involving especially those making higher salaries, the | lid is off in this legislation. I am in favor of seeing to it that Government employees shall continue to receive fair and decent pay. When the proper | time comes, I shall offer an amendment to the bill that in my judgment will be more equitable than the provisions of this bill.

Mr. Chairman, something was said with (2) respect to a bill that passed the House yesterday raising the salaries of postal employees. The amendment I expect to offer to this bill will do just about | the same for all the people in Government service as was done yesterday for the postal employees. Not only that, but the situation with respect to postal | employees is very different from that of these employees. In any event, we are not legislating for postal employees today. Our responsibility | today is to legislate for approximately two million employees of the Government. That is our job today, and that is the thing we are responsible (3) for in the consideration of this particular bill.

Is this bill right or wrong? That is the question. Should it be amended or not is the question involved, as I | see it.

Mr. Chairman, the pay raise bill, as reported by the majority of the members of the House Civil Service Committee, provides for pay raises that are | totally unjustified.

I favor granting some increases all the way along the line, but I do not believe that this House will approve the huge increases provided | for in this bill. I know there are many employees in the higher brackets that do earn the money; and I am in favor of granting increases to them, but (4) certainly not in amounts provided by this legislation.

Many of those who now receive high salaries came into the Government as war-service employees | but now receive $3,000 more than when they entered Government service. The Civil Service Commission, in testimony before the Civil Service Committee, | was unable to furnish the committee with information as to how much the average Government employee had received by virtue of promotions during | the war. It was admitted, though, that large promotions were the rule, and that most of the promotions were those in the $5,000 salary brackets and upward. (5) (1.56)

159

1.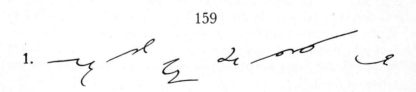

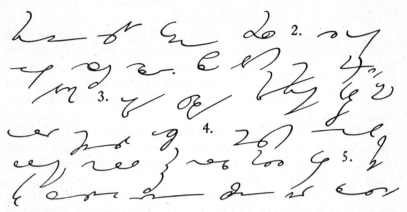

Key: (1) **Mr.** Speaker, duties, to perform, first, dictated, letters, volume, in addition to the, personal, variety. (2) Committee, legislative, knowledge, carefully, concerning, appear, testify, involved, formulated, discusses. (3) Reported, accepted, voted, participate, offered, length, in a few minutes, occasionally. (4) Informative, more or less, irrelevant, clearly, forcefully, currency, frequently, privilege. (5) Adjust, bodies, arguments, uncommon, assignment, one of the, selected.

Mr. Speaker, during these trying times, a Representative in Congress has many duties to perform. The people should have a true and complete picture of the work | that a Congressman does. A plain statement of his routine work may be helpful.

First, there is the everyday mail to look after. Every letter must be read and an | answer dictated. Then the answer must be read and signed. The number of letters received daily varies, but there is always quite a volume. In addition to the mail, | there are telephone and personal calls. The letters and requests received include a great variety of problems.

Then the Representative has regular and special (1) committee work. He may be a member of a special committee and at the same time serve on a regular legislative committee.

It is a matter of | general knowledge that all legislation is carefully considered and written by committees. Hearings are held. Witnesses who are interested and who have special | knowledge concerning the matter before the committee appear and testify, and they are questioned by members of the committee. Sometimes these hearings are very | long and involved.

After the hearings are closed, and a bill has been formulated, the committee reads the bill for amendments; discusses it from every angle; and (2) adopts such amendments as it thinks proper. When this has been done, the bill is sent to the House for consideration; and the bill as reported is often accepted | without change on the floor of the House.

Bills are discussed, read, sometimes amended, and then voted upon. A bill is usually discussed by members of the committee | that reports it, although others may participate. This is especially true when amendments are offered.

The time consumed in the consideration of a bill by | the House depends upon its length and importance. Some may be disposed of in a few minutes. Others take many days. Occasionally, some time is lost by talk that is (3) not always informative or interesting and which is more or less irrelevant to the issues involved. As a rule, however, the bills are explained clearly and | forcefully by those in charge of them.

I have been a member of the Banking and Currency Committee for many years and have been the ranking member | of that committee for almost four years, frequently serving as acting chairman. In some cases, the legislation reported by the committee has been in my charge on the floor of the | House.

As ranking member of the committee, it has been my privilege to serve on different conference committees. These committees are made up of representatives (4) from the House and the Senate who meet to adjust differences in bills as they passed both bodies. At these meetings, arguments and discussions lasting for weeks are not | uncommon.

In addition to this regular committee assignment, it was my honor to be one of the three persons selected by the Speaker to serve on the Special | National Economic Committee. I attended the public hearings of that committee for about eighteen months; and during that time, 442 | witnesses appeared and testified, some giving testimony of several days' duration.

Before this committee, people testified on a wide range of subjects. (5) (1.58)

160

Key: (1) Mr. President, privilege, Senator from Ohio, toward, economic, namely, welfare, establishment, exaggerated, system, inability, effectively. (2) Majority, acceptable, critical, increasingly, constructive, adopt. (3) Becomes, practically, discontent, unavoidable, serious, accomplished. (4) Constant, resources, decent, enactment, attainment, gentleman from Ohio. (5) Resolution, committees, investigate, education, reported, indicated, referred.

Mr. President, on Monday of this week it was my privilege to join with the distinguished Senator from Ohio in the introduction of a bill directed | toward the solution of what I regard as our most important economic problem; namely, housing.

In my judgment, no other problem before the Congress is | more important to the future welfare of this country. The necessity for the establishment by Congress of a sound housing policy and program cannot be | exaggerated.

Mr. President, the strength of our system of government centers in its ability to serve more effectively than any other system (1) the basic needs of the great majority of the people who are governed. When it fails to serve these needs, there are created the very conditions under which other | systems of government may falsely appear to be acceptable. We are still faced with a critical shortage of housing. There is every indication that, if | we fail this year to take necessary action, it will be more critical next year. It will become increasingly critical with each succeeding year until we face | the facts and take such constructive action. In addition to the shortage of housing, our Government has never tried to adopt a policy of replacing housing (2) that becomes inadequate. Our rate of construction has been so small in relation to the needs of our people for housing that we have had to keep in use practically | all our housing supply. This nation cannot safely face the difficult years of the future with the discontent that unsatisfactory housing places upon | its people. We cannot longer accept these conditions as unavoidable.

If we are to avoid them, we must decide now that we will face the issue and assume | the task of correcting the serious the housing shortage. It is an objective that cannot be attained in one or two years. It cannot be accomplished by treating housing (3) as a constant emergency. It is an objective that, as a nation, we must accept and accomplish through the full use of our resources in a sound housing | program.

We are late with such a program. We cannot turn back the clock, but we can avoid the price of further delay. We can accept now as the only satisfactory | objective the goal of a decent home for all our citizens. I believe that, by the enactment of the housing bill introduced this week, this Congress can provide | the means for assuring progress in the attainment of that objective.

This bill was started as a resolution introduced on March 1 by the gentleman from Ohio. (4) That resolution called for the establishment of a special committee of three members from each of these two standing committees of the Senate. It directed | this special committee to investigate and study every phase of the housing problem and the housing activities of the Federal Government. The | resolution went to the Education and Labor Committee, on which the Senator from Ohio was then serving, and was favorably reported to the Senate. |

The Senator from Maine then indicated that he did not desire to set up a special committee, and he referred the matter to the regular committee. (5) (1.61)

PART IX

130 WORDS A MINUTE

161

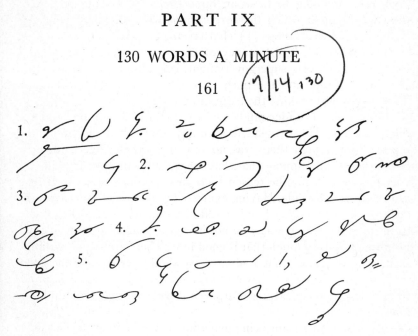

Key: (1) Extend, beyond, such a thing, Senator from Ohio, charters, corporations, circumstances, determine, upon which. (2) Creation, supergovernment, I understand, out of the, worth while. (3) I do not, so many things, undesirable, generous, some of the, sought, acceptance, substitute. (4) Everything, rewriting, word, proceed, I should like to say, last year. (5) Item, proposition, amount, 1 per cent, turned, United States, inquired, recollections, billions, outlined, previously.

Now, Mr. President, I submit that, if we do what has been suggested, we shall extend a principle beyond anything that has ever been done before. Never in the | history of this Congress has it authorized such a thing. The Senator from Ohio brought out the fact the other day, when questioning a witness, that there was no place where the | charters of these corporations were filed. The Senator wanted to know how it would be possible, in the circumstances, to

determine exactly what powers the corporations have | under the
law. Who is going to have an opportunity of looking at any of
the charters upon which the corporations were organized when we
do not know where those (1) charters are located?

I submit that, if the money of the people is going to be used
for the creation of a supergovernment, it is time that we took some
steps to | inquire into the purposes of those back of this demand.
That is why I am asking these questions today.

Of course, I understand the situation in which the Senator
finds | himself. He was glad to save anything out of the committee
report, even though there was not much worth saving. Under the
circumstances, I suppose that, having voiced a protest, I | will still
vote for the bill, for the reason there are certain features in it that
are really worth while. Having expressed my views of other features
of the bill, on the other hand, I still maintain (2) the right to vote
against the bill if I choose. I do not like to vote against the whole bill
because there is so much that is good in it. There are so many things
in it that we want | that I suppose we shall have to take the good
with the bad. It looks as if we just have to vote for the bill in order
to get the desirable features of it, even if we must take the | undesir-
able features as well.

Mr. President, I am being generous to the Senator, as he said I
should be; and certainly in all fairness to him I must say that |
he and his committee have worked out a measure that does define,
to some extent at least, some of the powers that were sought. To that
extent only, the acceptance of the proposed substitute (3) is more
desirable than striking out everything in the bill and rewriting
the whole bill.

I suppose the Senator wants to say a word before we proceed to
vote. | I shall be glad to give him part of my time, if he desires it,
after I have made a few more remarks upon the question before the
House. I should like to say that, generally | speaking, the bill makes
some additions to the authority granted in the act that was passed
more than a year ago. There is no question that additional authority
is granted. | What that additional authority is has been very well
stated by the Senator, but we all know that the situation has been
changed since last year. I shall not take the time to go (4) into each

item, but the principal proposition to which the Senator objects is what he calls the "catchall" clause, the last one in the measure.

The amount that is referred | to in the bill, I should like to say, is less than 1 per cent of the money which we turned over to the President of the United States under the various war bills, and for | which we have estimated. I just inquired of the Senator in charge of the bill, and his recollection agrees with mine, that we will spend billions in the program as now outlined. Part | of this amount will be spent during the next fiscal year. As I have previously said, the amount is limited to stated purposes. The right to make the loans expires on June 1. (5) (1.38)

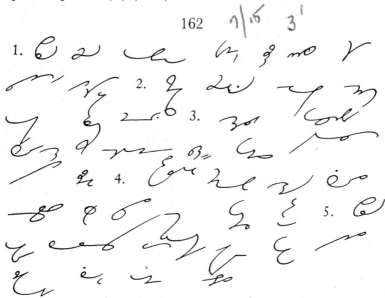

Key: (1) Appeared, word, listener, partisanship, exists, worth while, fortune, educated, to understand. (2) I shall not be able, firsthand, knowledge, unsuccessful, legislature, observation, something. (3) Constitution, practiced, articles, instrument, United States, personally, delegate, to do, existence. (4) Expenditures, fullest, consistent, hearty, materially, Associated Press, idea, involved, perfectly, speaker. (5) Appoint, report, eliminated, of course, to be done, proper, duty, established, hearings, reason, necessity.

This is the first time I have appeared before this body to say a word. I have been a patient listener to the proceedings of this House; and I know that, if some of my friends back | home could see the partisanship that exists here, they would wonder how we ever get any legislation passed that is worth while. It was my good fortune to be born in the West, to | be educated in the South, and to finish my education in the East. I think this has made me more tolerant of my fellow men. I have learned to understand men of the South, | and some are here today. I owe a great deal of whatever success in life I have attained to one who is now a Member of Congress here and Chairman of the Foreign Affairs Committee. (1) I am sorry he has not been able to be in the House more than he has, but he has been very busy with committee meetings that have prevented him from attending.

I | cannot let this bill pass by, however, without expressing to you my views on it, because we have a reorganization bill in our state that closely follows this bill. We have | had experience with it, and I can tell you from firsthand knowledge just how it has worked.

I say to you frankly that it has been the most unsuccessful law ever enacted in | our state. In fact, it has been so bad that the present legislature has wiped it out. As one who has had observation in political life, to some extent, and who knows something about (2) the Constitution, having practiced law for over thirty years and having written articles on that instrument, I feel that I know something about law; and it seems to me that | we are doing the wrong thing here.

The President of the United States is a very busy man. There can be no question about that. We are going to ask him to reorganize | this Government. He cannot do that personally; he must delegate it to somebody else to do. We created these different departments here, and I think we ought to be | able to take care of them when it comes to putting them out of existence if they are not satisfactory or if we do not need them any longer.

As I read the bill, the first (3) object is to reduce expenditures to the fullest extent consistent with the efficient operation of the Government. With that I am in hearty accord; and I think | possibly they could be reduced materially, and ought to be reduced materially, very soon. Yesterday, the Associated Press said that the Treasury figures | showed that the first eight months of the present fiscal year cost more than its income. It seems to me there is plenty of room for reducing the debt; and it must be reduced.

If this | reorganization will do it, of course the idea is a good one. The only question involved is how it ought to be done. I am perfectly willing to let the Speaker of this House (4) appoint a certain number of members to reorganize the departments of the United States Government; and, if they will bring in a report here and tell me what departments | ought to be eliminated, I shall vote for it. Of course, that is all very nice; but something ought to be done and has to be done; and I think the appointment of a committee of | Congress is the proper way to go about this reorganization.

It is said that such a committee would not bring in a report. Nevertheless, it is the duty of the | Members of Congress to do it. When a new department is established, we have hearings; and there is a reason given and some necessity shown for establishing that department. (5) (1.39)

163

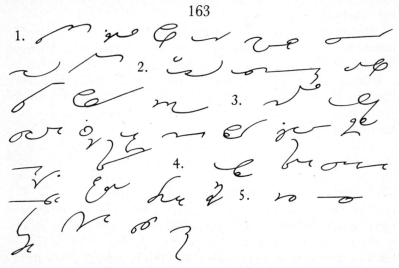

Key: (1) Education, history, appropriation, worked, compromise, amount, called, direction. (2) Overruled, recommendations, authorization, I did not, appropriated, school. (3) Country, larger, accordance, highest, respect, commission, ascertain, whether or not, effect, misunderstanding, voted. (4) Last year, voters, announcements, many things, expenditure, bureaus, sufficient. (5) Subcommittee, mind, benefits, dividends, without, considerable.

I was a member of the Committee on Education when the present bill was brought before this House, and I want to tell a little of the history of this matter.

At the | time this bill was before the committee, an annual large appropriation was made. There was a proposal in the committee, as a matter of fact there were a great many | suggestions made, to increase the amount of the appropriation. The committee finally worked out a compromise and brought out a bill that increased the original amount called | for in the bill. As a member of the committee, I did the best I could on the floor of this House to abide by the direction of the committee and hold the amount in the bill. (1) However, I was overruled by the membership of the House. I think that, as you have spoken on this matter, it is up to the committee to follow your recommendations | and to agree to the annual amount upon which you have decided.

Some reference has been made to the fact that it was stated in debate that this is only an | authorization bill. Here is a statement that was actually made during the debate. The gentleman asked me if I did not know that this was an authorization bill, and I told | him that I knew it is limited to three years and that the sums will be appropriated each and every year. That statement was made during the course of the debate.

The school people (2) of this country, hearing of and knowing about this bill, have prepared to carry on their work, using the larger sum. Schools have been built and other preparations have been made · in accordance | with what they believed to be the facts.

The gentleman for whose judgment I have the highest respect mentioned here that the President signed this bill and then appointed a commission | to ascertain whether or not he was going to put the bill into effect. I want to say to you that this is, indeed, a new theory in our form of government; and I | believe that there must be some misunderstanding of the matter.

Here is the situation (3) as I see it now in reference to this measure before us today. When we voted on this (3) bill last year, we were all facing an election. The House stood up here and told the voters, told the school children, and told the schoolteachers that we were going to give them a certain | amount of money for building purposes. The bill was signed; and announcements were made to the people of this country, again stating that we were going to spend a certain amount. It | is my belief that, at that time, we did mean what we said. Times have changed, however. Many things have happened since that time. This I know, but I want to get across to you just what took place | regarding this expenditure.

When the time came to live up to this proposition, the Bureau of the Budget found that there were not sufficient funds to take care of the matter. The Bureau, (4) therefore, did not increase the appropriation one cent.

I wish to say, on behalf of the subcommittee, that, if it had not been for their work, the schools would not now be receiving | what they are getting at the present time.

One of the facts that come to mind when we consider matters of this kind is that a great deal of money is spent for many other purposes. | I do not say that we should cease these expenditures where the money is carefully spent, but I do say that no money can be spent that will bring to this country the benefits and | dividends received from money invested for educational purposes.

I know this is a subject that is difficult to discuss without some considerable feeling. (5) (1.40)

164

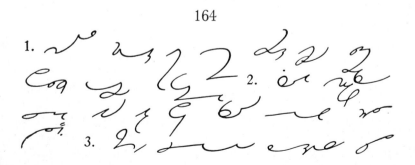

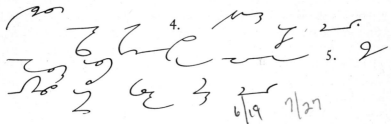

Key: (1) Country, solutions, to have been, Government, various, to find, universal, application, welfare, performance. (2) Hearts, co-operation, Americans, it is not, to speak, approach, pardoned, more or less, southern, diminishing. (3) Affected, similar, illustrate, idea, domestic, must be able, to become. (4) Districts, repeat, something, implications, recovery, ability, normal. (5) Afford, indefinitely, revenue, principal, furnishes, some of the.

The many problems that face our country today provide much thought for us all. There are many questions and many solutions. We must study them all. When we look very closely | at some of the answers that have been given, they appear to have been made along sectional lines. It is a fact that many of the solutions have been made by students of government | and history, with no thought of personal advantage. From the various opinions that we find, it rests with us, as representatives of the people, to find the true solutions. We must | find answers that will be of universal application. They must be for the welfare of all of our people and not for just a few. To the satisfactory performance of this (1) task, we must set our hearts as well as our heads. We must realize that success depends upon the understanding and the co-operation of all Americans in all walks of | life.

It is not my purpose today to speak of these problems, but rather to talk briefly of a method of approach that may enable us to deal with them. Before doing so, | perhaps I may be pardoned for saying that many questions that appear to apply only to one part of our country, and to be more or less local in character, may have a common | solution. For example, cotton presents a problem to the people of the South. It is the main crop of southern farmers; but bumper crops and diminishing markets have greatly decreased (2) the price of the cotton, and the entire country has been affected. In various parts of the country, farming has suffered in a similar way.

Let me illustrate the idea | I have in mind. As you all know, I am familiar with cotton because that is a product grown in my state. It is clear that, in addition to increasing the foreign demand | for cotton, we must increase the domestic use of it. The mere finding of such new uses is not the complete solution. The people of all the states must be able to become | purchasers of the new items that cotton will produce if the whole problem is to be solved.

The question is one of vital concern to each and every one of us, whether we (3) represent districts that are interested in producing raw materials or in making the finished product. Let me repeat, I have mentioned cotton only by way of | example because I know something about that product. The problem and the solution would be the same for any other product we might mention.

It is a fact that these sectional | troubles have national implications. They can be corrected only by general and national recovery. It seems quite clear that the ability of the people to | purchase depends upon their having a job that assures them the power to spend money. Now what is the natural and normal source of that job? The answer to this question is business. Business (4) is found in every district that we represent. We may not have cotton or corn or wheat in our own district, but we do have business of some kind. It is our one source of help. |

The Government cannot afford to employ a great many people indefinitely. We all know that such a course would dry up the revenue that must be collected for their pay. | Business is the principal source of national revenue; and I think it is true that, in the aggregate, small business furnishes more of it than big business and gives employment to | more of our people.

Some of the speeches made recently have pointed to this fact. The way to a normal condition is through normal operation. That sounds like good common sense to me. (5) (1.46)

165

1.

Key: (1) Observation, appropriation, encounter, difficulties, agricultural, constituents, absolutely, subcommittee, economy, budget. (2) Certain, enumerate, some time ago, secretary, complain, otherwise. (3) Projects, irrigation, completed, amount, mind, included. (4) Desert, vegetation, alongside, already, furnished, quantities, according. (5) Terms, congratulate, favorable, education, generally, schools, England, point.

It has been my observation that two appropriation bills usually encounter great difficulties in this chamber; that is to say the Interior bill and the | Agricultural bill. It happens that both those bills are of vital interest to my constituents; and that is why I am sorry when I see cuts made, unless such cuts are | absolutely necessary. I acknowledge the fact that we must make cuts in these days, but I fear some have been pretty extreme in this measure. I want to say to the chairman of the | subcommittee that, in his effort to protect the Treasury, he often cuts too deeply. I know of no subcommittee chairman who makes a clearer record for economy by (1) cutting under the budget estimates.

There are certain omissions from this bill that I have noted. Four minutes will not permit me to enumerate all of them; so let me begin | with this one. Some time ago we passed a measure here that authorized an additional assistant, because it was thought that the load of the secretary was increasing to such | an extent that he would need this assistant. Now, I do not find any provision for an appropriation for such an assistant. I do not know whether I should complain of this | particular omission from this bill, as it may be taken care of otherwise; but it is one of several omissions.

Last July several Congressmen went down to see the (2) head of that department. We told him that there were many projects for food production and irrigation projects on Indian lands and some others nearly completed. We also | mentioned that, if we could only get the stop order lifted and the green light given, these nearly finished projects could be completed and food production on them could begin at once. | Soon after that, a stop order was given. However, the necessary money has not yet been appropriated for all of them, even though the amount that is necessary | is small.

I have in mind one particular piece of land that I believe and hope is included in this bill, on page 34, if I read it correctly. On the Salt River Indian (3) Reservation near my home there are 3,000 acres of good land as level as this floor, now growing desert vegetation. It has a canal flowing alongside, with good | side ditches already provided. Nearly 90 per cent of the entire amount necessary to put this land in final condition has been expended, and yet the other | 10 per cent has been slowly furnished.

I have contended that these Indians, the best farmers of the Indian race in our entire country, could produce great quantities of food on that | land. I know that there are more than 3,000 acres that the Indian Bureau asked to have treated there, and I am wondering why the work has not been completed according to the (4) terms of the matter as we presented it a year ago. However, I do congratulate the committee on this degree of favorable action.

My friend from Iowa | speaks of education. I want to say to the gentleman that I feel he is right in regard to education of Indian children generally, that they should have the | benefits of our public schools. But I want to call attention to the fact that, with a reservation like the Salt River Reservation, larger than most of the New England states, it would | be impossible for the children there to go to the public schools.

We are far from the point where we can call upon the public schools of the states to furnish Indian education. (5) (1.49)

Key: (1) Privilege, I was not, majority, period, occasion, honeyed, words, supreme, sometimes. (2) Beyond our, few days, heard, demand, proposition, accomplished, little. (3) Forces, country, California, Ohio, constituents, Parliamentarian, we want, I should like to have. (4) To do, nothing, I should like to know, risen, opposition, prospered. (5) Manufacturers, hard, essential, editorial, rush, they are not.

I did not have the privilege last year of voting against this bill, because I was not here. In my campaign for election to Congress, however, I promised that, in the event ⏐ such a bill should be presented, I would vote against it. I received a majority of votes because of that pledge and other pledges that were made.

I was in the Senate of my ⏐ state for ten years; and during that period, I had occasion to listen to a lot of soft soap and a lot of honeyed words about various measures. They told us that certain measures ⏐ would do this and others would do that. Then we voted for them or we voted against them on those promises or statements, only to find the Supreme Court of the state, and sometimes the (1) Supreme Court of the United States, telling us that the bill we had voted for was outside the Constitution and that we had therefore gone beyond our powers.

The measure that is ⏐ now before this body has been debated here only a few days. It was stated yesterday that only a few copies of the bill were available last week. Thus far, we have ⏐ not heard a word from the nation. We have not heard from the people back home. We have had no demand whatever for this legislation. No one has asked us to vote for this proposition. | There is, therefore, no need for haste, it seems to me.

We have already spent weeks in debate and discussion of various kinds. We have accomplished very little in some directions, (2) I think; and yet the committee meets and forces this measure through without proper consideration. Now we already have it on the floor, just as if the whole country were demanding | that this be done.

There is no demand for it. You have had no word from back home. I do not care whether you are from California or from Ohio or from Maine; you have had | no word from your constituents asking for this measure. Then, why the haste? Where does this thing come from?

You say that our Parliamentarian, who comes from the Middle West and who is a very | good man, was the author of this legislation. Of course, he will prepare a bill for you or prepare one for me if we tell him what we want in the bill. But I should like to have word from (3) him as to who asked him to prepare this bill.

Some say that a certain man had something to do with it, while others say he had nothing to do with it. I should like to know what he did | have to do with it. In reply to the gentleman who said in his statement that we have been here several years and this is the first time the people have risen in protest, I say | that last year both parties had the good sense to rise in protest and say that this thing should not pass. It failed of passage, not because of opposition by one party, but because of the | opposition of both parties, who joined hands last year in opposing this bill.

I say to you that, in view of the fact that the only people who have prospered in the past several years have (4) been the manufacturers of red ink, we ought to think pretty hard when the taxpayers are called upon to pay further taxes. It is essential that we stop, look, listen, watch, and | pray about this proposition.

I read in the newspapers yesterday and today certain comments from editorial writers. Not many have learned about this bill, because they | do not know it is before us. When the people back home hear about the way in which it is proposed to rush this bill through Congress, they are going to tell us a thing or two. They are not | in favor of this reorganization bill, and I believe that they are not in favor of the section that authorizes the appointment of six administrative assistants. (5) (1.48)

167

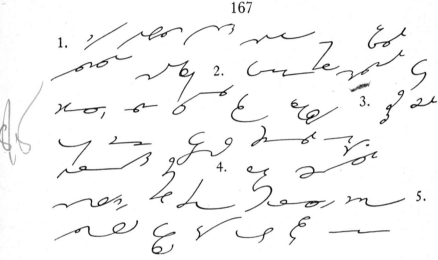

Key: (1) Supported, drastic, Democrats, control, engineer, opponents, dictator, countercharge. (2) Pronouncement, constituents, proof, statesmanship, anyone, admit, people, surprised. (3) Efficiency, words, legislation, someone, propaganda, few minutes, misunderstanding, tremendous, effectiveness. (4) Irrespective, candidates, congratulated, genial, reminded, school. (5) Declared, prepared, system, let us, exception, more and more.

I supported a much more drastic bill in the last Congress than the pending measure. Before that, I joined Republicans and Democrats alike in supporting such legislation | back in those days when the Republicans were in control. I voted to give the great engineer much more power than it is proposed to give the President in the pending bill, or | even in the bill defeated in the last Congress; and I did not hear all this opposition from the other side of the aisle. Where were the opponents then? In those days, we heard no talk | about a dictator or charges and countercharges that we were giving the President too much power. You see, it all depends upon who is doing the reorganizing.

I (1) do not agree that the gentleman's pronouncement to his constituents that he would oppose government reorganization, even before knowing what would be in such a bill, | is any definite proof or shows the essential marks of statesmanship. Of course, that is a matter of opinion. Never in the several years I have been here have I heard | anyone admit, much less boast, that he promised his people to oppose a bill before any of the provisions of the bill in question could possibly be known. Frankly, I am really | surprised that the gentleman now states that he made a promise that he would be against any kind of reorganization bill, even though the bill might save a great deal of money and (2) promote greater efficiency in government.

It is interesting to have the words of the gentleman, stating that he would want to amend his former statement. As to the | gentleman's statement that he is afraid this legislation might give someone more power, I realize that this propaganda has been spread so thoroughly for the past few months that some | of our friends in and out of Congress are still laboring under the misunderstanding that somebody around here wants to be a dictator. This bill, of course, grants no such power. May | I say, in passing, that, if I remember correctly, the President swept the great State of Ohio by a tremendous majority on one occasion and repeated with greater (3) effectiveness his smashing majority four years later.

I happened to be in and through that state during both campaigns. The good people of Ohio, like those in every | other section, irrespective of politics, have an abiding faith in their President. I was told that most candidates of the opposition tried their very best to win but were | unable to do so.

You boys are to be congratulated in establishing the record in the last campaign of being the champion promisers of the world. Not only in | your state, Sir, but in other states that I visited, I found our genial friends promising the world with a fence around it. They reminded me of the school teacher who, in applying (4) for a job, declared he was prepared to teach either the flat or the round system. He freely admitted he was prepared to teach any system, provided, of course, he could get | the job. Many apparently were for anybody's system that would get the votes.

But let us get back to the pending bill. In the years I have been in

Congress, I have noticed one | interesting fact that is true, regardless of who happens to be in power. When Congress has created a new agency of government, almost without exception that agency | has immediately begun to expand. Like a rolling snowball, the agency will keep on growing and, of course, demanding more and more money in order to expand further. (5) (1.51)

168

Key: (1) Survived, century, country, democracy, predicted, strength, distraction, to become, reflect. (2) Ourselves, civilization, fundamentals, careful, practical, management, sound, executive, contrary, enforcement. (3) Resolutions, expectation, gradually, structure, system. (4) Requirements, control, reported, to make, efficient, economical, one of the, assistants, undoubtedly, civil. (5) Accounting, favorably, calendar, chairmanship, gentleman from Missouri, congressional, upon the subject.

It is true that our form of government has survived for a century and a half while many different forms of government were being tried in many different countries | throughout the world. It is true that from time to time the death of democracy has been predicted by those who laughed at us. But it is good to know that the American system has matched | its strength against all the forces of destruction and has survived.

All this is true, and it means much to us. Because of this we cannot afford to become lazy. We cannot point to our | past and say that for 150 years American democracy has stood high among the governments of the world and that it will always be so.

Let us reflect for a (1) moment and ask ourselves how long the civilization of Greece lasted. The fundamentals of our Government are sound, we must admit, as they have always been; but we must be careful | that our Government stays on an even keel and does not become top-heavy.

In a practical country like ours, we insist upon and appreciate good management. Our people | demand not only sound laws but also the sound carrying out of those laws. It is not true, for example, that, in giving to the Executive Department the necessary | machinery of good management, the Congress loses its own powers by that much. On the contrary, the authority of the Congress is strengthened because the enforcement and (2) administration of our legislative decisions are made easier. The Congress does not pass laws in the spirit of New Year's resolutions, but in the just and confident | expectation that these laws will be put into practical effect in the best possible manner.

Beginning with the turn of the century, we have moved gradually into a | new era. During this time, the structure of the Government, with the exception of the introduction of the civil-service law and later the establishment of the Budget system, | has not been changed.

There is a weak link due to the changes that have taken place in this new age. The time has now come to face this problem and to arrange the machinery of the Government (3) so that it may meet the requirements of the new age and, in so doing, make certain that control by the people is not lost.

The proper House Committee has reported four | bills on the organization of the Government. The purpose of each bill is to deal with the one problem of management in the Government and to make it efficient as well | as economical. One of the bills gives to the President the power to reorganize the Executive Branch. Another bill provides the President with six administrative | assistants. These bills have already passed this House; but we shall undoubtedly have further opportunity to consider them in conference. The other two bills deal with civil-service (4) administration and our present accounting system. They have been reported favorably by the Committee and are now pending on the calendar, awaiting our | consideration.

The Committee mentioned, of which I have the privilege of being a member under the able chairmanship of the distinguished gentleman from Missouri, has | carefully studied the subject matter of all these bills. In addition to its own extensive hearings, it has had available to it the past hearings of many congressional | committees upon the subject, as well as a great deal of expert advice.

The committee very wisely divided the problem into four major parts for purposes of convenience. (5) (1.53)

169

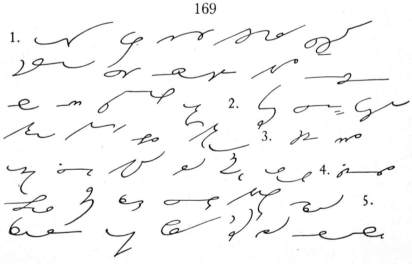

Key: (1) Long time, privilege, together, disagreed, acquainted, fundamental, another, milestone, destiny, men and women, anywhere, in the world, admiration, respect. (2) Beneficial, American, procedure, dishonor, directed, necessity, desirability. (3) Citizen, worthy, reasonable, himself, dependent, turned, sufferings, regardless. (4) Humanity, machinery, effective, serious, administration, distribution, concerned. (5) Parliament, legislature, appropriated, supervision, they want, millionaires.

Mr. Chairman, for quite a long time now I have enjoyed the privilege of working with many Members of this House. In committee and on the floor our activities have solved many | problems—large problems that have faced the country.

Many times we have stood together. Sometimes we have disagreed. During this time we have become acquainted with the fundamental | views of one another.

It is a long path that we have traveled. As I stand here today, at this milestone along the road of our country's destiny, I want all of you to know the | feeling in my heart. There is no group of men and women anywhere in the world for whom I have greater admiration and greater respect. Over and over again, you have shown your (1) faith in and love for your country. Your judgment and decisions have always been made on the basis of what is best for the country. Disagreement and debate over the best road for the | Nation to follow are beneficial to the country. It is the American way, and America always gains by this procedure. Different views are helpful in a free | country. There is no dishonor in disagreement that is directed toward finding a better road for our country to follow during these days.

Today, however, there is no | disagreement among the Members regarding the necessity and desirability of relief for the people who have been hit by the war. There is very little disagreement (2) among our people throughout the Nation regarding the question of relief. It is the natural desire of every good American citizen to see that every | worthy human being has food and clothing.

We are willing to go even further, to any reasonable extent, to aid any such individual to help himself and maintain | himself and those who are dependent upon him. Our people not only want to respond and are willing to respond—they demand that we respond. The American people | never have turned their backs to the needs and sufferings of others, regardless of who they were or where they might be.

The question facing us here today, however, is not whether or not we (3) shall respond to these demands of humanity in all parts of the world. The question arises as to what machinery we shall use and what methods we shall employ to render | the most effective and efficient relief service. This question of method is serious, perhaps more serious than most of us realize. The method of administration | and distribution of relief is the issue on which there is disagreement.

There are millions of Americans concerned with the method of relief. It is their money that is to | be used. It is their taxes that are to be increased to finance relief. It is the American people who will provide the money and goods for relief.

Do not be mistaken (4) about this fact. The parliament or legislature of no other country has appropriated any funds for direct relief. The American people, therefore, are very | much concerned about the supervision of these funds. They want to know who is supervising the relief throughout the entire project, all the way down the line to the persons actually | making the distribution. They want to know how these funds are to be used. They want to know where and from whom goods are purchased, and they want to know the prices paid. They do not want any | millionaires made out of relief paid for with American dollars.

Certainly every Member must have the interest and benefit of the American people in his heart. (5) (1.53)

170

Key: (1) Preceded, something, pertinent, democratic, privilege, to be able, legislation, imaginary, circle, determined, including. (2) Operate, mandates, remind, according, cabinet, delegates, efficient. (3) Certain, reorganization, nothing, boundaries, officer, tomorrow. (4) Moment, simply, effective, heretofore, accomplishing, instruct, empower, ratify. (5) Attempt, inject, functioning, conflict, conducted, in the world.

The gentleman who just preceded me said that something that was not pertinent to the bill was mentioned by one of the Members on the Democratic side. I feel it quite a | privilege for me to be able to follow a speech that was so carefully limited to the merits of this proposed legislation and struck so close to home the real point we have at | issue here.

I should like to draw an imaginary circle here in front of the House. It is supposed to represent the present scope of the powers of the Executive Department | of government. The limits of this circle have been determined by acts of Congress heretofore passed. Within this circle, the Executive Department, including the President (1) and other people who are working in that Department, is allowed to operate under the mandates the Congress has given it. The President, as I might remind the | House because we may have forgotten it, is the Chief Executive of the United States, according to the Constitution, and is charged with the task of carrying out as best | he can, with the assistance of his Cabinet, the laws that are passed. He is charged with the task of putting into operation those powers that the Congress delegates to him from time | to time. As the Chief Executive of the Government, the President is therefore responsible for the efficient operation of the Executive Department.

The bill we (2) have before us now is, in a certain very important sense, different from any other kind of legislation we could be asked to pass upon; for it has to do only | with the reorganization of the Executive Department in the interest of making of it a more efficient organization. There is nothing in this bill that | extends the boundaries of that circle I drew. There is nothing in this bill that gives the President or any other executive officer a single bit of additional | power he did not have before. There is nothing in this bill that states that Congress could not tomorrow, immediately after passing this bill, pass legislation to abolish (3) entire departments or set up new ones or change anything else it might have in mind to change.

As I said a moment ago, the President is the Chief Executive of this Government. | What we are saying in this bill is simply that we charge the President with the task of seeing to it that that job is done in a more efficient and effective manner than | it has been done heretofore. With a view to accomplishing this purpose, we instruct and empower the President to effect, within certain limits, such reorganization of | the various agencies and bureaus within that circle that I drew for you as he may deem to be wise—subject, however, to the power of Congress to refuse to ratify (4) the action he proposes to take.

Why do we have this bill? We have this bill before us because it represents an attempt on the part of a democratic legislative body | to prove to the world that it is possible to inject additional efficiency into the functioning of democratic government. We hear about the conflict in | the world between democracy on the one hand and dictatorship on the other. Well, the proof of democracy is going to be found in the ability of bodies like this | House of Representatives to see to it that democratic government is conducted in such fashion that it can match the efficiency of any other government in the world. (5) (1.56)

PART X

140 WORDS A MINUTE

171

Key: (1) Word, operating, interfere, various, itself, congratulate, opinion, knowledge. (2) Largely, reported, amendment, rendered, research, explained, compiled, millions, formulation, practical, gratifying. (3) Criticism, calendar, procedure, one of the most, impossible, usefulness, abused, doubtful, preliminary. (4) Duty, selected, qualifications, guard, expect, record, week ago. (5) Museum, introduced, rejected, justice, supreme, fraudulent.

As I said before, this bill is, in every sense of the word, an economy measure. It provides for a reduction of 25 per cent under the cost of operating the department | during the current year. The cuts are so carefully considered that they will not interfere with the efficient administration of the various agencies for which the bill provides. Of |

course, reductions cannot be made without giving rise to protests; but the bill speaks for itself.

I congratulate the chairman of the committee on the way in which the bill has been prepared. It is | a bill in keeping with the needs of the times. The chairman has the advantage of many years of experience in the preparation of such bills; and in my opinion, he has a wider knowledge (1) and a more intimate understanding of the various services and their needs than any other man who has served in this House. It is due largely to his management that the bill has been | reported to the House without amendment and is now on its way to final passage after a brief debate.

One feature of the preparation of the bill has been the service rendered by the | research staff of the committee. As was explained in the opening speech, the data compiled by the staff made possible the elimination of overlapping activities and the saving of | millions of dollars. It is the first time that the service of the staff has been enlisted in the formulation of the bill, and the results are both practical and gratifying.

Now, I shall digress (2) for a mild criticism of the manner in which the calendar was considered last week. As usual, the defect is not in the procedure of the House but in the manner in which it | is administered. It is one of the most useful of all the rules of the House. It offers opportunities for the consideration of bills of a minor character. This would be, to a | large extent, impossible if the ordinary procedure had to be followed. But the usefulness of this rule depends upon how it is used. The rule can very easily be abused; and, | if bills of doubtful merit are allowed to pass without preliminary examination, it will be necessary for members to object to all bills offered on the calendar in order (3) to insure rejection of such a measure as was permitted to pass when the calendar was last called.

As you know, it is the duty of six members to examine the bills that are filed in this | way. These men are carefully selected and are men of high qualifications. Knowing that these six men are on guard, the members of the House who have other pressing duties elsewhere can leave the Chamber, | secure in the knowledge that no objectionable legislation will be considered. That is what we expect. However, it is evident that things do not always work out that way.

If we | look at the record of a week ago, we find that a bill was passed by unanimous consent without a word from any of the six watchdogs supposed to be on guard. The bill had been before this (4) House for ten years. It is a bill that will take away certain property from the museum; and to my way of thinking, it should never have been passed. Eight times it has been introduced in the last three | or four years, and eight times it has been considered and rejected by committees of the House and Senate. A statement from the Chief Justice of the Supreme Court was read into the record about it, | describing it as a fraudulent claim. And yet the bill was allowed to pass without inquiry or notice of any kind to the museum or to the members who represent it here in the | House.

I cannot understand how those members who were charged with the protection of the calendar could have permitted such a measure to go through. The fact that such a bill passed requires investigation. (5) (1.46)

172

Key: (1) I did not, however, few minutes, American, happiness, worth, three million, temporary, surrounding. (2) Standard, comfortable, majority, facilities, of course, enact, families. (3) Findings, congressional, legislation, assistance, let us, construction, 10 per cent, volume. (4) It was not, private, sustain, emphasis, resources, obvious. (5) Concerned, equality, worse.

Mr. President, I did not intend to go into too many details on a subject that has been so extensively debated on this floor. However, I should like for a few minutes to | discuss the housing problem in the terms in which the American people think of it. They think of it in terms of their need for homes in which to live as Americans should, in which children can get | a fair start in life, and in which they can find the happiness to make life worth living.

I am thinking of the needs of nearly three million families who do not have any homes at all. There are many | who have only temporary housing such as trailers and rooming houses. I am thinking of the needs of the number of families in cities and surrounding areas whose homes fall below (1) decent standards of living. I am thinking of the families on farms whose homes are shacks that should be replaced or that need major repairs in order to make them comfortable. I am not | even counting the great majority of farm homes that do not have the sanitary facilities that have become so essential for safe living in our cities.

I realize, of course, that | even the best housing legislation we could enact is not going to solve the housing problem for these families overnight. That is why we must consider legislation that looks ahead into | the future.

If we really want to meet America's housing needs, we are going to need another eight million homes during the next twelve years. Despite the findings of the congressional (2) committees, there are still those who say we can solve this housing problem without enacting housing legislation. Despite the present poor housing situation, there are those who say that, if the Government | will just provide a little credit assistance and then let things alone, everything will work out all right!

Let us take a look at the record. The previous peak in home building was reached twenty-three | years ago. Then construction began to slide down, and it helped to take the whole economy with it. In 1933, homes amounting to only 10 per cent of the peak volume were | produced. Conditions twenty-three years ago were similar to what they are today. Homes were being built at prices that only a small portion of American families could afford to pay. When (3) that limited demand was filed, home building started to slide down again. The result was that production during the two decades before the war was

just enough to keep up with the increase in | families. It was not
enough to replace worn-out houses.

There are two ways of assuring enough housing for the American
people. One way is through a public-housing program. The other
way | is to bring the costs of private housing down so that there will
be enough demand to sustain the high rate of production that Amer-
ica needs. I think our emphasis should be on the latter. I | think the
Government should utilize its resources fully to help private enterprise get its costs down.

It is obvious that, if we leave the problem of housing to the local
communities, (4) it will not be solved. I believe that the Federal
Government, together with the local communities, has a responsi-
bility for the people's housing needs. I think it needs to be | concerned
with the health and character of its people. I think it has some responsibility of seeing that children start out in life with the equality of
opportunity that only | decent homes can provide.

If we accept the fact that we have a responsibility in this matter
of housing, and I believe that most of us do accept that responsibility,
then we must | take action and we must take it now. Every day that
we delay is a day lost in meeting the problem. Every day finds the
situation getting worse, with our citizens suffering more. (5) (1.48)

173

Key: (1) Committee, discussing, principle, refuse, admits, assign-
ments, removing. (2) Some of the, everyone, hampered, to do, colleague, qualified. (3) Perfectly, effective, gradually, two or three,

major. (4) Various, legislation, performed, years ago, reported. (5) Practically, controlled, difficulty, to supply, individual.

Mr. President, the number of Senators on the committee makes no difference. I am discussing the principle that is involved. We are going back again to the old practice, and we | shall continue to drift in that direction unless the Senate refuses to take sufficient action. Everybody admits that the number of members on committees ought to be decreased. | Under the present system Senators are members of five or six committees. These are mostly the older Senators. When new Senators come in, the older members keep their committee assignments; | and, in order to give the new members of the Senate an opportunity to be assigned to committees, we increase the number of Senators on the committee instead of removing (1) some of the older members. Everyone who has had any experience with the activities of the committees knows that their work is always hampered by the fact that many members, | the older members particularly, are on four or five other committees that are meeting at the same time. I am not stating anything new. Everybody here knows that is true. The right | thing to do, it seems to me, would be to take some of the older members off the committees. That applies to me just as it does to every other member of the Senate.

At the last session | of the Senate, in order to have my colleague appointed on a committee where he is particularly well qualified to serve, I gave up membership in a committee of which I was (2) a ranking member. I should have been removed from some of the other committees. I should be perfectly willing to give up those memberships if the same rule were applied to every other | Senator. If the membership of committees of the Senate were reduced to eleven, we would get much more effective service and the committees could do much better work than they are doing now. |

Also, Mr. President, the older members of the Senate gradually climb to the top of the important committees. The result is that one Senator will be chairman today of one of | the major committees, and he will also be the first in line on two or three other major committees. Then, when conference committees are appointed, he will be a member of conference (3) committees on bills coming from various Senate committees of which he is a member. That is a very important consideration in legislation. Often the most important work | of legislation is performed in conference committees, and the membership on conference committees should not be confined to a few Senators.

The situation is not so bad as it | was a few years ago, before we cut down the committees to some extent. No matter what the bills were that went to conference, if they had been reported by some of the larger committees of | the Senate, the same Senators were always on the conference committees.

The result was that, whatever legislation took place in conference committees—and a great deal of legislation (4) always takes place in such committees—there were Senators who practically controlled all the legislation, so far as conference committees could control it, and that often was the major part | of the work.

We are drifting into the same channel again, Mr. President, when we increase the membership of these committees. Two years from now we shall be facing the same difficulty. There will | be a number of Senators who do not wish to give up their committee memberships, and so the size of the committees will have to be increased again in order to supply the new Senators | with places on committees. There should be a definite ruling on this question. It should not be left to chance each year. It should not be left to the decision of the individual Senator. (5) (1.55)

174

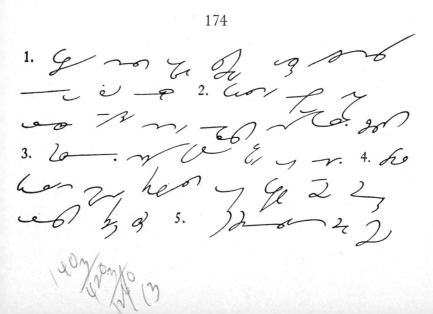

Key: (1) Preceded, connection, reports, advanced, occasions, designated, minority, heard, myself. (2) Protected, majority, trouble, remind, introduced, concluded, imperative, contemplating, executive. (3) Friday morning, custom, gentleman from Illinois, opposed, rush, nothing. (4) Purely, political, competent, jurisdiction, legislative, prejudice, interfere, functions, relative, justification, sides. (5) Few minutes ago, as soon as, convened, attitude, toward, to do so, I have been able, withstand, at all times, possession, complained.

Mr. Speaker, the gentleman who preceded me alleges that I have not kept faith with him and his colleague in connection with filing reports and resolutions that I do not favor but which | they favor or either of them favors. I remember that such a proposal was advanced. I do not remember that I made any agreement, nor have I any assurance; and I remember that | on two different occasions, when I designated them to call up resolutions, the committee minority was not given an opportunity to be heard properly. Therefore, in | the interest of protecting the committee minority, whether it be on our side at times or on the other side at times, I myself have continued to present resolutions looking (1) to consideration of bills, to be sure that the committee minority would be properly protected and heard, because I do not believe in taking advantage of the committee | minority, of which I was a member for many years. By "committee minority," I mean those on the committee not joining in the majority vote.

As to the resolution that has | caused all this trouble, I remind you that it was introduced last Thursday afternoon and, without any notice whatever, came before the Committee after we had concluded consideration | of two imperative matters and when we were contemplating going into executive session. This resolution was called up before members of our committee had an opportunity (2) to read it.

Copies of the resolution did not reach the office of the Committee on Rules until after the committee had begun its hearings of Friday morning. At the conclusion | of the business for which the committee meeting had been called, and, as I have said, when it was in order to

go into executive session, as is the custom, the gentleman insisted |
that we hear the gentleman from Illinois on his resolution immediately.

At that time I naturally opposed the rush on their part, because
I felt that members should have an | opportunity to read and study
the resolution before a hearing was called on it, to say nothing of
voting on it. /

From all I had noticed, I was under the impression that this (3)
resolution was introduced purely to create a political issue and place
us in an embarrassing position, especially when the subject was then
pending in a court of | competent jurisdiction. I felt that we should
not by any legislative action prejudice the case or interfere in any way
with the functions of the court. Last Monday, however, I | received
so much information relative to the untenable position of the company about all the favors they are receiving and have received at the
hands of the very group they | were opposing without justification
that I decided it would be best to probe this whole subject and get
all the facts from both sides. It was then I decided to favor the
resolution. (4)

I introduced this resolution a few minutes ago as soon as the
House convened and shall call it up as soon as the House will permit.
I changed my attitude toward this resolution not to | please men and
harmonize with occasion, not because, as has been stated by newspapers, I was forced to do so. So far I have been able to withstand
any and all pressure. I have at all times | done what I believed to be
in the best interests of the country.

I do very much regret that it became necessary for us to take pos-
session of the plant, although that act is, of course, | only nominal, as
everybody knows. I especially regret the fact that the Department of
Justice used two Army boys to carry out the action complained about
by the men. (5) (1.59)

PART XI

150 WORDS A MINUTE

175

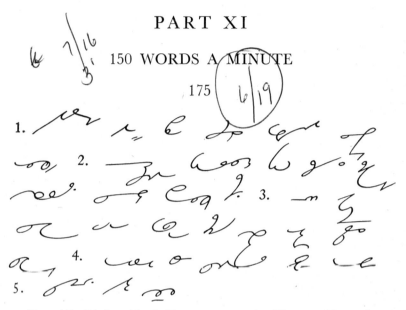

Key: (1) Distinguished, Texas, appear, families, presidents, imagination, required. (2) Manufacture, politics, board, exceedingly, established, guaranteeing, administration, application, everything. (3) In the world, to perform, ample, authority, priority, if you want, capable, respect, attorney, accomplish. (4) Lawyers, why not, actually, twice, listen. (5) I do not think, desires, quickly.

Mr. Chairman, yesterday the distinguished gentleman from Texas and I appeared on a radio program here in Washington. He and I both agreed, and I believe every Member of this House will | agree with us, that all Members of this body are eager to do their utmost to see to it that homes are built, especially for veterans and their families. We differ only on the methods to be followed. |

In his opening remarks, the gentleman who conducted the program made mention of the President's statement to the effect that we should use our imagination and referred to the manner in which the | people of the United States rose to the occasion when we were required to produce the materials of war.

I should like to call the attention of the Members of the House

288

to the fact that, when we were called (1) upon to produce these materials of war, the first thing that happened was that the President of the United States brought into Washington some of the most able men in the entire field of manufacture, | regardless of their politics. He set up the War Production Board and put in charge of it exceedingly able men, and they obtained the services of additional able men for the various | departments. We have now in this Government of ours a department that is established for the purpose of arranging the guarantee of loans on houses. That is known as the Federal Housing Administration. | Almost every homeowner who builds a home in the United States makes application for a loan, and this administration is required to approve everything in connection with the building (2) of the home before the loan is made.

Now is there any reason in the world why we need to place on top of the present agencies of the Government a new agency to perform just that function? If a | loan be approved by that administration, shouldn't that be ample authority for a builder to obtain priority to build a home? I just want to say this, that if you want to have a capable group | in the Government to direct this program, the most able and the most capable group in the Government is the Federal Housing Administration.

I have high respect and regard for Mr. John Turner. | He is a great salesman. He is a distinguished attorney. As mayor of a large city, he organized a housing program and appointed a committee to do the job; but the committee did not accomplish (3) very much. But we have many fine committees in this House, including the distinguished committee in charge of the bill, made up of a lot of fine lawyers, a few farmers, and some businessmen. Why not put | this program into the hands of men who actually know the building business? I suggest that this bill could be taken back into the Committee on Banking and Currency. They could call before it the men who | actually know what the building business is all about in the United States. In three days they could bring out a bill here on the floor that would build twice as many houses as are being anticipated | with present priorities, and we would all vote for it.

Every man in the House wants this program to get going and get going fast. Why not listen to these people and in three days bring back a bill that will (4) really produce homes? With all due respect to my colleague, the gentleman from Michigan, I do not think his bill will do very much more than the committee bill.

I am in favor of a bill that will actually | produce houses, and not one that will produce a lot of red tape and trouble for people in this country who are going to be responsible for carrying out any building program that this House and this | Congress desires to put in motion. Let us get busy and get the right bill, and get it quickly, and do away with all this discussion.

Because of the overwhelming importance of this entire matter, | I wish it were possible for me to go into it in somewhat greater detail. Unfortunately, I have a key meeting in a few minutes and, as a consequence, must terminate my remarks at this time. (5) (1.47)